THE WITNESS EXPERIENCE

This book provides the most comprehensive and scientific assessment to date of what it means to appear before war crimes tribunals. This groundbreaking analysis, conducted with the cooperation of the International Criminal Tribunal for the Former Yugoslavia (ICTY) Victims and Witnesses Section, examines the positive and negative impacts that testifying has on those who bear witness to the horrors of war, by shedding new light on the process. While most witnesses have positive feelings and believe they have contributed to international justice, there is a small but critical segment of witnesses whose security, health, and well-being are adversely affected after testifying. The witness experience is examined holistically, including witnesses' perceptions of their physical and psychological well-being. Because identity (gender and ethnicity) and war trauma were central to the ICTY's mandate and the conflicts in the former Yugoslavia, the research explores in-depth how they have impacted the most critical stakeholders of any transitional justice mechanism: the witnesses.

Kimi Lynn King, J.D./Ph.D., is a distinguished teaching professor at the University of North Texas (UNT), founding member of the American Moot Court Association, director for the Texas Undergraduate Moot Court Association, and coach of the nationally ranked UNT Moot Court team. Along with partner James David Meernik, she led the undergraduate/graduate study abroad courses that won the American Political Science Association (APSA) Award, and together they have coauthored 15 articles or book chapters on the Supreme Court and foreign policy, as well as in-depth research on the ICTY. Their greatest collaboration is their teenage daughter, who has traveled with them on all of their Hague trips since the beginning.

James David Meernik, Ph.D., is a professor of political science and Director of the Castleberry Peace Institute at the UNT. From 2003 to 2008 Meernik was Associate Editor of the flagship journal of the International Studies Association, *International Studies Quarterly*. He co-leads a UNT Study Abroad Program to the International Criminal Tribunal for the Former Yugoslavia that won the 2007 APSA award for the most innovative course in the United States. He has authored or coedited four books on international relations.

The Witness Experience

TESTIMONY AT THE ICTY AND ITS IMPACT

KIMI LYNN KING

University of North Texas

JAMES DAVID MEERNIK

University of North Texas

CAMBRIDGE
UNIVERSITY PRESS

CAMBRIDGE
UNIVERSITY PRESS

One Liberty Plaza, 20th Floor, New York, NY 10006, USA

Cambridge University Press is part of the University of Cambridge.

It furthers the University's mission by disseminating knowledge in the pursuit of education, learning, and research at the highest international levels of excellence.

www.cambridge.org
Information on this title: www.cambridge.org/9781108402729
DOI: 10.1017/9781108236065

First published 2017

Printed in the United States of America by Sheridan Books, Inc.

A catalogue record for this publication is available from the British Library.

Library of Congress Cataloging-in-Publication Data
Names: King, Kimi Lynn, author. | Meernik, James David, author.
Title: The witness experience: testimony at the ICTY and its impact / Kimi Lynn King, University of North Texas; James David Meernik, University of North Texas.
Description: New York, NY, USA: Cambridge University Press, 2017. | Includes bibliographical references and index.
Identifiers: LCCN 2017036745 | ISBN 9781108416214 (hardback) | ISBN 9781108402729 (paperback)
Subjects: LCSH: War crime trials – Social aspects – Netherlands – The Hague. | International Tribunal for the Prosecution of Persons Responsible for Serious Violations of International Humanitarian Law Committed in the Territory of the Former Yugoslavia since 1991. | Witnesses – Former Yugoslav republics – Attitudes. | War victims – Former Yugoslav republics – Attitudes. | Victims of crimes (International law) – Attitudes.
Classification: LCC KZ1203.A2 K56 2017 | DDC 341.6/90268–dc23
LC record available at https://lccn.loc.gov/2017036745

ISBN 978-1-108-41621-4 Hardback
ISBN 978-1-108-40272-9 Paperback

Contents

List of Figures   *page* vi

List of Tables   ix

Acknowledgments   xi

1   Introduction to the Survey and Survey Methodology   1

2   Exploring the Gender, Ethnicity, and Trauma
    Characteristics of the Witness Sample   37

3   The Witnesses and Their Encounter with International Justice   52

4   The Witnesses and Human Security: The Social, Economic,
    and Security Consequences of Testimony   85

5   The Impact of Testifying   118

6   Perceptions of Justice   149

7   Conclusions   178

Bibliography   197

Index   211

Figures

1.1 National and gender representation among eligible witnesses   *page* 14
1.2 Recruitment process outcome   16
1.3 Reasons for refusal   18
1.4 Interviewee behavior during the interview process   21
1.5 Geographic diversity   24
1.6 Education level   25
1.7 Interviewees by gender and age   25
1.8 Gender ratio – eligible VWS witness population and study
    population   26
1.9 Ethnic self-identification   27
1.10 Religious self-identification   27
1.11 Interviewee appearances by year   28
1.12 Interviewee trial appearances   28
1.13 Interviewees by trial and by calling party   30
1.14 Interviewee appearances as a proportion of all witnesses per trial 31
2.1 Ethnic self-identification   39
2.2 Ethnic identification among key ICTY nationalities   39
2.3 Ethnic identity and gender   40
2.4 Ethnic/religious minorities and mixed ethnic marriages in the
    immediate family   41
2.5 Mixed ethnic marriage in immediate family by geographic region   41
2.6 Wartime trauma experienced and witnessed by interviewees   44
2.7 Knowledge of wartime experiences by interviewees   45
2.8 Gender and wartime trauma by quintiles   46
2.9 Ethnicity and wartime trauma by quintiles   47
3.1 Knowledge about the work of the ICTY   54
3.2 Percentage of persons with greater knowledge about ICTY
    after testifying   55

3.3 ICTY knowledge before first time testifying and ethnicity 56
3.4 ICTY knowledge after last time testifying and ethnicity 56
3.5 Preparation, information, and satisfaction before trial 58
3.6 Reasons for testifying 60
3.7 Interviewee satisfaction with testimony when thinking about why they testified 64
3.8 Interviewees' reflections on satisfaction 65
3.9 Interviewee perception about treatment by the ICTY 67
3.10 Interviewee perception of treatment by type of witness 67
3.11 Witness perception of treatment by ethnicity 68
3.12 Interviewees' perceptions of the effectiveness of their testimony 70
3.13 Ethnicity and interviewees' perceptions of whether their testimony contributed to justice and truth 70
4.1 Relationship status 88
4.2 Impact on intimate relationships 88
4.3 Criticism, disassociation, and testifying 89
4.4 Persons who criticized and disassociated from interviewees 90
4.5 Positive and negative economic changes across time periods 91
4.6 Economic losses attributed to testifying across time periods 93
4.7 Satisfaction with ICTY financial entitlements during testimonial process 93
4.8 Threats to security by type 95
4.9 Whom interviewees believe were responsible for threats 96
4.10 Form of threat delivery 97
4.11 In-court protective measures of interviewees (using ICTY data on actual PMs) 101
4.12 In-court protective measures and feeling of overall security 102
4.13 Reasons behind interviewees' migration 103
4.14 Overall feeling of security today 104
4.15 Ethnicity and testimonial consequences 106
5.1 Interviewee health before testifying and within last three months (by gender) 124
5.2 Health issues before testifying and within last three months 125
5.3 Number of health issues before testifying and within last three months 126
5.4 Health worse because of the ICTY 127
5.5 Positive affect – before and after testimony 131
5.6 Negative affect – before and after testimony 132
5.7 Dispersion of positive and negative emotions – after testimony 135
5.8 Issues making testifying more difficult 138

5.9 Relieving emotional/physical distress during testimony process   139
5.10 Satisfaction with present and future life situation   140
5.11 Satisfaction with present and future economic circumstances   140
5.12 Satisfaction with present and future political circumstances   141
5.13 Satisfaction with present and future interpersonal relations in
     community   141
6.1 Interviewees who think the ICTY has generally done a "good
     job in . . ."   151
6.2 Perceptions of the administration of justice   152
6.3 Perceptions about sentences   153
6.4 Impact of international and national politics on the ICTY   154
6.5 Gender differences and the influence of international and
     national politics on the ICTY (in percentages)   154
6.6 Local courts are better suited to adjudicate war crimes (in
     percentages)   155
6.7 Fairness of treatment by the ICTY to defendants and witnesses   155
6.8 Interviewees who think the ICTY has generally done a "good
     job in establishing the truth"   159
6.9 Interviewees who think the ICTY has generally done a "good
     job in determining responsibility for grave crimes"   160
6.10 Interviewees who think the ICTY has generally done a "good
     job in determining punishment for those responsible"   160
6.11 Interviewees who think the ICTY has generally done a good
     job in "preventing grave crimes from occurring again in the
     former Yugoslavia"   161
6.12 Range of traumatic wartime experiences and support for
     ICTY goals   164

Tables

1.1	Witness sampling goals and interviewees surveyed	*page* 23
1.2	Survey respondents – by the numbers	29
2.1	Poisson regression estimates of the number of wartime experiences	50
3.1	Partial correlation coefficients for wartime trauma and motivation to testify	62
3.2	Strength of witness motivation to "speak for the dead" – ordered probit estimates	75
3.3	Strength of witness motivation to "put the past behind" – ordered probit estimates	75
3.4	Strength of witness motivation to "confront defendant" – ordered probit estimates	76
3.5	Strength of witness motivation to "tell my story" – ordered probit estimates	76
3.6	Ordered probit estimates of witness perception of their contribution to justice	79
3.7	Dichotomous probit estimates of witness perception of their contribution to justice	80
3.8	Ordered probit estimates of witness perception of their contribution to truth	81
3.9	Dichotomous probit estimates of witness perception of their contribution to truth	81
4.1	Ethnic minority status and testimonial consequences	107
4.2	Gender and testimonial consequences	109
4.3	Partial correlations between trauma and testimonial consequences	110
4.4	Explaining social consequences from the testimonial process	112
4.5	Explaining economic consequences from the testimonial process	113
4.6	Explaining security consequences from the testimonial process	114

5.1 Measures of interviewees' post-trauma symptoms in the last six
     months   120
5.2 Distribution of negative and positive affect – before and after
     testifying   130
5.3 Model – positive emotions after testimony   134
5.4 Model – negative emotions after testimony   134
5.5 Understanding witnesses' views on interpersonal relations in
     their communities   145
6.1 Support for ICTY goals among those who are ethnic minorities
     in their communities   162
6.2 Support for ICTY goals and level of importance placed on
     reasons for testifying   166
6.3 Support for ICTY goals among those who feel they have
     contributed to justice and truth   167
6.4 Testimonial consequences and support for the ICTY   168
6.5 Establishing the truth model   170
6.6 Determining responsibility model   171
6.7 Punishing those responsible model   172
6.8 Preventing crimes from occurring again model   173

Acknowledgments

Professors Kimi Lynn King and James David Meernik wish to thank many individuals at the International Criminal Tribunal for the Former Yugoslavia and at the University of North Texas who made this project a reality. We appreciate the support and encouragement of all the units of the ICTY that were involved in assisting this project, especially the ICTY Registrar John Hocking, Deputy Registrar Kate Macintosh, and Chief of Court Support Services Gregory Townsend. A very special thank you to Jan Kralt in Public Affairs, who was the first person we met at the ICTY many, many years ago, and who has worked patiently with us ever since. There have been so many people who helped not only with this project, but have also assisted us in a myriad of ways over the years with our visits to the ICTY. We extend our most heartfelt appreciation and thanks to all of you.

We especially wish to call attention to the role played by a group of amazing ICTY staff who drove this project through to completion. Adisa Agić and Marija Marković should be especially commended for their tireless efforts and ethic of care for witness well-being during interviews in the field. Invaluable assistance has been provided by the VWS interns in the Sarajevo Field Office Amela Jakubović, Jasenko Jašarević, and Rafaela Tripalo.

At the University of North Texas we appreciate the coding and data entry work of Melissa McKay, Sabra Messer, Taylor Ledford, Savannah Leigh Shuffield, Kara Hoffpauir, Ayal Feinberg, Roman Krastev, Rachel Ferris, and Eliza Kelly. Dr. Mark Vosvick and Eliot Lopez in the Department of Psychology and the Center for Psychosocial Health Research provided invaluable insight and assisted with advice related to psychological, physiological, and trauma-related survey items. Thanks also to administrative support provided by Sharon McKinnis and Cece Hannah. We must also acknowledge a vital partner, Marlene Meernik, who has traveled faithfully with us on these journeys to The Hague throughout almost her whole life.

Drs. King and Meernik extend our most profound and heartfelt gratitude to our partners in this adventure, three amazing women: Helena Vranov Schoorl, Sara Rubert, and Tiago de Smit of the Victims and Witnesses Section. We worked with our colleagues for six years to carry this project through to the end. When the workload or the complexities of running this operation would begin to wear on us, we could always count on the dedication and inspiration of these women who have given so much to this project and to all the witnesses who have come through the ICY doors. Their commitment to witness well-being inside the confines of an international institution and the ethos of care they provide should be the standard and role model for all tribunals everywhere.

This book is based in part on a joint publication by the Victims and Witnesses Section (VWS) of the International Criminal Tribunal for the former Yugoslavia and University of North Texas (UNT), *Echoes of Testimonies: A Pilot Study into the Long Term Impact of Bearing Witness before the ICTY*. The VWS contribution entailed development of the research tool, provision of anonymized witness data to UNT, collection of research data through interviews with witnesses, and provision of contextual background of ICTY witnesses and VWS work experience.

The views expressed in the book are those of the UNT authors alone and do not necessarily reflect the views of the International Tribunal or the United Nations in general.

Finally and most importantly, international tribunals depend critically on *all* witnesses to carry out their mandates, and the ICTY is no exception. The brave men and women who have come forward over the last twenty years have given much of themselves in this quest for truth and justice. The study could never have been accomplished without the willingness of the interviewees who gave so generously of their time and voices to share their experiences yet one more time. Their contributions are more than anyone could have ever asked for and exceeded all of our expectations.

It is to *all* the witnesses and their families that this study is dedicated.

1

Introduction to the Survey and Survey Methodology

INTRODUCTION

This was never going to be an ordinary survey project. Surveying individuals who have experienced the horrors of war and lived to tell their story to an international tribunal is no easy undertaking. Yet such compelling research is necessary if we are to understand fully the "justice cascade" and how transitional justice mechanisms can be used to hold accountable those who have violated human rights (Sikkink 2011). While great strides have been made in developing the rule of law and international legal institutions to discourage governments and rebels from violating humanitarian laws and human rights, there is an intensely personal component to the judicial proceedings that can often be overlooked. The witnesses – whose experiences are the foundation of a tribunal's search for truth – are vital for exonerating or convicting the accused, and their testimony helps establish the historical record. They are the indispensable stakeholders for whom the core mission of the International Criminal Tribunal for the Former Yugoslavia (ICTY) is to ensure that equity and fairness are applied throughout the testimonial process. And as critical and as difficult as the testimonial process is, the witness experience does not end with the court's final judgment. The witnesses go back to their lives and face the consequences of returning home to shattered communities after testifying. What paths and pain take the witnesses from war and its aftermath to the rarified courtrooms of an international tribunal? How do the witnesses' experiences and perceptions in the post-testimonial phase help us better understand and develop justice systems that ensure justice is done? How can we better gauge the short-term and long-term impacts on witnesses who testify? And most especially, how can legal institutions ensure that these individuals are not re-traumatized by the process and protect those who have come forward from backlash within their communities?

Our most fundamental purpose of this unique survey was to examine more fully the witness experience by exploring these and other questions through an in-depth survey and short interview with a cross-section of witnesses who have testified before the ICTY.

The initiative to implement a survey project about the witness experiences of those who appear before a war crimes tribunal came from both the ICTY (the Victims and Witnesses Section – VWS) and a team of faculty and graduate students at the University of North Texas (UNT). Since 2001, UNT scholars had regularly interacted with VWS because of study abroad and faculty research programs. When the ICTY put out a call for a research partner, UNT responded with a proposal and was ultimately selected. Negotiating the Memorandum of Understanding (MOU) and seeking multiple approvals through the Institutional Review Board (IRB) (which included a review of both national and international requirements needed to conduct this type of unique research) were only the beginning. Utilizing focus groups with VWS personnel, both in the region and in The Hague, we took more than 18 months to develop a comprehensive approach toward the survey. The survey needed to be witness-centered, and the process itself was intended to provide an opportunity for witnesses to let the ICTY know the impact that testifying had on them. The collective wisdom of those who had testified was needed to provide insight about testifying so that future generations of war crimes victims and witnesses might better know what to expect. Of paramount importance was guarding against having the survey process trigger traumatic memories as witnesses recounted what testifying had meant to them. Moreover, protecting the identity, security, and confidentiality needs of those witnesses who had received protective measures during the time of trial was also critical, resulting in the need for additional protocols. All of these practical considerations were constrained by the need to conduct a survey consistent with scientific evaluations about the impact of testifying on witnesses and providing an ethic of care to witnesses in the post-testimonial phase, as we describe in this chapter. Ultimately, our goal has been to contribute to a broader, interdisciplinary understanding about what it means to bear witness, as research is relatively embryonic in this field.

To be sure, there have been other relevant studies on individuals who have appeared before international tribunals investigating human rights violations. Stover (2005) interviewed 87 prosecution witnesses from the ICTY, as well as ICTY personnel and affiliates through a structured interview process. While witnesses were mostly positive about their experience, the study highlighted criticisms about the testimonial process and the Tribunal itself. Cody et al. (2014) also examined victim-witnesses from the International Criminal Court through an interview survey instrument prior to testifying, soon after testifying, and 6–12 months after testifying. The witness testimonial process was found to be positive overall, with women being slightly more positive than men. Women, however, felt less secure than men did in the post-trial phase and were less likely to think that their testimony contributed to truth or justice.

Perhaps the most important research has come from the wealth of information provided by in-depth interviews conducted at the Special Court for Sierra Leone. Researchers found that witnesses were more likely to have a positive experience if they felt respected by court personnel and found cross-examination to be a positive experience (Horn et al. 2009b, 2011). Witnesses have both public and personal reasons for why they testified (Stepakoff et al. 2014, 2015), such as contributing "to public knowledge about the war," desiring "retributive justice," and as part of a "moral duty to other victims." The study found that four out of five witnesses described the consequences of testifying as primarily positive (compared to negative or neutral), with more than three times as many positive as negative consequences.

The present study, different from the previous seminal pieces, is groundbreaking in many respects. No survey research has utilized a systematic and scientific sampling process by independent analysts of all types of witnesses in the testimonial process – those called by the Office of the Prosecution (OTP), Defence, and Chambers. Additionally, the human security needs of witnesses who testify with protective measures (those whose identities cannot be revealed because of the security risks they would face if their full identity was known) meant that only authorized Tribunal personnel could have access to them. Nonetheless, the partnership between the VWS and UNT meant that we were able to survey these individuals, thus being able to expand on previous work and delve more deeply into the witness experience than other research has been able to do (Stover 2005).

The present study also builds on research done with smaller samples of prosecution witnesses (Stover 2005) to provide a more in-depth analysis of the multifaceted experiences of witnesses, such as their physical and psychological well-being and their perceptions about international justice (Stepakoff et al. 2014, 2015; Stover 2005; Cody et al. 2014). This project helps enable the ICTY and other international criminal tribunals to assess more fully the post-testimony needs of witnesses and to develop best practices in witness management and well-being, because as other research has argued, there is still much that needs to be known about bearing witness (Horn et al. 2009b, 2011; Henry

2009; O'Connell 2005; Mendeloff 2009; Stepakoff et al. 2014, 2015; Stover 2005; Cody et al. 2014).

The survey was designed to gather information across multiple aspects of the witnesses' experiences before, during, and after the testimonial process. The 32-page survey instrument includes 149 multiple-choice questions along with 37 follow-up questions and 31 opportunities for witnesses to write in their own short answers to questions throughout the questionnaire. In five sections, the survey evaluates: (1) witness background and reasons for testifying (28 questions with 2 follow-ups); (2) socioeconomic impact on witnesses (8 questions with 7 follow-ups); (3) security concerns for witnesses (10 questions with 21 follow-ups); (4) physical and psychological health and well-being of witnesses (82 questions with 3 follow-ups); and (5) witness perceptions about justice and the ICTY's legacy (21 questions with 4 follow-ups). A sixth section asks three open-ended questions that are audio-recorded at the conclusion of the written survey. This section provides witnesses with an opportunity to elaborate more freely on concerns or issues about the testimonial process, their advice for future witnesses in war crimes trials, and their feedback to the ICTY about what they would change about the proceedings or the process of testifying.

Our more specific objectives were several. First, we sought to provide a comprehensive analysis of the effects on witnesses that result from having participated in criminal proceedings before the ICTY. Interviews with victims and witnesses reveal that participating in a judicial process can contribute to and/or aggravate the psychological recovery process of survivors of violence. Many existing studies recommend further research into the long-term impact of giving testimony, with an emphasis on victims' and witnesses' well-being, to provide adequate assistance during the post-trial period (Horn et al. 2009b, 2011; Henry 2009; O'Connell 2005; Mendeloff 2009; Stepakoff et al. 2014, 2015; Stover 2005; Cody et al. 2014). Second, we and the ICTY in particular sought to assess witness needs. Information from the study enables the VWS and witness support structures at other tribunals to better assess witnesses' needs during and following testimony to assist in identifying the appropriate course of action for those who require additional support. Third, the project was designed as part of the ICTY efforts to assess its legacy and to provide useful information/guidelines for future witness support structures. The conclusions and recommendations drawn from this study would be the first comprehensive analysis of the effects and consequences of witnesses' involvement in international criminal proceedings, therefore contributing to the legacy of the ICTY and assisting in the development of best practices at other international and domestic tribunals.

UNDERSTANDING THE WITNESS EXPERIENCE THROUGH
ETHNICITY, GENDER, AND EXPERIENCE

Our goal, however, is not just to review the descriptive statistics from this extraordinary trove of information about the witness experience. We advance scholarship and theory on international justice, conflict, and the micro-level impact of major international institutions; address critical gaps in the literature and our theories on transitional justice; and provide new theoretical insights into the meanings of bearing witness and delivering justice. Specifically, we analyze how witnesses experience the testimonial process through three key factors – ethnicity, gender, and trauma – as the principal, although not the exclusive, lenses of analysis to advance our knowledge and theory of the witness experience and international justice. Why the focus on these three factors?

First, issues of ethnicity, gender, and trauma figure prominently in the jurisprudence of the ICTY. The charges of genocide (always) and crimes against humanity (frequently) are based on the intent of the perpetrator to target a population because of its ethnicity (as well as other characteristics). A strong gender component has been part of the ICTY's work as the Tribunal has delivered key precedents regarding liability for sexual assault, including holding commanding officers responsible for violence committed by their subordinates; prohibiting sexual enslavement as a violation of international law; and finding liability for sexual violence committed against males. Perhaps most pointedly the traumas suffered by the witnesses were the primary impetus for establishing the tribunal. These traumatic experiences helped determine which perpetrators the OTP chose to indict, while the traumatic impact of the crimes is a defining feature of the sentences handed down for those convicted. The gravity of the crimes – the trauma suffered by the witnesses – is an ever-present reality in international justice and judicial decision-making. Thus, understanding the witness experience along the axes of ethnicity, gender, and trauma is critical in explaining how the Tribunal and its legacy are experienced and understood.

Perhaps the most important rationale for examining the impact of testifying on witnesses through their ethnicity, gender, and trauma suffered is that these factors weigh heavily as defining features of who the witnesses are and why they are called to testify. Victims were typically singled out for abuse or left alone because of their ethnic identity. The targeting of women (and men) for sexual violence is thought to be a routine consequence of war, with human victims as weapons of mass conflict and as the bounty for conquering armies. These traumatic experiences can shape the lives of the witnesses, their physical and emotional health, and their social relations in the community. Using a witness-based framework regarding the experience of testifying, we contend these three foci provide both depth and breadth for understanding the witness experience before war crimes tribunals.

Ethnicity

The wars of the former Yugoslavia, like many intrastate conflicts, were fought along key markers of identity, of which ethnicity was the most salient and encompassing. Each of the principal ethnic groups – Bosniaks (or Bosnian Muslims), Serbians, Croatians, and Kosovar Albanians – struggled to define a political, geographic, and social space in which they felt secure. Bosnian Muslims battled Serbs; Croats fought Serbs; Bosnian Croats fought Bosnian Muslims; and Kosovar Albanians fought Serbs.[1] Ethnicity also correlates highly with religion (Bosniak Muslims, Catholic Croatians, Orthodox Serbians, and Kosovar Albanian Muslims), language (the Bosniak, Croat, and Serb populations each lay claim to distinct languages, even though there are substantial similarities, while Albanian is quite distinct from all the others), history (especially given the subjugation of the various groups by distant empires, e.g., Ottoman Empire, Austro-Hungarian Empire), and wealth (poverty tends to increase the further south one goes in the region). Indeed, the term "ethnic cleansing" was coined during the Balkan wars to describe the expulsion of people from their homes and their replacement by members of another ethnic group who laid claim to these lands.

Ethnicity is critical for understanding not just the Balkan wars but many civil conflicts. Some estimates indicate that almost two-thirds of all civil wars stem from ethnicity and identity issues (Denny and Walter 2014; Seymour et al. 2016; Themnér and Wallensteen 2012). Identity, and in particular ethnic identity, has been prominent in studies of civil conflict, especially in the post–Cold War era with the decline of international conflicts (Mason and Meernik 2006). Despite recognition that ethnicity is a critical marker in dividing populations, there is debate regarding whether ethnicity is nearly so dominant in explaining conflict (Seymour et al. 2016) and whether it is too crude a mechanism for understanding complex conflicts with dynamic and opportunistic alliances that often transcend ethnic identity. Violence in local theaters

---

[1] We recognize that there were also brief conflicts in the breakup of Yugoslavia that involved Slovenes (1991) and Macedonians (2001), but because there were no trials regarding the former and just one regarding the latter, there are no Slovenes and only two Macedonians in our sample.

of conflict can often be rooted in local divisions and less driven by "supralo-cal" identities (Kalyvas 2003). To be sure, ethnicity does not always provide the sole motivation. The opportunity or the support necessary to wage civil war along identity lines, greed, and grievances are also powerful motivators. Ethnicity, however, provides the organizing concept that may not only lead to violence but also foment greater levels of violence in war-fighting, and espe-cially human rights abuses against civilians. There are incentives to target the coethnic nationals of one's adversaries to create ethnically cleansed lands (Cederman et al. 2011) or as a strategy for undermining support in the popula-tion for one's adversaries (Fjelde and Hultman 2014).

The conflicts in the former Yugoslavia were fueled by long-standing ethni-cally based rivalries that often caused many observers to argue there was little the international community could do to stop the cycles of violence (Kaplan 1994). At the same time, political leaders such as Slobodan Milošević and Franjo Tudjman exploited these tensions for their own ends. Gagnon (2004) shows that these leaders actually "demobilized" and sidelined populations largely reluctant to embark on campaigns of ethnic violence and cleansing through fearmongering, circumscribing political space for their opponents, and buying the acquiescence of key players. Nonetheless, whether individuals define and fight conflicts based on ethnicity and kinship ties, or their underly-ing fears of the other are exploited by instrumentalist political leaders for their own ends, violence assumes strong ethnic dimensions. Efforts at addressing the causes of these conflicts and prosecuting those responsible for taking eth-nic conflict to the extremes of crimes against humanity and genocide must recognize these divisions as well. As Seymour et al. (2016: 49) write, "Ethnicity is thus a potent cleavage around which to organize collective action because it is prone to manipulation from above and because ethnic homogeneity induces more cooperative behavior from below."

Gender

Gender has been shown to be a critical dimension along which the horrors of war and the challenges of post-conflict peace-building occur (Hudson et al. 2012). Yet research that explicitly focuses on the gender dimensions in transi-tional justice has been lacking (cf. King et al. 2016; King and Greening 2007; Brounéus 2010). It is striking in the development of gender-based approaches within traditional interational relations (IR) behavioral theories that research questions connect gender identity and female roles within the community to increasingly interdisciplinary questions about women's roles in international law, conflict, and organizations. Gender and the role of women in post-conflict societies bring women's unique "voices" to the table, and gender-based analyses provide insight into traditionally male-dominated arenas (King et al. 2016; Tickner 2001; Enloe 1993; Menkel-Meadow 1985; Gilligan 1982). Feminist IR research has moved from "margin to mainstream" (Kelly 2005: 474) and has developed a more relativist sense of women as "socially positioned citizens" whose relationship to power-based males makes women both subjects and objects (Youngs 2008: 697). Whether as soldiers in civil conflict, victims of war, or arbiters of the peace, women's roles are reconceptualized inside different contexts providing opportunities to examine gender inside institutions and communities (McBride and Mazur 2010; Al-Ali and Pratt 2009; Kelly 2005).

The creation of the ICTY and the other ad hoc tribunals, however, has advanced international law about sexual violence and increased the prominence and presence of women as prosecutors, defense counsel, and judges. The expansion of the presence of women was also thought to help ensure that allegations of sexual violence would be vigorously prosecuted and punished (King et al. 2016; Askin 2003; Copelon 2000; Hoefgen 1999; Bunch 1995), after centuries of wars where such crimes were marginalized. Individuals were targeted with gender violence throughout the 1990s Balkan wars as a tactic to destroy a population by destroying female fertility (preventing future births, damaging women physically and psychologically, and forcing impregnation by the enemy). Rape allowed warring males the opportunity to dehumanize the population and gave soldiers the "spoils" of war (Stiglmayer 1994; Ray 1997). Whether it was because they were women singled out for sexual abuse and enslavement or men who were selected for elimination during genocidal massacres, there were gender-conscious political and military strategies employed in these conflicts. This connection between sexual violence and ethnicity is clear from patterns in cross-national data examining state militaries and their role in carrying out sexual violence in conflict zones (Seymour et al. 2016: 53; Cohen and Nordås 2014). Gender plays a prominent role in conflict violence, and thus is a crucial lens through which to understand the witness experience.

Experience and Trauma

The Prosecution, Defence, and Trial Chambers typically call their witnesses to testify about their wartime experiences.[2] These experiences, or the witnessing of such events, include extreme deprivation of food or healthcare, destruction of home and community, detention, separation and disappearance of

---

[2] To be sure, there have been many expert witnesses called to testify about the historical background and the events of the 1990s, but our focus in this survey, as we describe subsequently, is on the fact witnesses.

family members, severe beatings, sexual violence and rape, torture, and the killing of others. These events represent the very reason for the establishment of the ICTY and the need for witness testimony.

One cannot overstate the impact of this trauma in terms of the physiological and psychological health of those persons who are responsible for "bearing witness." It means that not only did they endure significant levels of trauma, with which they still cope on a daily basis, but the very process of having to testify in one or more trials required them to recall these painful memories, to cope with waiting periods (which can last years) before being called to testify, and to deal with the residual impact of having testified.

In addition to the painful relevance of these wartime experiences for both the witness and the ICTY, we are particularly interested in the extent to which the amount and type of trauma witnesses have undergone affects their perceptions and opinions about the testimonial process and the ICTY itself. There are two particularly compelling questions of theoretical and practical importance that we can gain leverage over through our focus on witness experiences and trauma. First, there has been a number of publications in the last 10 to 15 years on the emotional and psychological well-being of witnesses, victims, and persons who have survived the conflicts in the former Yugoslavia. There has been debate about the impact of testifying on psychological healing (Bandes 2009; Henry 2009, 2010; Herman 2003). Does the process of testifying do more harm than good to the emotional state of those who testify given the level and kinds of wartime traumas the witnesses endured? Some have argued that the process of testifying could provide a healing, closure, or catharsis to help overcome traumatic events (Moghalu 2004: 216; Stover 2005). Others have argued that evidence is limited and questionable when it comes to the impact on victims (Bandes 2009: 16), and that this is particularly true for the ICTY witnesses (Clark 2009a, 2009b, 2009c, 2009d, 2014). The reality is, however, that little is known about "the individual psychological and emotional effects of national truth-telling and accountability mechanisms, or about victims' experiences with criminal justice more broadly" (Mendeloff 2009: 596). We examine the impact of wartime trauma on witnesses to understand why some witnesses may be able to better withstand the rigors of the testimonial process and why others may not.

The witnesses' type and range of traumas associated with war can also help us understand one of the most interesting findings to emerge from research on the micro-level impacts of trauma. In a fascinating piece of research that surveys a number of articles across several social science disciplines, especially economics, Bauer et al. (2016) find that people who are exposed to violence are more likely to become cooperative, participate in social activities, take leadership roles, and give altruistically. Indeed, there is a burgeoning field of cross-national research on how violence affects people's psychology and social relations that demonstrates, as we would expect, that these singular events exercise an important impact on our lives. The counterintuitive finding is that these experiences can often generate positive effects. If indeed the silver lining of war is that it does help many people act on the better angels of their nature afterward, then we should find evidence of it in our data.

Thus, these three foci – ethnicity, gender, and trauma – are chosen for their practical relevance, their institutional significance, and their theoretical leverage to help us shed light on the critical questions scholars seek to understand about the witness experience. Throughout we examine how ethnicity, gender, and trauma have influenced the reasons why witnesses testify, their personal experiences with the testimonial process, and their views of international justice. We analyze how the three factors influence the types of negative harms experienced by witnesses, such as economic losses, security threats, and impacts on psychological health. Research on these questions has largely been anecdotal, exploratory, and generally not reflective of the diversity of factors that shape the witness experience, nor has research done an adequate job of connecting the testimonial process to the post-testimonial phase (cf. Cody et al. 2014; Brounéus 2010; Stover 2005). In this book and through the use of these unique survey data, we not only provide a practical understanding of the witness experience that can be utilized by other international and national tribunals, but we can also begin to answer some of the most vexing questions facing those interested in transitional justice. We begin by briefly reviewing the history of the establishment of the ICTY.

BACKGROUND TO THE ICTY

The end of the Cold War from 1989 to 1991 led to the collapse of multiple communist governments, like that of the former Yugoslavia. The communist ideology and the dictatorial rule of longtime Yugoslav president Joseph Tito had been the glue that held together the disparate peoples of Yugoslavia through his death in 1980. Without these binding agents, nationalist leaders like Slobodan Milošević of Serbia and Franjo Tudjman of Croatia played upon the fears of uncertain times and established authoritarian governments to enforce their notions of ethnic purity. In their quest for power, nationalist leaders across the region propounded virulent propaganda and divide and conquer politics, and inspired the creation of brutal paramilitary groups. This violent nationalism, a history of conflicted regional and ethnic relationships and rivalries across the former Yugoslavia, a collapsing economy, and changes to the global world order led to violent quests for ethnic purity and territorial expansion (Woodward 1995). Ethnic cleansing, concentration camps, sexual enslavement, the obliteration of religious and cultural objects, genocide, and the destruction of interethnic trust were the result. Roughly 150,000 were killed in the wars of the 1990s in the former Yugoslavia, mostly in Bosnia-Herzegovina, but also in Croatia, Kosovo, and Serbia.[3] Approximately four million more fled their homes, becoming refugees either internally or abroad. The United Nations, the European Union, and the United States engineered a massive international response to rebuild the war-ravaged region, as well as establish a transnational justice mechanism to hold accountable those persons most responsible for the violence (Clark 2014; Roper and Barria 2006).

Created by United Nations Security Council Resolution 808[4] in 1993 and located in The Hague, Netherlands, the ICTY was tasked to bring to justice those most responsible for serious violations of international humanitarian and human rights laws in the course of these conflicts, and to help establish peace in the region. Crucial to the fulfillment of the ICTY's mandate is the testimony of those directly affected by the conflict – the victims and witnesses who appear to provide testimony after having been called by the OTP, Defence counsel, or Chambers. The numbers of those testifying at the ICTY – more than 4,650 individuals[5] – attest to the "the crucial nature of witness testimony" (Wald 2002: 219). The VWS – created via Article 22 of the ICTY Statute and Rule 34 of ICTY Rules of Procedure and Evidence – is the first unit of its kind to have authority to provide services for victims and witnesses, including making logistical and security arrangements for witnesses to appear in The Hague, counseling, support, and the capacity to make recommendations regarding protective measures. Its mandate requires the office maintain "the highest levels of integrity, impartiality, and confidentiality," so that witnesses are aware of their rights and entitlements. In 2010 as part of its "counseling and support" mission, the VWS sought to examine the impact of testifying in the post-testimonial phase, and it was as a result of this mission that the survey was developed.

The role of victims and witnesses in providing accountability and legitimacy for transitional justice in post-conflict situations has become increasingly more important in recent years (Findlay 2009), yet research about the

---

[3] In fact, there has been debate over the number of deaths from throughout the former Yugoslavia. Some list 140,000 and more (www.ictj.org/publication-type/fact-sheet), while others find higher or lower numbers, such as the Humanitarian Law Center (www.hlc-rdc.org/?cat=266&lang=de).

[4] As found at http://bit.ly/2gbICTY (September 12, 2016).

[5] As found at http://bit.ly/2fVICTY (September 12, 2016).

long-term impact of the testimonial process on those who actually testify has remained limited (Doak 2011b). Steadily, a variety of stakeholders including social scientists, psychologists, social workers, and law professionals have begun to empirically measure and assess witness well-being. As the ICTY draws into its final phase, examining the testimonial process and the impact on its constituents is also important to fully understand the ICTY's legacy (Arzt 2006; Elcheroth and Spini 2009; Ford 2012; Hagan and Ivkovic 2006; Meernik 2014; Meernik and Guerrero 2014; Meernik and King 2013).

DEVELOPMENT OF THE SURVEY

During the year-long process of developing the survey, all VWS personnel (employed at that time) participated in multiple focus groups to provide insight into the witness experience. Sixteen videoconference calls and meetings took place between the VWS (The Hague), the VWS Sarajevo Field Office (SFO), and UNT (Denton, Texas) to develop the survey (January–December 2012). The team included 19 VWS members (The Hague), 3 members from the SFO, and 7 faculty members and graduate students in the UNT Departments of Political Science and Psychology. Protocols for survey administration, witness contact, outreach, and security were developed based on field research best practices and ICTY historical experiences.

From the inception of the project, UNT consulted with and eventually received approval through its Institutional Review Board (IRB) to ensure the survey complied with national and international standards.[6] The survey and all documents needed for implementation were submitted through the ICTY Conference Language Services Section (CLSS) for official translation into Bosnian-Croatian-Serbian (BCS) (January–May 2013) and into Albanian (November 2014). All items on the survey instrument were reviewed independently by the VWS Hague office, the CLSS translation unit, the VWS SFO offices, and UNT to ensure that the instrument's language, terminology, and measurement structure were all aligned to reflect the witness experiences. All language and terms used in the survey instrument, the protocols, and the consent form were designed to be read by witnesses who had at least an eighth-grade education as was required by the IRB.

The VWS maintains a database for daily operations that tracks information on all individuals who have received VWS's services, and these data are

---

[6] IRB 13200-R15 approved March 2013 and annually renewed. Currently in effect from April 2015 until May 2016 – on file with the University of North Texas along with National Institute for Humanities Human Subject Training certificates for all VWS and UNT personnel.

linked to other ICTY witness records management systems that populate important witness information driven by judicial decisions (e.g., protective measures, subpoenas, safe conduct, etc.). Thus, the VWS database provides a rich depository of witness information. VWS, through this extensive database, produced an anonymized witness list that allowed UNT to filter and identify an eligible pool of potential respondents. From these data, random and quota samples were drawn for those in the region (Bosnia and Herzegovina, Croatia, Serbia, and Kosovo) for VWS to begin initiating contact. Support and dependent persons (family, friends) who accompany witnesses and do not testify were excluded as were expert witnesses (those with knowledge about military doctrine, forensic science, population demographics, and other topics). We did not include those living outside of the former Yugoslavia in order to focus on those still living in the post-conflict region. Witnesses from the last four ICTY trials (Ratko Mladić, Radovan Karadžić, Vojislav Šešelj, and Goran Hadžić) were excluded to prevent interference with ongoing trials. Finally, for practical reasons, those who testified from 1994 to 1998 were mostly excluded because all contacts from this period were maintained by the local authorities in the former Yugoslavia, and as such their contact details are unknown to the VWS.

UNT generated first a quota sample for country, gender, and side appearing (OTP, Defence, or Chambers), and then relied on random sampling to yield a survey population to resemble the characteristics of the target population of witnesses from the former Yugoslavia. Lists of witness identification numbers were sent to the ICTY VWS to make contact. This process continued throughout the survey administration as we worked to ensure our sample characteristics matched the characteristics of all witnesses in the ICTY database.

The focus of the study predicated that certain types of witness be contacted – namely the general fact witnesses population – while other types of witnesses were excluded. The study also sought to protect vulnerable or at-risk populations from potential exposure to risk that might result if they were to participate in the survey. Witnesses were eligible for inclusion if they testified from 1999 or later and if they physically appeared before the ICTY or testified via videoconference link from a remote location in at least one trial. Witnesses were *not* eligible if they: (1) had been accused or convicted of crimes (defendants); (2) were high-level politicians or other high-level officials; (3) were current or former ICTY staff; (4) had security issues (the Protection Unit reviewed all files); (5) had a legal matter pending before the ICTY; or (6) had concerns about their well-being because of ongoing physical and psychological health issues. Exclusion was the result of a holistic review of the individual witness case by VWS staff consistent with their mandate of post-testimonial care while

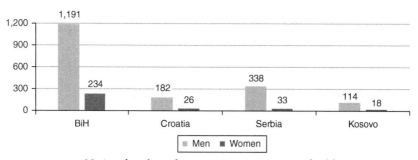

FIGURE 1.1. National and gender representation among eligible witnesses.

being cognizant of the need for a scientific selection of the sample population. In total, 61 witnesses from the UNT sampling list were excluded because of the foregoing reasons.

The final number of eligible witnesses in the region is 2,136 (Figure 1.1). Ensuring adequate gender representation was critical because war tends to be men's work, and thus the ICTY witness populations reflect a predominantly male set of witnesses. Eligible women from the region range from less than 9% in Serbia to more than 16% in Bosnia and Herzegovina. Target goals of 80% male to 20% female were used, which oversampled the number of women because their eligible numbers were lower (approximately 13% of *all* ICTY witnesses were female).[7] VWS focus groups voiced concerns that women might be less likely to participate because of both cultural and societal constraints on women regarding appearing before the Tribunal. This meant that the attempt was made to contact the vast majority of females from Croatia, Serbia, and Kosovo (Bosnia and Herzegovina had larger numbers of women testify).

The Recruitment Process

Concern for witness security, safety, and most importantly well-being necessitated that only VWS personnel could administer the surveys, which were all conducted on the territory of the former Yugoslavia. At no time did any survey personnel from outside the ICTY ever know the identities of these individuals or have contact information. VWS social workers who could respond effectively if the survey or interview process created any emotional or other difficulties for the witnesses were trained in survey techniques and administered

[7] As found at www.icty.org/en/about/registry/witnesses/statistics.

the surveys over a two-year period. Additionally, the post-testimonial survey offered many the opportunity to raise questions they had or address outstanding issues that might still have remained (getting specific documents, seeking additional support mechanisms, etc.). These safeguards ultimately resulted in a lengthy, but safe survey process that put the interests of the witnesses as paramount. VWS staff received training on presenting information about the study in a secure and sensitive way to victim witnesses who may have been out of contact with the ICTY for years. Operational guidelines were prepared and videoconferences were organized with the SFO Project Coordinator, resulting in a "recruitment script" and "operational instructions" for tracking data, and protocols for making referrals, answering questions, and sharing information.

After an initial phone call explaining the survey goals (following protocols to protect witness security and confidentiality), a second phone call was made if witnesses needed time to think about participation and to consult with other persons. If witnesses confirmed their participation, the VWS arranged for a meeting at a location selected by the witnesses where they felt comfortable and secure. Witnesses *could refuse to do the survey at any point in the process, including after arrival at the location for the interview and even if the survey had been started.*[8]

The first recruitment calls began in July 2013 by two to three staff members in The Hague and Sarajevo offices, and over time (March–December 2014), 14 Hague staff members were involved with recruitment calls on a daily basis. To reach a pool of 300 eligible persons, staff contacted approximately 1,200 witnesses seeking participation. Figure 1.2 provides information on the outcomes of the recruitment calls.

Accessibility of witnesses is a challenge whenever one is seeking to reach people in war torn countries. We found that 38.4% of witnesses had outdated contact details and 4.7% of calls resulted in no one ever answering after multiple attempts. Sadly, approximately 4% of the witnesses (43) had passed away in the intervening years (over 15 years for some witnesses). VWS used multiple efforts to obtain up-to-date contact information by checking all available open

---

[8] Five witnesses terminated interviews after arrival at the rendezvous point and before the survey began. One witness interview was terminated after 20 minutes because of VWS staff concerns regarding witness fragility. Referral materials were provided, along with VWS follow-up to ensure witness well-being. Two witnesses refused to complete the interview due to their disappointment with the Tribunal. Two witnesses did not want to sign the Informed Consent form before starting, and therefore could not be interviewed under IRB regulations. Two witness surveys were excluded after the interviews were completed as the witnesses were unexpectedly called to appear in an ongoing trial, and the MOU with the ICTY required that all information from witnesses in current trials be excluded from results.

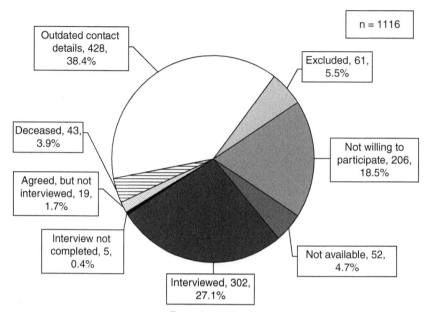

FIGURE 1.2. Recruitment process outcome.

sources for those *without* in-court protective measures. For those *with* in-court protective measures, security protocols mandated the use of only internal sources (OTP was consulted to see if they had updated contact details).

Phone calls from the ICTY may produce some apprehension among witnesses who may not have been in contact for years, and hence it was necessary to provide appropriate reassurances. Using established ICTY protocols for contacting witnesses, the VWS staff immediately informed and reassured witnesses that the reason for VWS contact was not related to court appearances, but rather concerned optional participation in the survey to provide feedback to the ICTY about their experiences. Some witnesses needed several calls to have time to think, or to consult with family, lawyers, or others, before deciding whether they wanted to participate in the study. Other witnesses found it difficult to refuse participation out of a long tradition of loyal cooperation with the Tribunal, and kept postponing their final answer. VWS staff consistently maintained during the recruitment process that this was voluntary with no legal obligation or consequences for refusal. VWS personnel let witnesses know that the ICTY was seeking to find out how they were doing and allow them the opportunity to provide constructive criticism about their experiences. The VWS, at all times, empowered witnesses to make a decision that was in *their* best interests while also being sure that if witness fragility was a concern the witness received follow-up. These multiple calls slowed the pace of the recruitment, but highlight the importance of adopting a witness-centered approach that focuses on witness well-being as its first priority.

Overall, Figure 1.2 illustrates that the survey had high response rates. When considering the responses of just those individuals the VWS was able to speak to (that is, excluding those who were deceased, those for whom contact information was incorrect, and those who were excluded for other reasons before any contact was made), the cooperation rate was approximately 55% (comparing those who accepted to those who refused to participate). Conversations during the recruitment calls lasted from a few minutes to half an hour, depending on the witnesses' needs. The reactions from witnesses ranged from gratitude for the renewed contact and for the opportunity to participate in the research, to others who were less positive about the survey. Among those witnesses who chose not to take the survey, most mentioned psychological or physical health reasons, while others expressed dissatisfaction with the ICTY. Reasons for refusal were recorded as shown in Figure 1.3. Altogether, 206 former witnesses refused to participate.

Witness responses to being contacted varied widely. Health, stress, and a busy schedule were among the top reasons for refusal. Approximately 19.7% gave no reason for declining, and there were five calls that ended abruptly (coded as "no answer" given). A number of interviewees expressed dissatisfaction with some aspect of the Tribunal – 17.7% did not wish to be contacted again; did not want to associate with or trust the ICTY; were disillusioned with the ICTY; or were unhappy with OTP, Defence, or Chambers. Security concerns were raised by 5% of contacts. Many witnesses requested more general information in writing and were provided with the study information leaflet *The Echoes of Witnesses and Testimonies* (a majority of recruits agreed to participate after reading it). A large number of witnesses were elderly, and indicated their willingness to participate, but for mobility reasons asked if they could be visited at home.

While there was a script for recruitment calls, for a number of witnesses, this sudden, renewed contact was a welcome opportunity to share other concerns and questions, to seek additional assistance, or to inquire about an ICTY staff member whom they remembered fondly. For some witnesses, the ICTY seemed to have a reputation as a powerful, international institution, and therefore some believed they could be assisted in one way or another in their current situation. These requests were related mostly to their economic situation, like unsolved property matters, housing, unemployment, or other various benefits that do not fall under the mandate of the Tribunal. Where

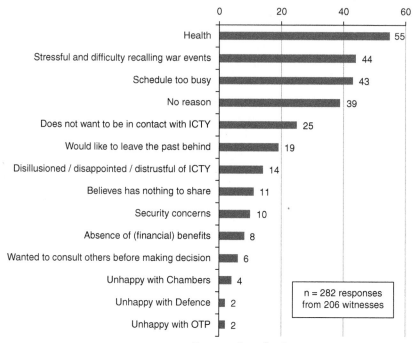

FIGURE 1.3. Reasons for refusal.

possible, the VWS referred witnesses to the relevant group or organization that could help resolve the request or provided assistance in navigating requests for information from the ICTY.

In view of the VWS Policy on Privacy and Confidentiality, only qualified VWS staff were eligible to conduct interviews. Only VWS staff with a relevant professional background were selected to conduct the in-person interviews so that prompt intervention could occur if a witness became emotionally and/or physically distressed.[9] The VWS has access to a range of personal information about victims and witnesses that might not be available to others within the Tribunal or even others in the witness's life. This information includes details on psychological or physical health or other personal matters affecting families and friends. Witnesses disclose this information with their trust and confidence knowing it will be respected by VWS staff. Because of this privileged position in the lives of witnesses, it is incumbent upon the VWS to demonstrate the highest possible standards of confidentiality and privacy in relation to the handling of information.

[9]   All four interviewers have backgrounds in psychology or social work.

Particular attention was paid to witnesses who were granted in-court protective measures during trial.[10]

Failure to adhere to high standards might have compromised the witnesses' privacy and security, and could also affect the operations of other ICTY functions (witnesses may refuse to cooperate with ICTY/MICT (Mechanism for International Criminal Tribunals) in the future if they do not feel their privacy is protected). Thus, only trained VWS personnel have direct access to witnesses' personal data (e.g., address, phone numbers, and personal history). Throughout the study the VWS ensured that UNT was not privy to any confidential and/or identifying witness information.

Locations of interviews ranged from urban centers to very remote rural areas. In order to include witnesses of all profiles, the VWS staff travelled extensively throughout Bosnia and Herzegovina, Croatia, Serbia, and Kosovo. This enabled the interviewer to gain important information on the witness environment and living conditions. Each interview was conducted at the witness place of residence or any other place participants deemed appropriate to meet. Sometimes witnesses did not wish to be seen with ICTY officers publicly, or they did not wish their family to know that they had testified. The VWS accommodated witnesses' requests by ensuring appropriate locations and safe environments for each interview. Consequently, interviews were completed in public venues (restaurants, hotels, café bars) as well as in private spaces (witness workplaces or homes) or UN field offices. Some witnesses could only be met at their home due to their distance from residential areas, age, health issues, or psychological fragility. This witness-centered practice also ensured a proper environment where witnesses felt they could express themselves freely, and it facilitated the smooth completion of the interview.

The Interview

During each in-person meeting, interviewers compiled an interview diary noting down technical problems (questionnaire wording, recording problems, etc.) as well as any behavioral or emotional reactions that the interview might have triggered. A statistical analysis of all interview diaries shows that participants were mostly positive and willing to contribute to the study.

One key goal of the study was to provide witnesses with an opportunity for some type of closure in their relationship to the ICTY. In addition to collecting

---

[10] Witnesses who received protective measures pursuant to Rule 75 of the ICTY Rules of Procedure and Evidence were scrutinized closely to ensure the survey did not present a risk (http://bit.ly/2gZICTY).

qualitative data on the testimony impact, VWS interviewers also facilitated reflection on the testimony experience and provided an opportunity for witnesses to express their views and feelings. Adapting the process to address witnesses' needs, health, and security was paramount. Each interview occurred in a context unique to that witness, determined by their personal histories, local and cultural traditions, gender sensitivity, as well as current economic and political situations. Each case file was reviewed before witnesses were met so that they would be approached respectfully and with understanding.

Interviewers were trained on how to help the interviewee understand the questionnaire (so as not to influence witness answers) and how to proceed during the recording of open-ended questions. When witnesses expressed specific reactions to the interview, the interviewer allowed for a more free dialogue. Therefore, the total time needed to complete an interview varied from 40 minutes up to 4.5 hours. As originally envisioned the survey was only to have taken approximately 75–90 minutes. There were some difficulties involved in completing the interview because of witness literacy, health and dexterity with writing, and reactions to the survey. Because the recalling of traumatic events can trigger emotional and physical reactions, it was agreed that interviews could be terminated at any moment if it was not in the best interest or welfare of the witness.

To better assess witness well-being during the interview process, interviewers monitored witness behavior and emotions throughout the process and coded witness reactions and temperament. Figure 1.4 reveals the diverse array of witness behaviors during the interview process. Witnesses experienced a variety of emotions as a result of the interview process, including both positive and negative emotions triggered by particular questions (n=95). While a number of witnesses were talkative (n=77), many were more businesslike in their approach (n=23), this was not a universal experience. The survey triggered emotions in 96 witnesses (including disappointment, crying, anger, agitation, frustration, and nervousness). A number changed behaviors during the interview (n=40), and some witnesses experienced physical reactions (n=31).

After the Interview

Generally, all emotional reactions that emerged during the interviews were dealt with and handled on-site. As per VWS protocol, witnesses who made requests that did not fall under the VWS mandate were referred to local institutions and organizations. Reasons for referral were not rooted in the

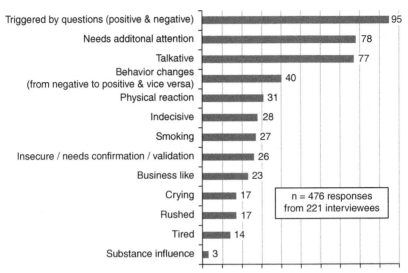

FIGURE 1.4. Interviewee behavior during the interview process.

interview itself, but generally came from unresolved war-related issues that witnesses were dealing with (trauma consequences, property issues, legal matters, etc.). After the interview 6 witnesses were referred to local non-governmental organizations (NGOs) for psychological assistance in regard to their war trauma; 12 were referred to relevant organizations for legal assistance (e.g., to establish their status as civilian victims of war, to initiate a legal lawsuit for compensation, or to sort out property issues); 7 witnesses requested a video recording of their testimony; and 12 requested other documents related to their court appearance. Thus, there are a small, but critical number of witnesses interviewed who are still facing issues in the post-conflict and post-testimonial phase for whom the ICTY was able to provide assistance.

After each interview, VWS interviewers reviewed and redacted any sensitive information on each survey related to the identity of the witnesses. Each audio track was transcribed and reviewed by two different persons, and revised transcriptions were sent to the ICTY CLSS for official English translation. Thirty-four witnesses did not want to be recorded during the final three open-ended questions.[11] In some cases witnesses requested and were given the possibility to answer in written form to the open-ended questions (n=7).

---

[11]   There were 15 in Bosnia-Herzegovina, 4 in Croatia, 10 in Serbia, and 5 in Kosovo.

Selection Effects

One important issue regarding the survey population is the possibility that more emotionally and physically resilient individuals participated in the survey than those who are in the larger witness population. Recall that health and emotional distress were the top two reasons witnesses gave for refusing to participate in the study. It is certainly possible that there may be some type of selection bias occurring, with more healthy witnesses being more likely to take part in the administration of surveys such as this. It may also be possible that those individuals who were most satisfied with the ICTY were more likely to take the survey, while those witnesses who had more critical opinions did not wish to be bothered by Tribunal personnel and refused to take the survey. Our sample may include an emotionally and physically healthy population of individuals who are more likely to have positive views of the ICTY than the actual witness population. Where possible, we compare our survey results on some key items to another survey the VWS has been administering to all witnesses, which should help alleviate concerns regarding selection bias (see Heckman 1976).

In 2009 the VWS began implementing a completely anonymous survey that is administered to all witnesses after they have testified and before they leave The Hague. This survey, while limited in its scope and intended for VWS internal use, used multiple measures to ask witnesses about their experiences with the overall logistical and psychosocial support provided by the VWS. This internal survey can be used to compare with our larger survey project. Therefore, we believe it is possible to address potential biases, which can better help us understand the interviewee population.

We also acknowledge another issue the reader should consider as one digests our findings. With the exception of information on the trials in which the witnesses testified, our survey taps into the witnesses' memories and opinions. We cannot guarantee that these recollections are always accurate or that witnesses are truthfully recalling their experiences and emotions. Indeed, many are commenting on events and experiences that have taken place more than a decade before the survey was administered. We caution the reader that while these data may not be perfect, they represent the best possible accumulation of knowledge about the ICTY witness experience.

In addition, there are issues associated with endogeneity in our analyses as we seek to understand the relationships that exist among the many variables our survey covers. Many opinions and recollections may not be fully independent attitudes and thus cluster together. For that reason, we try to avoid as much as possible analyzing these data in terms of causality. We approach the

TABLE 1.1. *Witness sampling goals and interviewees surveyed*

	BiH	Croatia	Kosovo	Serbia
% ICTY witnesses	62%	15.60%	8.30%	14.20%
% study interviewee goal	50%	20%	10%	20%
% interviewees (total number)	54.3% (n=163)	20.7% (n=62)	8.3% (n=25)	16.3% (n=49)

data analysis with an abundance of caution, and with the hope that whatever the nature of these relationships – correlative, causal, or something else – we have much to learn from the witnesses about what testifying has meant to them. It is a fundamental tenet of our research that the witness experience matters, and that practitioners, activists, and scholars must begin to systematically include witness voices in our understanding of the impact tribunals and all transitional justice mechanisms.

THE STUDY POPULATION

Who are the witnesses who agreed to participate and were surveyed? They are a diverse group of individuals from all parts of the former Yugoslavia who have given their time[12] and energy to provide invaluable feedback about their experiences, concerns, and insight into what it has meant to testify before a war crimes tribunal and the impact it has had in their lives. We begin by exploring key demographic characteristics

The VWS and UNT, relying on VWS statistics, evaluated and set target numbers for the sampling process to ensure that adequate numbers of persons (including women) from different parts of the former Yugoslavia would be included in the study. The target goals are listed in Table 1.1 – with the percentage of witnesses eligible from each geographic area in the top row and the percent target goal in the second row. The last row summarizes actual number of witnesses surveyed for the study. The majority of surveys (54.3% or 163) took place in Bosnia and Herzegovina, followed by Croatia (20.7% or 62 interviews), Serbia (16.3% or 49 interviews), and Kosovo (8.3% or 25 interviews).

One of the more important goals of the sampling process was to ensure a broad geographic representation of witnesses across the region. As the results

---

[12] Total time for all interviews – 532.1 hours: 300.5 hours with witnesses in Bosnia; 81.1 hours in Croatia; 101.7 hours in Serbia; and 49 hours in Kosovo (average time of interview=1.8 hours – shortest=45 minutes and longest=4.5 hours).

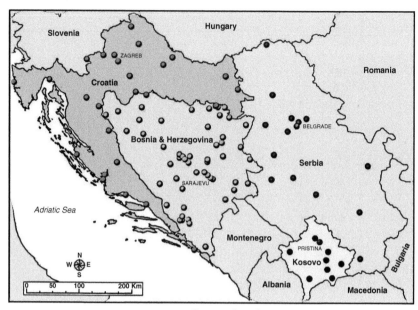

FIGURE 1.5. Geographic diversity.

from Figure 1.5 illustrate, there is also a diverse array of witnesses across the geographic target areas, including interviewees from urban and rural areas.[13] For purposes of providing comparisons to the broader population, we also examined witness educational attainment levels. More than 23% of respondents have a high school diploma (71), 100 individuals have a college degree, and 41 individuals indicate they have some form of advanced college degree (Figure 1.6).

It has been especially important to undertake this survey to reach a population of aging witnesses. Capturing what it means to "bear witness" is vital – especially for males.[14] The average age of the interviewees is 59.3 years old – with ages ranging from 28 to 94 years. There are significant differences with gender as women are, on average, seven years younger than men who

[13] Using the international standard of cities as those areas with 100,000 and more residents, 154 interviewees live in urban areas and 146 live in rural areas, smaller cities, and settlements. Looking at the 146 interviewees in the rural areas, we find that the breakdown of these is as follows: 24 in cities and settlements < 100,000, 54 in cities and settlements < 50,000, and 78 in cities and settlements < 25,000.

[14] Indeed, 4% of the witnesses that were reached for recruitment calls had passed away, while one witness passed after the recruitment call and before the scheduled interview.

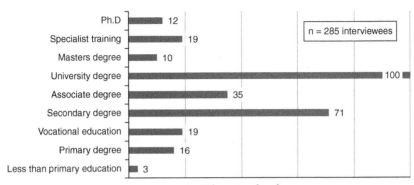

FIGURE 1.6. Education level.

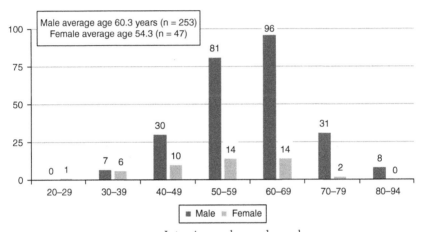

FIGURE 1.7. Interviewees by gender and age.

testify. There are also noticeably fewer women in the 60 years and more categories (Figure 1.7).

Women comprise approximately 13% of all the witnesses who have appeared at the Tribunal. As indicated earlier, women were sampled at higher rates (80% male and 20% female) than the overall eligible witness population (83% male and 17% female) to ensure adequate gender representation (Figure 1.8).[15] The sampling process produced a representative pool of respondents. While women constitute 16.4% of the eligible pool of witnesses in Bosnia and

[15] The percentage of eligible witnesses who are female is slightly higher than the percentage of witnesses who are female listed on the ICTY website because the overall witness population also contains other groups, such as expert witnesses, that we do not study.

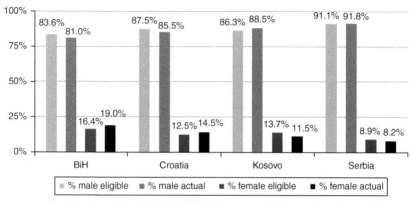

FIGURE 1.8. Gender ratio – eligible VWS witness population and study population.

Herzegovina, because we oversampled women, we have a slightly higher percentage of women in our sample population. A difference of means test reveals no significant differences between any of the gender eligible and the gender actual pools from any geographic area.

In recognition that witnesses might not want to identify their ethnic and religious affiliation, respondents were provided with the option to give their ethnic and religious identities or to choose not to provide any information (Figure 1.9). These self-identified responses reveal an ethnically diverse sample of persons, with 81 individuals (27%) describing themselves as Croat; 78 persons (27%) indicating they were Bosniak; 95 persons (31.7%) identifying as Serb; 25 persons (9%) identifying as Albanian; and a handful of others, including Macedonian (n=2), Croat-Bosniak (n=1), and "Earthling" (n=1), also recorded. Figure 1.9 provides the breakdown, and we note that more than 6% of the respondents chose not to respond and one interviewee identified as dual ethnicity.

As with ethnicity, the sample includes a diverse array of religious affiliations among the witnesses (Figure 1.10). There are 70 Catholics (23%), 92 Muslims (31%), and 82 Orthodox (28%), while the remainder are Atheists (9 or 3%) and Agnostics (4 or 1%).

Interviewees and ICTY Trials

Witness respondents have appeared across all the years of the Tribunal's history. Even though we did not have contact information for persons who testified from 1994 to 1998, we were able to survey some of the witnesses who testified in those years if they also testified in later trials. The interviewees have

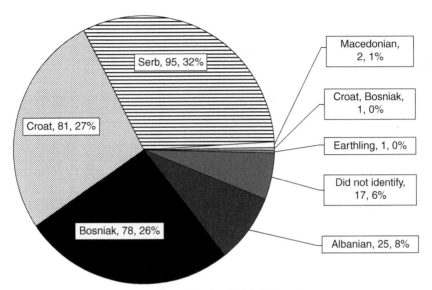

FIGURE 1.9. Ethnic self-identification.

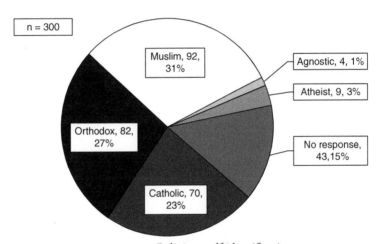

FIGURE 1.10. Religious self-identification.

come from across the life cycle of the Tribunal, from almost the beginning until 2012, although a majority testified between 2000 and 2009 (Figure 1.11).

There are multiple ways to analyze witness participation in the trials (Figures 1.12). Witnesses may testify more than once in any given trial, or testify multiple times in multiple trials, and indeed may appear for one or more of the calling parties (OTP, Defence, or Chambers) in the same or different trials. Regardless of how it is measured, the sample represents a vast range of

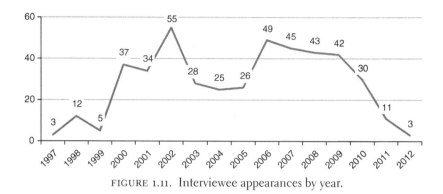

FIGURE 1.11. Interviewee appearances by year.

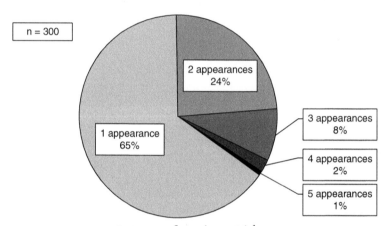

FIGURE 1.12. Interviewee trial appearances.

experiences through time, across all trials, trial types, and defendants. The 300 respondents have appeared 448 times (20 of those have appeared twice in the same trial).[16]

The overall picture that emerges from the interviewee profiles is that the appearances by witnesses are representative of the Tribunal's work as a whole for the time period being examined (Table 1.2). Approximately two-thirds have appeared on behalf of OTP, with the remaining one-third appearing for Defence. Uniquely, there have been 45 appearances by 17 witnesses who have appeared for both the OTP and Defence. Four Chambers witnesses also

---

[16] Note that "Witness Appearances," "OTP Appearances," and "Defence Appearances" do not add up to the total number of respondents because witnesses can testify multiple times for different sides (OTP, Defence, Chambers), or testify on the same side in the same case more than one time. The 20 witnesses who appeared twice in a trial appeared across a number of trials.

TABLE 1.2. *Survey respondents – by the numbers*

Total interviewees as *both* fact and expert witness	3
Total interviewees with written testimony (not viva voce testimony)	7
Interviewees appearing in two roles (OTP, Defence, & Chambers)	45
Number of different trials	41
Number of total defendants	90
Total Chambers appearances (all also appeared for OTP)	4
Total Defence appearances	151
Total OTP appearances	293
Interviewees appearing only once	195
Interviewees appearing 1+ times	105
Number of interviewees	300
Total interviewee appearances in unique trials	427
Total interviewee appearances (includes same trial more than once)	448

appeared for OTP. Approximately two-thirds of the witnesses have appeared only once to testify (n=195), with about one-fourth having appeared two times and 11% having appeared three or more times (Table 1.2).

Finally, we surveyed witnesses from a wide range of trials (Figure 1.13). We note that there were some limitations because of the necessity of excluding witnesses from trials that were still in progress at the time of the study. Figure 1.13 breaks down interviewees by trial and the side for which the individual testified – OTP, Defence, or Chambers. As is to be expected, larger, more complex trials with a higher volume of witnesses have greater representation. The Kordić and Čerkez, Milutinović et al., Popović et al., Prlić et al., and Slobodan Milošević trials utilized between 240 and 350 witnesses, while earlier trials like Dokmanović, Aleksovski, Jelisić, Sikirica et al., and Kunarac et al. had lower numbers of witnesses called (approximately 40 to 70 witnesses total in each of the trials). To compare witness representation by percentages, we have also provided data about the total number of interviewees that participated in each trial (Figure 1.14).

CONCLUSION

The witness survey project was designed to provide a witness-centered and critical analysis regarding the impact of testifying for one of the most vital stakeholders of a tribunal – its witnesses. The survey and interviews were conducted by VWS personnel who have extensive experience and training in psychology and social work as well as more than 55 years of combined experience

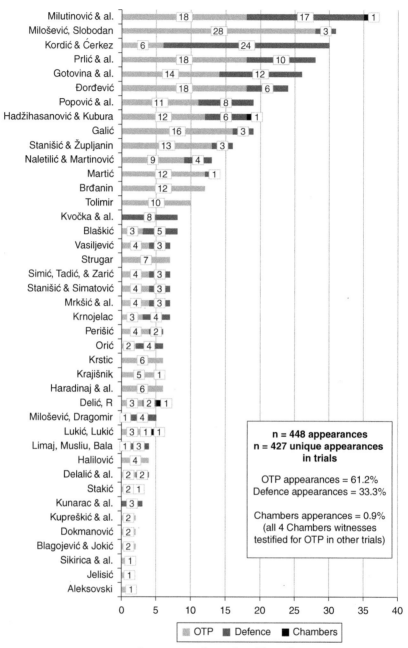

FIGURE 1.13. Interviewees by trial and by calling party.

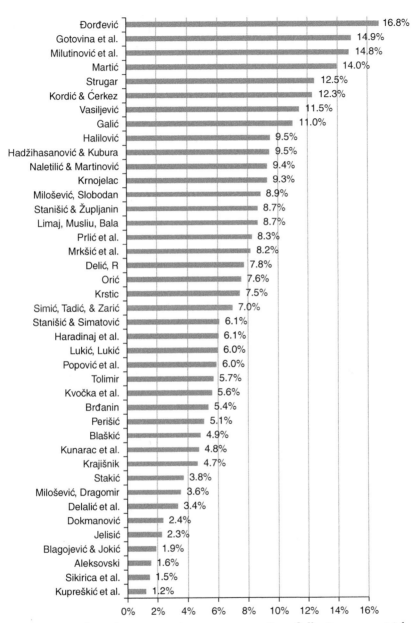

FIGURE 1.14. Interviewee appearances as a proportion of all witnesses per trial.

at the ICTY. Thus, the highest ethic of care was provided to witnesses while protecting witness identity. The VWS also protected the anonymity of interviewee responses to reassure witnesses that their feedback was confidential by relying on anonymous codes that cannot be linked by the UNT researchers to witnesses' identity.

This is the first time in the history of international justice that a war crimes tribunal has contributed to systematic and scientific research into the long-term impact of testimony in different areas of witnesses' lives, while providing witnesses with an opportunity for closure and feedback. This project enables the ICTY and other transitional justice mechanisms to assess more fully the post-testimony needs of witnesses and to develop best practices in witness management, care, and well-being. This project also contributes toward a better and more informed understanding of the legacy of the ICTY.

The theoretical dimensions and contributions of this project are equally important. The survey was designed to help address some of the most critical debates in psychology, sociology, criminology, and political science regarding the impact of testimony on witnesses and how the witness experience informs their views on a range of subjects from their own personal encounter with the ICTY to their views on reconciliation and international justice. We use the theoretical foci of ethnicity, gender, and experience to gain leverage on these theoretical questions and provide scholars of post-conflict studies and transitional justice research with insights into a unique population. Our plan for this book is as follows.

Chapter 2: Gender, Ethnicity, and Wartime Trauma

We begin by reviewing what we know about the witnesses and their gender, ethnicity, and wartime traumas. This chapter presents both basic descriptive statistics about these three characteristics of the witnesses, as well as analyses of the degree and type of overlap among the three parameters. We also explore related topics such as whether witnesses are ethnic minorities in their communities and whether they or their close family members are married to individuals from another ethnic group.

Chapter 3: Personal Views of Testifying and the Witness Encounter with International Justice

This chapter concerns the witnesses' own personal views on the judicial process and their motivations for testifying. We examine why witnesses testify as well as their perceptions of their treatment by the ICTY, including satisfaction with their testimony. Other research has found that witnesses at tribunals tend to be more positive and satisfied about their personal reasons for testifying (Horn et al. 2009b; Stepakoff et al. 2014; Stover 2005, 2014), but this project represents the first time that there has ever been a systematic attempt to link personal satisfaction and motivation to other types of indicators to empirically evaluate what it means to witnesses to testify, given their identity and their experiences. One of the most interesting findings that emerges is that witnesses are largely pleased with their performance in court, especially given the reasons they cite for being important motivators for testifying. Moreover, witnesses note that they believe they personally have been treated quite well by the ICTY. As well, those witnesses who suffered the most during the wars of the former Yugoslavia tend to report the highest levels of satisfaction with their performance, which also supports the emerging research findings on the positive impact of war on attitudes and social engagement.

Chapter 4: Social, Economic, and Security Consequences of Testifying

Chapter 4 concerns the consequences witnesses face as a result of being called to testify and after they return home following their testimony. The act of testifying before the ICTY can pose human security risks for witnesses, and these effects have social, moral, and political dimensions for the VWS, for the ICTY, and most especially for those who experience threats to their socio-economic and physical safety. This chapter examines the scope and severity of social, economic, and security concerns that result from testifying. While a substantial majority of interviewees did not experience personal, economic, or security harm as a result of their testimony, there is a significant, important group of witnesses who endured negative consequences in their lives as a result of their affiliation with the ICTY. These negative effects range from criticism and loss of association, to economic consequences through loss of income or property, to threats to their physical safety. While a substantial majority of witnesses report feeling secure today, a smaller, but critical number of witnesses report continuing to perceive threats to their economic and physical well-being.

Chapter 5: Physical and Psychological Consequences of Testifying

In Chapter 5 we engage the theoretical debate regarding the physical and psychological consequences of testifying. Witnesses are typically called to testify about their war-related experiences, and the results here show that 99% of the interviewees survived a broad range of trauma including shelling,

combat situations, murder and disappearance of loved ones, torture, detention, extreme deprivation of food and shelter, and the destruction of homes
and communities. In particular, we examine two questions of critical theoretical importance in the field of transitional justice. The first concerns whether
those who appear before legal venues are helped or harmed because of recalling horrific events (Doak 2011b; Brounéus 2010; Stover 2005). Does legal intervention exacerbate the fragile status of the witness or victim (Bandes 2009: 13;
Herman 2003; Henry 2009)? Does the testimonial process do more harm
than good to the emotional state of those who testify? Some have argued that
testifying can provide healing, closure, or a catharsis to help overcome traumatic events (Moghalu 2004: 216; Stover 2005). Others argue that evidence
is limited and questionable when it comes to the impact on victims (Bandes
2009: 16), and that this is particularly true for the ICTY witnesses (Clark
2009c, 2014). The reality is, however, that little is known about "the individual psychological and emotional effects of national truth-telling and accountability mechanisms, or about victims' experiences with criminal justice more
broadly" (Mendeloff 2009: 596). Empirical research into this critical component of the testimonial process is just now emerging (Stepakoff et al. 2014,
2015; Doak 2011b; Mendeloff 2009). The second issue concerns witnesses'
opinions about interpersonal relations in their community. While the ICTY
was not charged with promoting reconciliation in the former Yugoslavia, the
Tribunal is intended to help ensure peace and security, which may well hinge
on the degree to which formerly warring parties can resolve their differences.
Thus, we also investigate which factors are associated with witnesses' attitudes
regarding interpersonal relations and reconciliation (Clark 2014; Meernik and
Guerrero 2014; Meernik et al. 2016).

Chapter 6: Perceptions of Justice and the Impact of the ICTY

This final analytical chapter seeks to answer some of the most difficult and
contentious issues presented regarding the role of tribunals and what they
contribute to post-conflict societies. The purpose of this chapter is to analyze
witness perceptions of the impact of the ICTY in realizing the broad goals
of its mandate to provide truth, accountability, punishment, and deterrence
of future war crimes. There has been no shortage of studies that use different measures regarding public opinion and support for the work of international tribunals and national courts (Ivković and Hagan 2015, 2016; Arzt 2006;
Elcheroth and Spini 2009; Ford 2012; Meernik 2015a; Meernik and King 2013;
Saxon 2005). This chapter is unique in terms of linking both identity (ethnicity and gender) as well as experience to views about transitional justice,

the role of national courts, and whether the ICTY has treated witnesses and defendants fairly. We make several important findings in this chapter that both confirm and challenge perspectives on the Tribunal's legacy.

First, our findings reveal that such broad measures of support for international justice should be broken down into their constituent elements as witness perceptions of international justice differ depending on what aspect of the tribunal's mission is being evaluated. We do not rely on broad measures of assessment about the ICTY, but instead dig deeper into different dimensions to specifically analyze the different components of the ICTY's goals. Witnesses do not generally treat these goals – establishing truth; determining responsibility; meting out punishment; and advancing deterrence – as an undifferentiated whole. Rather, they discern critical differences in how the ICTY has approached and advanced these goals and adjust their evaluations accordingly. The deterrence mission tends to attract the most support, while the witnesses give the ICTY the lowest marks for its performance in sentencing the guilty (especially those who have pled guilty for sentencing). We also find that there are two factors that stand out above all of the other influences on witness perceptions of international justice – ethnicity and efficacy. Consistent with other research, not only does ethnicity exercise a direct impact on witness perceptions of the ICTY's effectiveness – Bosniaks are more likely to support the ICTY and Serbs are more likely to not support the ICTY across most dimensions – it is also highly correlated with other determinants of ICTY support. Of special importance is our finding that the greater one's belief that one has contributed to the ICTY's mission of justice and truth, the more likely an individual is to support the ICTY. International justice is, in many respects, like domestic justice. Those who take part in it, and those who are affected by it, want to feel that they have made a difference in it. This in turn has an impact on how they evaluate whether the judicial body has accomplished its mandate.

Chapter 7: Conclusions

The concluding chapter seeks to comment on the importance of the findings both for scholarly research and for the work of other international and national tribunals. We specifically compare and contrast findings from other emerging research to suggest a more comprehensive approach to understanding what it means to bear witness and why scholars need to think more broadly about the unique, complex, and varied testimonial experiences. We also offer recommendations based on the practical implications of this research and how the findings can inform approaches and methods of witness support at other tribunals. As we look to the future of tribunals and their contributions, witnesses will always be indispensable for international justice, and we suggest several ways to identify witnesses who are most at risk because of human security concerns (key for international justice) as well as strategies for dealing with witnesses who may be especially vulnerable psychologically and physically to the rigors of testifying. We conclude this final chapter by suggesting further avenues of research inquiry for both theory and practice.

2

Exploring the Gender, Ethnicity, and Trauma Characteristics of the Witness Sample

INTRODUCTION

As discussed in Chapter 1, the principal axes through which we seek to understand the opinions and experiences of the witnesses are gender, ethnicity, and the type as well as range of trauma experienced during the Balkan wars. These three characteristics are key issues in the ICTY jurisprudence; they have helped define the nature of the conflicts and the crimes committed in the former Yugoslavia; and they are an integral part of the witnesses' identities and the basis for their appearances on the witness stand. In this chapter, we take the reader through an exploration of how these characteristics help describe who the witnesses are, and we also analyze the extent to which there is overlap and other relationships among the three dimensions. For example, we find that wartime trauma is not evenly distributed across our witness sample, but varies in part based on witness ethnic identity and gender.

To better acquaint the reader with the witness sample we begin by providing a brief overview of witness characteristics along these three dimensions. Second, we explore in-depth how the nature and scope of trauma experienced by witnesses vary by gender and ethnicity. We conclude by assessing the utility of the three witness dimensions and how they can help us understand witness recollections, perceptions, and opinions.

GENDER, ETHNICITY, AND WARTIME EXPERIENCE: AN OVERVIEW

We begin by reviewing the key sample parameters of our witness database. Of the 300 ICTY fact witnesses in the sample, 253 are male witnesses (84.33%), while 47 are female witnesses (15.67%). Women were distinctly less likely to be called to testify by the ICTY, and our sample reflects this. Women comprise approximately 13% of all ICTY witnesses – a strikingly small sample of the witnesses who testify – and we note our sample size of 15.6% closely approximates their actual proportion. We sought to oversample women, given their low numbers and also because ICTY personnel indicated that women might be more reluctant and thus less likely to agree to be surveyed.

The wars in the former Yugoslavia were the direct result of partisan leadership advocating separatist autonomy for homogenous ethnic and religious groups, and in turn, this has consequences for post-conflict society and reconciliation (Clark 2014). In recognition that witnesses might not want to identify their ethnic and religious affiliations when surveyed, respondents had the option of providing their ethnic and religious identities or choosing not to provide any information. As is the case in multiple areas of the survey, witnesses were allowed to write in their responses to allow them to provide their self-perceived identity. The results indicated that 81 individuals (27%) described themselves as Croat; 78 persons (27%) said they were Bosniak; 95 persons (31.7%) identified as Serb; and 25 persons (8%) identified as Albanian. There were other witness-provided identities including Macedonian (n=2), Croat-Bosniak (n=1), and "Earthling" (n=1). Figure 2.1 provides the breakdown, and we note that 17 (5.7%) of the respondents chose not to respond (12 from Bosnia, 4 from Croatia, 1 from Kosovo, and none from Serbia).

Figure 2.2 provides the percentages and frequencies of ethnicity combined with information from witnesses' country of origin. For example, while Croats may have written on the survey they were "Croat," by looking to their national origin we can determine how many are Croats from Croatia and how many of these witnesses are from Bosnia. We can see that while Bosniaks are the largest single group, there are more Croats and Serbs when we consider those from Croatia and Serbia, respectively, as well as those from Bosnia.[1]

Figure 2.3 provides a breakdown of ethnicity by gender. We see that female witnesses are most likely to indicate they are Bosnian (21%) or Bosnian Serb (19%), or they either did not indicate an ethnic identity or listed another group (23%). In most of our graphs we distinguish among Bosniaks, Serbs, Bosnian Serbs, Croats, Bosnian Croats, Kosovar Albanians, and others, including those who did not choose to identify with an ethnic group. In our statistical analyses, we utilize five of these categories – we generally place Bosnian Croats in

---

[1] The reader will note that there are sometimes slightly smaller numbers of witnesses from ethnic groups from the various nations when compared to the number of people who claim a particular ethnicity. This is because some individuals, such as Serbs, do not reside in either of the nations with which they are usually associated, such as Bosnia or Serbia for the Serb witnesses (they may reside in Croatia or some other nation).

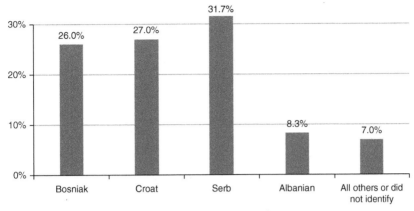

FIGURE 2.1. Ethnic self-identification.

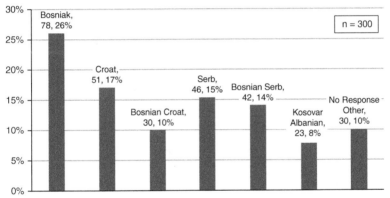

FIGURE 2.2. Ethnic identification among key ICTY nationalities.

the remainder category of "non-response and other" in order to have a more diverse reference category.

One of the more interesting findings from the respondent sample concerns the large numbers of persons who have mixed marriages in their immediate family, as well as the number of witnesses who are ethnic minorities where they live. The communities in the former Yugoslavia had varying rates of intermarriage among the various ethnicities, and rates of interethnic marriage differ depending on the ethnic group under inquiry (Smits 2010). Conventional wisdom is that intermarriage between ethnicities was rather common, but statistical analyses of data before the wars do not bear this out (Botev 1994). Perhaps this perception persists because of ethnic polarization or perceptions about how "other" identities are determined (Buric 2012). Interviewees were

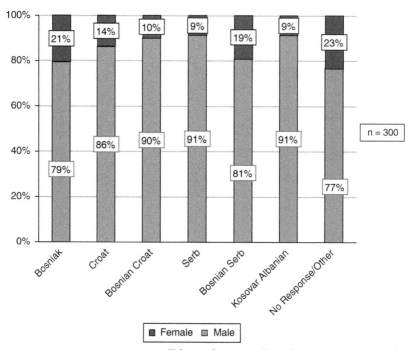

FIGURE 2.3. Ethnic identity and gender.

asked two questions regarding ethnic identity that may have some bearing on their testimonial perspective. The questions ask: (1) whether the witness is an ethnic or religious minority in the community where he or she lives; and (2) whether the witness is himself/herself in an ethnically mixed marriage or has an immediate family member (parents, intimate partners, siblings, or children) who is in an ethnically mixed marriage. Approximately 13% (n=39) of the respondents are ethnic minorities where they are living, and notably 39.3% (n=118) of respondents have immediate family members or are themselves in mixed ethnic marriages (Figure 2.4).[2] There is overlap between the

---

[2] The issue of minority status and "constituent peoples" is complex in the former Yugoslavia, particularly in Bosnia and Herzegovina, where the Constitution established following the Dayton Peace Accords provides structural representation based on ethnic identification. For this reason, some participants might refuse to identify as part of a minority if they are member of one of the constituent peoples, because such identification might "diminish" their importance. For more critical commentary regarding the impact this has had, see Minority Rights Group International (2003) and O'Brien (2010). Increasingly, persons in the region are resistant to traditional labels of identity that are based on national comparisons (see Grim et al. 2015 and Bieber 2015).

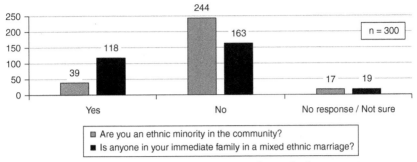

FIGURE 2.4. Ethnic/religious minorities and mixed ethnic marriages in the immediate family.

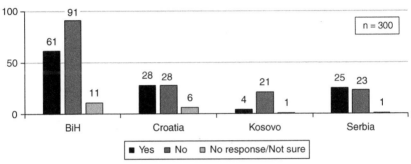

FIGURE 2.5. Mixed ethnic marriage in immediate family by geographic region.

two groups – 17 persons *both* are an ethnic minority in their community and have ethnically mixed marriages in their immediate family. Thus, 46.7% of the survey respondents are either an ethnic minority in their community or have a mixed ethnic marriage in their own or immediate family.

Most striking about the interviewees is the high number of interethnic marriage across the region (Figure 2.5). Notably, in both Croatia and Serbia, there are roughly equal numbers of survey respondents who have a mixed ethnic marriage in the immediate family. In Bosnia and Herzegovina, the numbers are quite high as well (61 persons). Other research has found that exogamous marriage (outside one's ethnic group) declined in the years 1990–2005, particularly in Croatia (Mrdjen 2010). The difference between our rates of intermarriage may be owing in part to generational differences (given the average age of the interviewees here). Indeed, we find significant correlations between older witnesses and mixed marriage (meaning that the older an interviewee is, the more likely they are to have someone from their immediate family in a mixed marriage). We note that our results are consistent with Mrdjen (2010) as they pertain to gender – female interviewees are less likely than their male counterparts to be in mixed marriages.

Witness Wartime Experience

It is important to understand the war experiences of the interviewees to understand the nature of the events they are called upon to describe at testimony. We discuss in Chapter 5 how the witnesses have been affected by these wartime traumas and the interaction between such experiences and the testimonial process. Such difficult events are likely to be pivotal in understanding the human security challenges faced by the witnesses as they exonerate or implicate those involved in these events, who in turn may seek to influence the desire and ability of witnesses to testify before the ICTY. We suspect that wartime trauma plays a substantial role in the emotional and physical health of witnesses, as well as the nature of their experiences on the witness stand as they are asked to recall these events and may even be challenged by aggressive attorneys. Finally, we expect that the quantity and quality of the wartime experiences will influence how witnesses perceive their own role in the testimonial process, as well as the effectiveness of the ICTY.

Here, we begin by describing the type and extent of the trauma these witnesses experienced during the war. As some witnesses have shared with the VWS, with the passage of time and the inclination of people around them to put the wartime events behind them, sharing their experiences of what happened during the conflicts in the former Yugoslavia is not always welcomed back home. Some have difficulties in articulating all they have seen, felt, or been through, or they simply may have chosen not to share their experiences as they do not want their loved ones to know what happened.

Once in The Hague, witnesses often used the opportunity to share their experiences and feelings with the VWS staff members or other witnesses after they felt it was safe and appropriate. As a number of VWS staff members recalled, witnesses' stories were diverse, ranging from memories of happier times to recollections of horrific events and the loss of loved ones for whom they still grieve. While recalling painful memories, some witnesses said they felt they were reliving the events, even going so far as to share that they were experiencing intense physical and emotional pain directly linked to injuries and experiences, including difficulty sleeping and eating. Some described how, even after the passage of many years, the memories and images became so clear that they felt as though they were real and happening in the present.

Others reported different types of stress, and yet others indicated they were not experiencing such problems.

The levels of war trauma endured by these witnesses are significant and substantial, as the data illustrate. Consistent with one of the largest studies to date in the region that examined wartime experiences,[3] the witnesses in this study have experienced extreme forms of physical and mental trauma. Interviewees were asked to indicate whether they had "Experienced"; "Witnessed"; "Heard stories"; or had no knowledge about multiple types of trauma that civilians and military personnel experienced during the armed conflict.[4] The results are divided into two figures: Figure 2.6 contains the number of responses of those who selected "Experienced" and/or "Witnessed," while Figure 2.7 contains the number of responses of those who chose either "Heard stories" or the final category of "None," which indicates that the witness did not experience, witness, or hear stories about the type of trauma present during the Yugoslav conflict. The results are ranked from highest to lowest for the "Experienced" and "Heard stories" categories, respectively.

Some wartime experiences are more prevalent than others among the study population, indicating common traumatic experiences across our respondents – more than 200 of the interviewees selected shelling, being close to death, and feeling as if their lives were in danger as common wartime experiences. Indeed, 78% of the witnesses indicated they experienced shelling. There were 185 interviewees who indicated they experienced combat situations, as well as a lack of food and water. In sum, the 300 interviewees reported they directly experienced a total of 2,876 events (of these, 2,813 were specifically asked about on the questionnaire, and the remaining events were described in short answers provided by the interviewees).

Figure 2.7 shows responses of those who either heard stories or knew nothing of these events. Notably, the frequencies in this figure are fewer than in Figure 2.6, indicating that interviewees were much more likely to have indicated they directly experienced or witnessed the violence and destruction of war. Nonetheless, there are still sizeable numbers who did not experience,

---

3   The South-East European Social Survey Project provides social survey data to study the sociology and social history of the Western Balkans. The survey, conducted by the Norwegian University of Science and Technology from 2003 to 2004, allows for basic analyses of overall cross-national and cross-ethnic group differences within the region, and contains information about 23,000 respondents with 1,000 variables and 32 different samples. Information was collected through a 75-minute survey instrument and interviews (http://bit.ly/2gNSEES).

4   The study relied on a modified version of the Harvard Trauma Questionnaire, which lists events or activities common in times of conflict (Palić et al. 2015). For more information see http://bit.ly/2grLHTQ. Witnesses could choose more than one option.

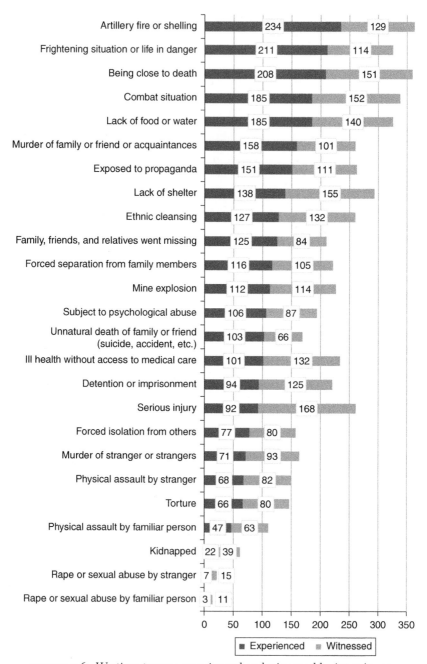

FIGURE 2.6. Wartime trauma experienced and witnessed by interviewees.

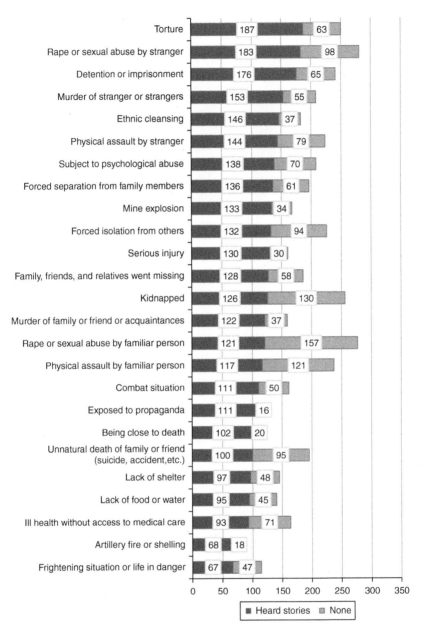

FIGURE 2.7. Knowledge of wartime experiences by interviewees.

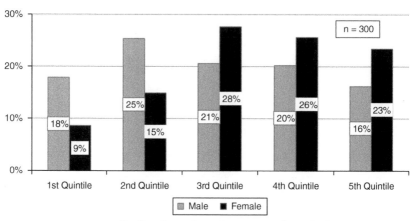

FIGURE 2.8. Gender and wartime trauma by quintiles.

witness, or even hear stories about common war events. For example, despite the prevalence of sexual assault during the wars in the former Yugoslavia and the attention accorded to these crimes by the ICTY as well as the media, 157 interviewees indicated they knew nothing of such crimes as committed by someone who was familiar to the victim, and 98 interviewees said they knew nothing of such assaults committed by strangers. Despite the trauma suffered by a large percentage of the interviewees, there are still significant numbers of these individuals who seem to have emerged from the wars with little knowledge of its violence and destruction.

We next look at wartime trauma along gender and ethnic lines. To do this we created an ordinal measure of the number of traumatic experiences the interviewees suffered during the war. The ordinal measure consists of five categories of levels of responses based on which quintile an interviewee's number of experiences falls into. Figure 2.8 breaks down wartime trauma along the gender dimension. Most obviously we see that female witnesses tend to be more likely to report more frequent types of trauma. While 18% of the men fall into the first quintile, or report fewer types of reported harm, and 25% fall into the second quintile, female witnesses are more likely to report levels of harm in the third, fourth, and fifth highest categories. For example, 23% of the female witnesses report experiencing the highest number of wartime traumas, while 16% of male witnesses report such high levels of traumatization. On average, female witnesses report 11.8 wartime traumas, while male witnesses report 9.5 such experiences with a t-test indicating that the difference is statistically significant. Female ICTY witnesses in this sample are indicating that they were generally subject to more harm than male witnesses.

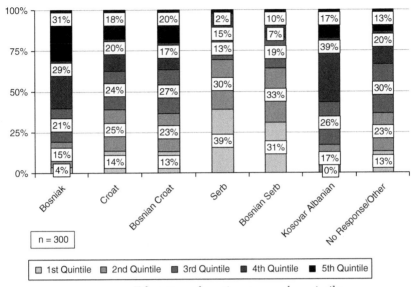

FIGURE 2.9. Ethnicity and wartime trauma by quintiles.

We next turn to examining the level of trauma reported by the different ethnic groups. The violence of the wars in the former Yugoslavia was not typically widespread and affecting people throughout the former constituent republics of Yugoslavia. Rather, such violence often tended to occur in particular areas (such as eastern Bosnia and along the border between Croatia and Serbia), and tended to focus on particular groups of people. Indeed, 80% of the civilian deaths during the Bosnian war were Bosniaks (Borger 2016: xxii). We see ample evidence of this in the survey sample (Figure 2.9). As the darker shading at the top of the Bosniak category shows, this ethnic group reports experiencing the highest level of trauma – 31% of Bosniaks fall into the fifth or highest quintile for experiencing trauma. In total, 60% of all Bosniaks fall into the fourth and fifth quintiles. This demonstrates quite clearly what we know from studies of the war in Bosnia as well as the cases at the ICTY – that Bosniaks generally experienced the highest amount of suffering during the war.[5] Kosovar Albanians also tend to cluster into the two highest categories of trauma – 56% are in the fourth and fifth quintiles. Serbs report the least level of trauma among the groups. For example, only one Serb reported

---

[5]   The ICTY has documented for the historical record locations where war crimes occurred. That map too reveals the majority of the violence during the wars was in Bosnia and Herzegovina, Croatia, and Kosovo (http://bit.ly/2gRICTY).

experiencing the highest level of trauma in the fifth quintile. Bosnian Serbs also report relatively low levels of traumatic wartime experiences compared to the other groups – just 17% (like Serbs in Serbia) fall into the two highest categories. Approximately 37% to 38% of Bosnian Croats and Croats report being in the two highest categories. When we conducted t-tests on the ethnicity variables and range of trauma experienced, we found that Bosniaks and Kosovar Albanians were statistically more likely to report higher levels of trauma, while Serbs and Bosnian Serbs were analogously less likely to report high levels of wartime suffering.

We must remind the reader, however, that our measure of wartime experiences tells us only the frequency with which interviewees indicated they underwent particular experiences. The data do not tell us of the severity of these events, the number of people affected, or other critical indicators regarding just how traumatic these events were. We do not look to develop a scale of human suffering or imply that some people's suffering was more severe or harmful than another's. Rather, we can indicate only the range and frequency of these traumas.

As we analyze the impact of both ethnicity and wartime trauma on our other variables of interest, we must remain mindful of the degree to which Bosniaks and Kosovar Albanians are more likely to report more trauma, as well as the lower levels of trauma typically experienced by the other ethnic groups. While research on the Bosnian conflict and the ICTY has often focused on ethnicity (Clark 2014; Ford 2012), it is important to remember that ethnicity may also be capturing some portion of the impact of wartime trauma because being Bosniak or Kosovar Albanian is associated with a greater likelihood of experiencing wartime suffering. Whatever political attitudes might generally characterize membership in these groups, it may not always be easy to disentangle the degree of influence contributed by either variable.

To better understand the types of experiences witnesses had during the wars of the former Yugoslavia, we conducted factor analyses of the experience measures. We sought to discover if certain groups or types of experiences tended to be reported together. The factor analysis revealed five distinct dimensions of trauma as reported by the witnesses. To identify these constellations of variables we selected out only those factor loadings where the Eigenvalue was at least "1." Factor 1 variables that tended to cluster together and that were responsible for explaining the most variance included the following wartime experiences: (1) being held in detention; and (2) being imprisoned. We label this factor loading group "detention." Factor 2 variables include: (1) family, friend, or relative who went missing; (2) murder of family, friend, or acquaintance; and (3) unnatural death of family member or friend. This category we label "suffering of family and friends." Factor 3 wartime experiences include: (1) ill health without access to medical care; (2) lack of shelter; and (3) lack of food and water. We term this category "deprivation." Factor 4, which we label "sexual assault," involves: (1) rape or sexual assault by a familiar person; and/or (2) rape or sexual assault by a stranger. Factor 5 we term "war violence" and includes: (1) combat situation; (2) artillery fire or shelling; (3) being close to death; and (4) mine explosions.

To begin, we sought to determine if some witnesses were more likely to experience certain types of trauma than others as well as more trauma in general. We estimated five regression models to evaluate the impact of ethnicity, gender, and other factors on the likelihood of witnesses experiencing these five types of trauma. In most of the models there were no statistically significant coefficients (results not shown). In the model of the likelihood of individuals being held in detention we found Bosniaks were statistically more likely to experience this type of trauma. The estimates for the second factor of "suffering of family and friends" and for the fourth factor "sexual assault" did not generate any statistically significant coefficients. When we modeled the fifth factor, "war violence," we found that older individuals were less likely to experience this trauma. It is only in the estimates for the third factor of "deprivation" that we find a more reasonable fit. Serbs, Bosnian Serbs, and Croats were all *less likely* to report that they went without the basic necessities of life, while women were more likely to have experienced these problems. The coefficients for these four variables are all statistically significant. The wars of the former Yugoslavia generally spared individuals living in most of Croatia and to a lesser extent Serbia (with the exception of the 1999 NATO air war regarding Kosovo), which is not altogether surprising. Otherwise, we did not find statistically significant and substantively meaningful results when we estimated the proclivity of individuals to report these specific types of traumas.

We next turn to looking at which factors are related to the amount of trauma suffered by the witnesses. The results here help us understand the ways in which the impact of war is felt disproportionately along ethnic lines and gender. We ran a Poisson regression model using the total number of wartime traumas witnesses indicated they experienced during the war, which was as few as zero and as many as 25 (results in Table 2.1). The coefficient for the Bosniak variable is statistically significant and positive, while the coefficients for the Serb and Bosnian Serb variables are also statistically significant, but negative. In terms of witness reporting, it is clear that Bosniaks experienced a broader range of traumatic experiences and the deprivations of war. Indeed, across the three-and-a-half-year and multisided war, ethnic conflict meant

TABLE 2.1. *Poisson regression estimates of the number of wartime experiences*

Variable	Coefficient	Standard error	Z score	P value
Bosniak	0.281	0.058	4.860	0.000
Serb	−0.394	0.077	−5.100	0.000
Bosnian Serb	−0.359	0.079	−4.530	0.000
Croat	0.030	0.068	0.440	0.663
Kosovar Albanian	0.332	0.077	4.330	0.000
Ethnic minority	0.184	0.058	3.170	0.002
Female	0.120	0.056	2.150	0.031
Education level	0.000	0.013	0.010	0.991
Age	−0.005	0.002	−2.680	0.007
Constant	2.516	0.134	18.840	0.000

n=270

Bosniaks fought with various ethnicities. The conflict saw Bosniaks versus Bosnian Serbs (1992–1995), as well as Bosniaks versus Bosnian Croats in 1993 to 1994 and even against other Bosnian Muslims (i.e., Fikret Abdic and his autonomous zone in the northwest of the country). Given such multisided violence, we see as expected that Bosniaks tend to report experiencing the greatest number of wartime traumas. We also see that Kosovar Albanians report higher levels of trauma than the other groups – the coefficient for this variable is positive and statistically significant (the reference category is Bosnian Croat and others). Not surprisingly, the two groups that were targeted by superior military and militia forces report the most trauma. We note that individuals who are ethnic minorities in their community also report higher levels of trauma. Indeed, much of the fighting in the Bosnian war, especially in the east, concerned Serb forces looking to create ethnically pure enclaves. Those who stayed behind, or left and returned, probably experienced some of this archetypal violence.

We also found that women are more likely to report more trauma than male witnesses. As we discussed earlier in this chapter, women report higher levels of traumatic wartime experiences than males, especially those involving our factor of "deprivation." The reader will recall that female witnesses report 11.8 wartime traumas on average, while male witnesses report on average 9.5 such experiences. Lastly, we see that there is a negative relationship between age and the number of reported wartime traumas. The more elderly witnesses were less likely to experience the ravages of war, perhaps because they may have seemed to pose less of a "threat" (e.g., elderly Bosnian Muslim males were not specifically targeted during the Srebrenica genocide), or because their activities and mobility may have prevented them from coming into conflict with opposing armies.

CONCLUSION

We saw in this chapter that the ethnic, gender, and experiential profiles of the witnesses in the sample are quite distinct. There are roughly approximate distributions of individuals from the principal ethnic groups and across gender given the characteristics of the total witness population, which is critical in order for us to generalize from these findings. At the same time, we also saw that the witnesses experienced a great diversity of the number and types of war-related trauma. In general, we see that the typical witness is a Bosniak, Serb, or Croat (as they were sampled in similar percentages), is male, and has experienced almost 10 different wartime traumas, especially if he or she was Bosniak or Albanian.

We also found that there are important relationships between our ethnicity and war trauma measures. Bosniaks and Kosovar Albanians reported experiencing much higher levels of trauma than did the other ethnic groups. Serbs and Bosnian Serbs were likely to report fewer such traumas, while Croats and Bosnian Croats were not statistically dissimilar from the mean. In addition, female witnesses were more likely to report experiencing higher levels of trauma than male witnesses. As we proceed through the analytical chapters it will be important to bear in mind that ethnicity implies more than the use of cultural/linguistic markers. For many of these witnesses, it may also connote greater wartime suffering.

Now that we have described these basic characteristics of the witnesses, we can begin to analyze the data to find out the opinions and perceptions these individuals have about their experiences and the work of the ICTY. The witnesses in this sample, as well as the large population of witnesses in general who have appeared before the ICTY, represent a unique and complex group of individuals whose traumatic experiences formed the essential raison d'être for the existence of the Tribunal. In the subsequent chapters we draw upon this blend of ethnic, gender, and war experience to best describe what the process of testifying has entailed for the witnesses and how they view the work of the ICTY.

3

The Witnesses and Their Encounter
with International Justice

INTRODUCTION

There is a tendency to think of witnesses who testify before an international criminal tribunal in terms of how the individual is affected by the experience. The witnesses, however, are not passive vessels whom the Tribunal shapes. Witnesses appear before the ICTY with their own unique set of experiences, reasons for testifying, and interpretations of what this testimonial process has meant to them. Their personal encounters with the international justice system are the subject of this chapter as we seek to understand the reasons that motivate individuals to testify, what they know about this foreign court that has called on them to bear witness, and how they perceive their own personal treatment by the ICTY. We examine the micro- or individual-level impact of the ICTY to ultimately understand what this process means to the individual. We take up separately in Chapter 6 the witnesses' assessments of the ICTY as an international institution that is charged with administering justice, advancing deterrence, and promoting peace.

This chapter proceeds as follows. First, we look at witness knowledge and preparation regarding the testimonial process before describing the reasons why individuals testify, their own assessments of the fairness with which they were treated by various actors involved in the judicial process, and finally, their own sense of personal satisfaction with their performance on the witness stand. The second part of the chapter focuses on an in-depth and multivariate analysis of two of the most critical issues pertaining to the witness experience. We examine how ethnicity, gender, and wartime trauma are related to the reasons why some individuals feel more compelled to testify than others. We find that while individuals who identify as Croatian or Serbian are less likely to report being motivated to testify because of a desire to "tell their story," almost all witnesses regardless of ethnicity report being motivated to testify because of larger, external concerns such as "speaking for the dead" and "as a moral duty to all victims of wars." Those individuals who suffered the most trauma, however, are more likely to report testifying for both external reasons and internal reasons.

We also analyze witnesses' opinions on whether their testimony contributed to the discovery of the truth or to justice. We find that individuals are significantly influenced by their perceptions of treatment by the Office of the Prosecutor – a positive impression of the OTP seems to help influence or perhaps solidify individuals' positive assessments of their own performance. We also find in all but one set of estimates that those witnesses who are strongly motivated to testify are also more likely to feel positive about their contributions. We begin by describing witnesses' experiences leading up to their testimony.

PREPARATION AND TESTIFYING BEFORE AN INTERNATIONAL TRIBUNAL

The magnitude of the crimes alleged and the complexity of holding trials in a multilingual environment in a court outside the region of the former Yugoslavia where a majority of the witnesses reside create difficult challenges in preparing witnesses. Witnesses need sufficient information and adequate time to prepare for testifying for the sake of their own well-being and to ensure the integrity of the trial process (Cody et al. 2014; Wald 2002). The preparation process for the witness starts as soon as the ICTY contacts the witness for the first time to determine if the individual is willing and able to testify. There are a myriad of considerations involved in bringing witnesses – many of whom may have never been in any court before, let alone a tribunal in a faraway country – to testify about traumatic wartime experiences (War Crimes Justice Project 2010). The VWS has a mandate to provide all witnesses with information about their rights and obligations, as well as practical, logistical, and legal information that will be needed during the course of their testifying.

For some witnesses, testifying before a war crimes tribunal is a daunting, alien prospect because the ICTY structure is new to the international system and is a sui generis, hybrid legal system drawing from both common and civil law traditions.[1] The level of knowledge witnesses have can vary substantially

---

[1] A key difference between common law and civil law is the role of the judge. In common law systems, judges are neutral arbiters and leave advocacy to the parties. In contrast, judges in civil law systems have broader authority to take a more active role as a questioner or an investigator in the proceedings (Crawford et al. 2013).

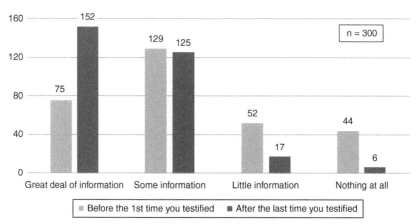

FIGURE 3.1. Knowledge about the work of the ICTY.

depending on their background and experiences with courts and how closely they have followed, if at all, the legal and political developments occurring in The Hague and the former Yugoslavia. To ascertain the level of knowledge witnesses had about the ICTY as an institution, interviewees were asked how much they knew about the ICTY before the first time they testified and after the last time they testified (Figure 3.1). A large number of interviewees (68%; n=204) knew a great deal or had some information even before they testified, while a substantial proportion (75%; n=277) knew a great deal or had some information after the last time they testified. It appears that the process itself contributes to an increase in knowledge about what witnesses know about the ICTY. This still leaves open the question of whether certain individuals learned more or less from the experience than other groups.

Turning to that question we find that gender differences exist between the levels of information that women report having learned after having testified as compared to men. Figure 3.2 compares interviewee knowledge before the first time and after the last time they testified by gender. For more than 40% of women and 52.6% of men, there was no increase in what they knew about the ICTY between the first time they testified and after the last time they testified. Notably, five individuals (one woman and four men) thought they knew *even less* about the ICTY after they testified for the last time. Finally, according to a t-test comparing genders, women were significantly more likely than men to indicate that they knew a great deal about the ICTY after the last time they testified (Figure 3.2). Perhaps women are more inclined to acknowledge the net increase in information they learned. Alternatively, women may have had less access to information about the ICTY before having testified for the first

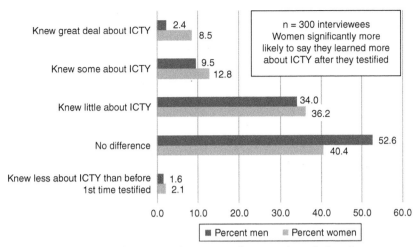

FIGURE 3.2. Percentage of persons with greater knowledge about
ICTY after testifying.

time as a result of their views about criminal and international justice issues
(Barberet 2014) or because of cognitive processing differences between men
and women more generally (Halpern 2013). Either way, the survey reflects that
there may be a steeper learning curve for women as compared to men.

Among the major ethnic groups, Bosnian Croats indicated the greatest
level of knowledge beforehand (30% indicated they knew a great deal about
the ICTY), while fewer Bosniaks, Serbs, Croats, and Bosnian Serbs claimed
to know a great deal (Figure 3.3). Kosovar Albanians were most likely to indicate they knew nothing before they testified. We see in Figure 3.4 that when
queried about their knowledge after having testified for the last time, Kosovar
Albanians indicated the greatest level of knowledge (65% indicated they knew
a great deal). Only 33.3% of Bosnian Serbs claimed to know a great deal,
while 55% of Bosniaks and Croats knew a great deal; 40% of Bosnian Croats
and 50% of Serbs responded that they knew a great deal. We ran t-tests on the
different ethnic groups and whether their knowledge, before or after the last
time they testified, varied along this dimension. There were no statistically
significant t-tests when we analyzed ethnicity and ICTY knowledge before
the first time witnesses testified (results not shown). Similar results were
obtained when we assessed the relationship between ethnicity and ICTY
knowledge after the last visit to The Hague, except that Bosnian Serbs were
statistically more likely to know less after their last time on the witness stand.
We also looked to see if there were any relationships between the level and
type of trauma a witness experienced and their level of knowledge, but found

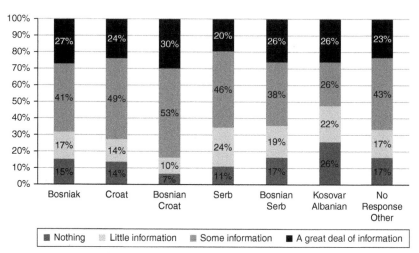

FIGURE 3.3. ICTY knowledge before first time testifying and ethnicity.

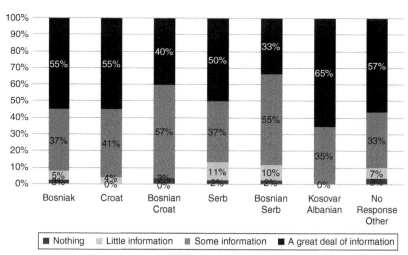

FIGURE 3.4. ICTY knowledge after last time testifying and ethnicity.

no statistically significant relationships between knowledge and the level of trauma. We found one instance where those individuals whose trauma tended to be characterized by deprivation (e.g., food, shelter, healthcare) appeared to be less likely to know more about the ICTY before testifying for the first time (results not shown). Since this was the only instance where we found a statistically significant correlation, we hesitate to make too much of this finding.

Witnesses need adequate time and preparation to be ready for testifying, and the VWS provides witnesses with information and briefings about testifying that begin from the first telephone call. The first in-person meeting typically occurs at the witness's hotel in The Hague unless the VWS has assessed that the witness needs to be briefed in their home country before departure. Witnesses are provided assistance, where appropriate, in the BCS or Albanian languages, with briefings tending to focus on the logistics and practical information needed during their stay in The Hague (e.g., accommodation facilities, the role of the VWS, medical assistance, and other matters). VWS personnel do not coach the witnesses about the substance of the testimonial process, but instead provide briefings that cover logistical issues, such as scheduling matters, the technical procedures in the courtrooms, explanations about simultaneous interpretation, the roles of the parties, and protective measures to ensure the witnesses have the information they need. The information about the legal process can be complex, especially because the Tribunal does not typically employ the civil law tradition in use in the former Yugoslavia. Moreover, the process can be easily misunderstood, especially for those who receive protective measures. Even when a witness receives protective measures the Prosecution and Defence teams and the accused still know the witness's identity, and it can be disconcerting for witnesses to come face to face with the accused in the courtroom or to find that the public can follow the proceedings from the gallery (Elias-Bursać 2015; Stepakoff et al. 2014; Cody et al. 2014; Stover 2005; Wald 2002) and via online streaming.

Interviewees were asked whether they: (1) had sufficient time for preparation; (2) had adequate information needed to testify; and (3) were satisfied with the assistance provided by the VWS. As Figure 3.5 illustrates, women are somewhat less likely to agree that they had sufficient time to prepare – 89.4% of women and 92.1% of men agreed (or strongly agreed) that they had sufficient time to prepare. There are also other gender differences as 85.1% of women and 93.7% of men agree they had adequate information about testifying, and 87.2% of women and 94% of men agree they were satisfied with the VWS's assistance. This is in contrast to Cody et al. (2014), who found women were more satisfied with victims' and witnesses' assistance at the International Criminal Court (ICC). Regarding ethnic differences, overwhelming majorities of witnesses across the ethnic groups report they had adequate time and information about testifying and were satisfied with the work of the VWS in helping them to get ready to testify. We again estimated a series of t-tests to discern if there were meaningful differences on these three measures across the ethnic groups (results not shown). There was no statistically significant difference in the tests for ethnicity regarding whether the witness believed she

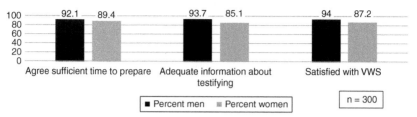

FIGURE 3.5. Preparation, information, and satisfaction before trial.

had sufficient preparation time or between ethnicity and whether the witness believed the process of testifying had been adequately explained. However, Bosnian Serbs were statistically less likely while Bosnian Croats were statistically more likely to indicate that they were satisfied with the information and assistance they received from the VWS. Female witnesses were statistically more likely to be satisfied with their assistance from the VWS, although gender does not appear to play a statistically significant role in distinguishing satisfaction on the first two measures.

Beyond the legal and logistical concerns that witnesses face, there are more personal factors involved in both the reasons for and the impact of having participated in the process of testifying.

WITNESSES' MOTIVATIONS FOR TESTIFYING

In the last decade, a systematic inquiry has begun into the reasons why witnesses decide to testify (Stover 2005). The importance of the role of witnesses in war crimes tribunals dates back to the Nuremburg trials, where there was criticism that victim witnesses were not used as widely as perhaps they should have been to testify directly about Nazi crimes (Arendt 1963). Given that witnesses are the "soul" of the ICTY's work, examining in detail what motivates and influences them to testify is vital for the practical consequences of the Tribunal's mandate (Wald 2001).

Perhaps the most comprehensive research to date on witnesses' motivations comes from the interviews of 109 men and 38 women who testified before the Special Court for Sierra Leone (SCSL) (Stepakoff et al. 2014). Researchers identified two broad aspects of motivations to testify: (1) helping oneself; and (2) helping others. The top reasons included denouncing "wrongs committed against me during the war"; contributing "to public knowledge about the war"; desiring "retributive justice"; and providing a "moral duty to other victims."

The results highlight common themes that have emerged from earlier research – the need for witnesses to tell their story; the need to find out more about what happened to themselves and loved ones; the pursuit of justice; and the desire to contribute to the historical narrative about war crimes (Stover 2005; Stover et al. 2011). A study of Rwandan prosecution and defense witnesses (n=60) who testified before national courts – the Gacaca courts[2] – and the International Criminal Tribunal for Rwanda (ICTR) echoed similar reasons. Like in other studies, witnesses indicated multiple reasons including: (1) an obligation to bear witness to the genocide; (2) a moral obligation to tell the truth and to know more about what happened (e.g., finding family and friends, identifying perpetrators, etc.); (3) public acknowledgement of suffering and wrongdoing; and (4) a commitment to rebuilding the post-conflict society (Clark and Palmer 2012). Finally, victims of sexual violence may have distinctive motivations. Such women appearing before the SCSL stated it was important for them to testify in order to provide evidence about what atrocities had been committed and to give a narrative of their experiences (Staggs-Kelsall and Stepakoff 2007). Sexual violence victims testifying before the ICTY and the War Crimes Chamber of the Court of Bosnia and Herzegovina noted a need to hold perpetrators responsible, to prevent future crimes, and to tell the truth about what happened (Mischkowski and Mlinarević 2009).

All of these reasons are evident in the experience of ICTY witnesses. Because of the breadth and range of motivations and the intensely personal nature of testifying, the survey contained specific and open-ended questions about these matters (Doak 2011b; Bonomy 2007; Wald 2002). Interviewees could choose more than one explanation for testifying, and many did (Figure 3.6).

We combined responses of "agree" and "strongly agree" in Figure 3.6. When examining this level of agreement regarding witnesses' motivations to testify, the most prevalent reasons were "to help the judges reach an accurate decision" (97.7%); "because I do not want the war events in the former Yugoslavia to ever happen to anyone else" (97.6%); and as a "moral duty toward all victims of war" (95.3%). These reasons mirror the conclusions of Stepakoff et al. (2014), who found significant external motivators for testifying. It is interesting to note that the responses that elicited comparatively lesser levels of support were those rationales that pertained more to the individual's personal stake in testifying. While 81.3% of the witnesses agreed or

[2]   The Rwandan government established the Gacaca courts after the 1994 Rwandan genocide to help resolve the backlog of pending criminal cases. These courts were holistically focused, including components of Western law practices and traditional African dispute resolution, to facilitate victim participation in the justice process. Commentators both lauded the Gacaca courts as efficient (more than one million cases were resolved by the time all trials ended in 2012) and condemned them for lacking due process and assigning "collective responsibility" that may contribute to continuing rifts within Rwanda society (Bornkamm 2012).

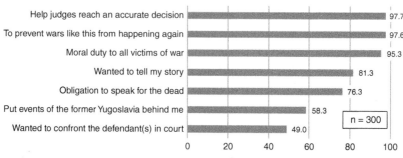

FIGURE 3.6. Reasons for testifying.

strongly agreed it was important to testify because, "I wanted to tell my story,"
only 58.3% indicated they did so to "put the events from the wars in the
former Yugoslavia behind" them. A smaller percentage, mostly OTP interviewees (49%, or 147 persons), agreed or strongly agreed that it was important for them to testify to confront the defendant in court, while 28%, or 54
persons, disagreed or strongly disagreed that confronting the defendant was
an important reason for testifying. Gender does not appear to play a role
in helping us understand witness motivations. While female witnesses were
more likely to believe in the importance of testifying to speak for the dead,
there were no statistically discernible gender differences across the other witness motivations.

   Witness motivations to testify varied across the ethnic groups. While nearly
all witnesses regardless of ethnicity believed it was important to testify to help
the judges reach an accurate decision and as a moral duty, there was significant variation when they were asked about confronting the defendant in court
(results not shown). Majorities of Bosniaks and Kosovar Albanians (approximately 73% in both cases) agreed with this rationale. Among all the other
ethnic groups only a majority of Croats agreed with this statement. Substantial
majorities of all groups expressed concurrence with the notion of wanting
to tell their story, to speak for the dead, and to prevent wars from happening
again. Majorities of all groups, except Serbs, also believed it was important to
testify to put the events of the past behind oneself.

   The t-tests to distinguish whether witnesses differed on the intensity of
their rationales for testifying across ethnicity were quite revealing. Bosniaks
stood out dramatically as they were statistically more likely to report greater
intensity of motivation across all seven measures. Regardless of their reasons
for testifying, Bosniaks are more highly motivated as a group to appear at
the ICTY. Conversely, Serbs scored distinctly lower in terms of motivation
to testify across all categories, with the exception of the variable measuring

whether witnesses testified because they felt a moral obligation for all victims of war. Bosnian Serbs were less likely to indicate that it was important to testify in order to "tell my story"; to "speak for the dead"; "as a moral duty for all victims of war"; and to "confront the defendant." There were no statistically significant differences among Croats to distinguish their motivations for testifying. Bosnian Croats did not reveal any noticeable differences from the other groups except that they were statistically less likely to be motivated to testify because of the need to help judges reach an accurate decision. Finally, Kosovar Albanians also did not reveal any discernible differences in the reasons they testified when we examined t-tests for the motivation variables.

There are strong relationships among the seven reasons for testifying and the level and type of trauma witnesses experienced. First, the partial correlation coefficients (Table 3.1) demonstrate a strong and positive relationship between amount of trauma experienced and motivations for testifying. The more trauma witnesses suffered, the more highly motivated they were to testify. As well, the experience clusters we created for "detention," "suffering of family and friends," and "deprivation" were almost all positively related to strong motivations for testifying. Only the rationale pertaining to the prevention of war was not correlated with these three types of trauma. In general, the greater the level of trauma a witness experienced during the war, the more highly motivated they are to testify.[3]

Certainly, witnesses understand their role in the larger context of advancing truth and justice and deterring war crimes. Their multidimensional perspective encompasses their sense of duty toward others (Clark 2014; Doak 2011b), as well as more personal reasons for testifying. Interestingly, the findings here mirror in some respects those of studies of witness motivations at the SCSL (Stepakoff et al. 2014) and the ICC (Cody et al. 2014). The overall picture emerging is that witnesses have broader and more complex motives for testifying, which are driven by both internal but, more dominantly, external factors. We return to this topic in the second half of the chapter when we develop a multivariate model to provide a richer explanation regarding the motivations impelling witnesses to testify.

---

[3] The survey allowed witnesses to give their own motivations for testifying through an open-ended short-answer question. A number of interviewees gave answers similar to those given for the close-ended questions. Witnesses tend to cite external, altruistic motivations rather than more internal, self-focused reasons (Stepakoff et al. 2014). Witnesses tend to cite a general concern for society as a whole and a need to tell the truth about what happened. The next most common answers relate to a higher duty, namely ensuring the accused receives a just punishment or exoneration, as well as a moral obligation to testify.

TABLE 3.1. *Partial correlation coefficients for wartime trauma and motivation to testify*

	Tell my story	Speak for the dead	Put past behind	Prevent war	Moral duty	Confront defendant	Help judges
Total wartime trauma	0.298	0.416	0.307	0.191	0.215	0.350	0.183
	0.000	0.000	0.000	0.001	0.000	0.000	0.002
Detention	0.172	0.257	0.225	0.095	0.138	0.281	0.124
	0.004	0.000	0.000	0.103	0.019	0.000	0.033
Friends/family suffering	0.224	0.275	0.204	0.077	0.084	0.160	0.110
	0.000	0.000	0.001	0.184	0.154	0.008	0.059
Deprivation	0.159	0.249	0.107	0.164	0.117	0.209	0.075
	0.007	0.000	0.084	0.005	0.046	0.001	0.200
Sexual assault	0.030	0.081	0.046	0.052	0.051	−0.006	0.007
	0.615	0.178	0.461	0.376	0.383	0.923	0.912
War violence	0.059	0.073	0.041	−0.015	0.033	0.054	0.050
	0.322	0.225	0.506	0.804	0.580	0.375	0.396

n=300

PERSONAL SATISFACTION WITH TESTIFYING

While witnesses' motivations pertain more to their personal values and experiences, witnesses' satisfaction with their testimony seems to be related more to multiple factors that may not be within the witnesses' control. Witnesses' satisfaction with their testimony more likely depends on whether they thought the experience was positive or negative (Clark 2014; Horn et al. 2009b; Stepakoff et al. 2014; Stover 2005); cathartic or traumatizing (Brounéus 2010; Mendeloff 2009; Dembour and Haslam 2004; Stover 2005); important in truth-telling (Findlay and Ngane 2012; Doak 2011b); or important for telling a personal narrative ("tell my story") (Hodžić 2010; Horn et al. 2009b). While research on witnesses' satisfaction has increased, there has been less theoretical development regarding what contributes to or undermines witnesses' satisfaction. We suggest that testifying is more likely to be satisfying if it was a meaningful encounter for the witness (Doak 2011b); if the witness felt respected by court personnel; and if the perceived cross-examination was a positive experience (Horn et al. 2009b).

Witness satisfaction among those surveyed varied widely. Witness satisfaction with their own performance was distinct from satisfaction with the trial itself. Whether a witness left the courtroom satisfied tended to depend on what he/she was expecting to gain from the experience. Some witnesses went in confident and came out agitated, particularly if they felt they were unable to tell their story and were repeatedly interrupted, or if they were challenged aggressively and/or accused of lying in cross-examination. Infrequently, the judges allowed witnesses to say something at the end of the testimony, which may or may not have been important for the latter's satisfaction (Moffett 2014). When releasing a witness, the Trial Chamber often thanks the witness for coming to testify, and in some cases, acknowledges the suffering the witness endured. In rare instances, the Trial Chamber may invite a witness to give a victim impact statement as part of the sentencing process.[4] VWS personnel noted that such gestures by the Trial Chamber and the consequent briefing by the calling party enabled witnesses to address concerns about their in-court testimony.

To gauge witnesses' satisfaction as it related to their motivations for testifying, interviewees were asked to reflect on their reasons for testifying and whether they were satisfied with their testimony.[5] Interviewees overwhelmingly (91%) indicated that they were satisfied with their testimony in light of their motivations for testifying, with 4.7% indicating dissatisfaction, while the remaining 4.7% had either no opinion or no response (Figure 3.7). Satisfaction did not vary with gender or ethnicity. Such findings are consistent with those of recent research on witness testimony (Cody et al. 2014). There were no significant differences between those who testified for the Prosecution or the Defence in terms of satisfaction. Both OTP and Defence witnesses are about equally likely to be satisfied with their testimony (93% and 90%, respectively), although OTP witnesses were a little more likely to indicate they were dissatisfied with their testimony (7% versus 1% for the Defence witnesses). As well, we found no real substantive differences among the ethnic groups, although "only" 88% of Croats were satisfied with their testimony, which is slightly less than the overall 91% satisfaction level. Female witnesses, however, were somewhat less likely to be satisfied with their testimony compared to men (85.1% versus 91.7%). There were no statistically significant correlations between the

---

[4] Victim impact statements are written or oral statements that are part of the process of allowing crime victims an opportunity to tell the court what the crime has meant personally to them and to what extent they were affected (Rule 92 *bis* ICTY Rules of Procedure and Evidence, IT/32/Rev.50, July 8, 2015). They have been limited in usage at the ICTY (Moffett 2014), and the usefulness of such statements has been both touted (Ciorciari and Heindel 2016) and questioned (for an extended discussion see Ochoa 2013: ch. 4).

[5] See question A20a in Annex III from the survey, available on line at www.icty.org/x/file/About/Registry/Witnesses/Echoes-Full-Report_EN.pdf.

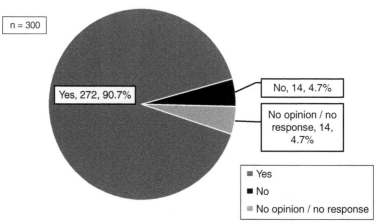

FIGURE 3.7. Interviewee satisfaction with testimony when thinking about why they testified.

level and types of wartime traumas witnesses experienced and satisfaction with their testimony (results not shown).

Interviewees could also summarize why they were satisfied or dissatisfied with their testimony and provide multiple reasons. This question prompted the highest response rate of any of the short-answer questions in the survey (n=253). The responses varied widely, but reflect other themes emphasized in previous research on witnesses, as well as the experiences of the VWS staff who support witnesses immediately after their testimony (Stover 2005, 2014; Stepakoff et al. 2014). What is striking about the results is that the open-ended questions reflected positive, as opposed to negative, reasons for testifying. As we discuss further in the book, these results support what is a consistent finding – namely, when witnesses look back on their experiences, they are more positive than negative about the process.

Overwhelmingly, interviewees' satisfaction stems primarily from feelings related to telling the truth (n=108) and contributing to fact-finding and the historical record (n=105) (Figure 3.8). Beyond these, there are a variety of reasons that relate most closely to contributing to or to participating in the administration of a just outcome. These reasons relate to witnesses feeling like they contributed to the judges' decisions or the judgment; that they had held the defendant accountable or exonerated the defendant; or that they had facilitated the advancement of justice. Not all witnesses were as sanguine about their testimony. Some felt they had been unable to tell their story or were unhappy with the Prosecution or the Tribunal more generally. Still others felt as though they did not contribute to the judgment.

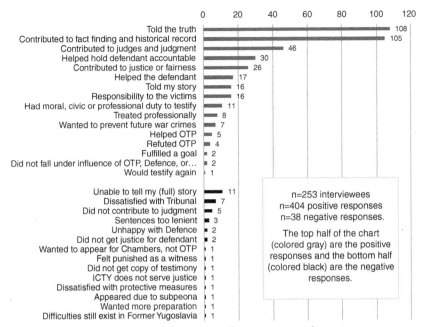

FIGURE 3.8. Interviewees' reflections on satisfaction.

WITNESSES' PERCEPTIONS OF ICTY FAIRNESS

One critical determinant of individuals' evaluations of their encounters with justice, whether national or international (Tyler 1990; Tyler and Darley 2000; Tyler and Huo 2002), is their perception of treatment. Those individuals who believe that they were treated fairly by a court are more likely to believe in the legitimacy of the court (Tyler and Darley 2000: 716). Therefore, we next examine how the individual witnesses perceived they were treated by four critical actors in the testimonial process – the Trial Chambers, the Prosecution, the Defence, and the VWS. The results show that large majorities of witnesses believe they were treated fairly.

It is the role of the Trial Chambers to control the proceedings and address violations of the code of conduct during the examination in chief and cross-examination. Witnesses appreciate it when a Trial Chamber intervenes on their behalf. Similarly, they have positively welcomed statements made by the Chambers at the conclusion of their evidence in which they acknowledge the witness's personal suffering (Stepakoff et al. 2015). Additionally, many witnesses ask at the end of their testimony if they can make a final statement to the court (Bandes 2009). The VWS experience is that these are usually short and that witnesses appreciate it when they are given permission to speak at the end of their testimony.

The witnesses' perceptions of their treatment by the parties is often influenced by their perceptions of courtroom dynamics and their preparation for the difficult act of testifying (Stepakoff et al. 2014, 2015). It is the calling party that usually determines what topics will be covered during the testimony, but some witnesses may find it hard to focus on a certain segment of their war experience and disregard other parts that they consider important. The VWS noted that sometimes witnesses consider the courtroom as the right arena to tell the whole truth about what they survived, and they may feel offended when they are interrupted while talking about very important life events. When witnesses are asked to reply only with "yes" or "no" to a series of questions posed by the parties and/or Trial Chamber, the VWS noted that they may feel that the complexity of their experience and the emotional suffering attached to it is not being properly acknowledged. Others have also confirmed such observations (Wald 2002).

Witnesses are often surprised when an opposing party tries to undermine their credibility. Some felt outraged and reported to the VWS they felt as if they were the ones in the dock. Particularly, witnesses who testify about their own experience of abuses and violence (sexual violence, torture, loss of close family members, etc.) may be deeply hurt during cross-examination if they feel that the opposing party is questioning their evidence. Moreover, witnesses can be severely distressed when the questioning goes into details they might have preferred to forget.

Witnesses were asked about their perceptions of treatment by the four units (Figure 3.9). The VWS and Chambers received the highest marks from witnesses regarding fair treatment (95% and 93%, respectively, believed they were treated fairly by these actors). Overall, 79% believed they were treated fairly by the OTP; and 71% believed they were treated fairly by the Defence. Further analysis examined whether these opinions depended on which party called the witnesses (Figure 3.10). The percentages change slightly when looking at treatment by the OTP and Defence – while 88% of the witnesses called by the OTP believed they were treated fairly by the OTP, only 63% of the Defence witnesses expressed that opinion of the OTP. Opinions are reversed when examining perceptions of how witnesses were treated by the Defence – with 89% of Defence witnesses indicating they believed they were treated fairly by their calling party, while only 60% of OTP witnesses believed they were treated fairly by the Defence. In general, however, large majorities of witnesses believe they were treated fairly by *all* parties.

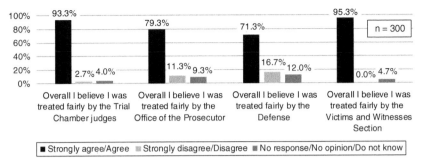

FIGURE 3.9. Interviewee perception about treatment by the ICTY.

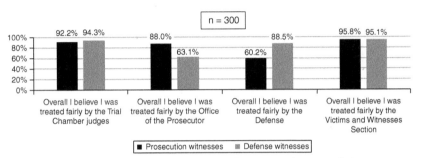

FIGURE 3.10. Interviewee perception of treatment by type of witness.

Some of the usual trends we have come to expect when we look at the role of ethnicity in shaping opinions are in evidence in Figure 3.11. Bosniaks and Kosovar Albanians are more likely to believe they have been treated fairly by the OTP, while Bosnian Croats and Serbs more readily indicate that the Defence was more likely to have treated them fairly. Interestingly, Croats were more likely to believe the OTP was fairer to them than the Defence, while Bosnian Serbs did not evince a clear preference for either party. There was little difference between male and female witnesses regarding their opinions of fair treatment by the OTP, while male witnesses were significantly (according to a difference in means test) more likely (74%) than female witnesses (59.5%) to believe they were treated fairly by the Defence. There were no statistically significant relationships between the level or type of trauma witnesses experienced during the war and perception of treatment by the opposing counsel. Because opinions were overwhelmingly positive about witnesses' treatment by Chambers and the VWS, we chose not to explore these two variables any further.

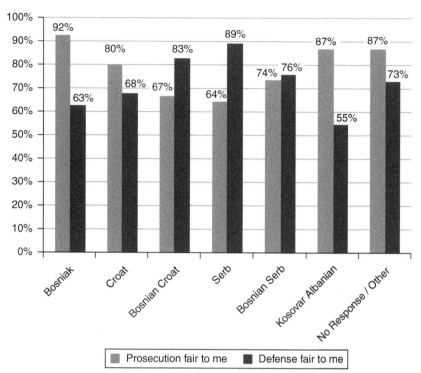

FIGURE 3.11. Witness perception of treatment by ethnicity.

Interviewees were also given the opportunity to express opinions in more detail about the Trial Chambers, Prosecution, Defence and VWS (results not shown) in the open-ended questions. Interviewees believed the judges were professional and acted properly in their comments (38 interviewees wrote this type of response), while 12 believed the judges were not. Interviewees also frequently mentioned that they felt the judges believed them (10) and cared about their well-being (8). When asked specifically about their treatment by the OTP, a number of interviewees also believed that the OTP cared about their well-being (39); that the OTP was professional and acted properly toward them (12); that they were allowed to testify without interruption (17); and that the Prosecution protected them from hostile cross-examination by the Defence (13). There were, however, nine interviewees who thought the OTP defamed or degraded them during their testimony. While the most frequent response about the Defence from those who made such comments was that the Defence cared about their well-being (39 interviewees), 38 interviewees said that the Defence attorneys acted unprofessionally. Numerous interviewees also mentioned that the VWS treated them professionally (44 interviewees) and paid the unit a compliment of some sort (10 persons). It should be mentioned, however, that some interviewees would comment on the performance of judges and the Defence, for example, when asked for their comments about the OTP and VWS. For instance, when given the opportunity to comment on their treatment by the VWS, 53 interviewees instead wrote that they believed they were treated unprofessionally by the Defence.

WITNESS PERCEPTIONS OF THE EFFECTIVENESS OF THEIR TESTIMONY

Lastly in this section of the chapter, we look at how witnesses perceive their own contribution to justice by having testified. Previous research has shown that people are more likely to accord legitimacy and provide support to institutions of justice when they believe that they have some voice or influence in the institution (Doak 2015; Tyler 1990; Tyler and Darley 2000). It is a cornerstone of modern tribunals that the witness must be a stakeholder in the process of transitional justice if justice is to be served (Wald 2001; Hoefgen 1999).

Most interviewees when asked about whether, upon reflection, they believed that their testimony (1) contributed to providing justice and (2) contributed to the discovery of the truth about the wars in the former Yugoslavia (Figure 3.12) strongly agreed or agreed (67%) that their testimony contributed to justice, and 71% believed their testimony contributed to the discovery of truth. Only small percentages strongly disagreed or disagreed with these statements in either category (8% and 6%, respectively), while a number of interviewees did not know or were not sure. This is an especially critical finding for the long-term prospects of international justice, as such feelings of efficaciousness are key to establishing the legitimacy of institutions of justice, both national and international.

Ethnicity helps differentiate among witnesses' beliefs in the efficacy of their testimony (Figure 3.13). Bosniaks and Kosovar Albanians were most likely to believe their testimony contributed to truth and justice, while Bosnian Croats and Serbs were much less likely to reach such conclusions. Indeed, Serbs were more likely than not to believe their testimony did not contribute to either truth or justice (perhaps because, as we show later, they are less likely to believe the ICTY in general contributes to these goals). Approximately 74% of women and 70% of men believed their testimony contributed to the discovery of the truth; while 64% of women and 68% of men believed their testimony contributed to justice (results not shown). There are also positive and statistically significant relationships between the level of trauma and believing that

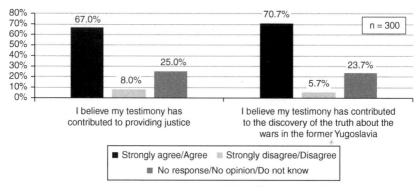

FIGURE 3.12. Interviewees' perceptions of the effectiveness of their testimony.

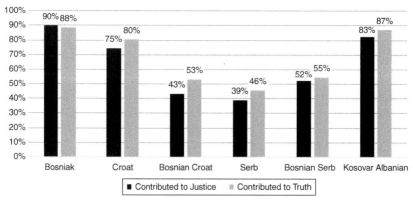

FIGURE 3.13. Ethnicity and interviewees' perceptions of whether their testimony contributed to justice and truth.

one contributed to truth and justice, which we explore in more detail in the multivariate model. We also find that those who experienced detention or imprisonment were statistically more likely to indicate they were satisfied with their contributions to truth and justice.

Witnesses care whether their testimony will help in reconstructing the truth about the wars in the former Yugoslavia. As revealed in their written comments, sometimes witnesses feel confused and insecure about how they performed in the courtroom and doubt the usefulness of their testimony. In addition to being given the opportunity to publicly tell their stories, witnesses are pleased when their contribution is acknowledged by the Tribunal and when they see that their testimony is relied upon in the final judgment. In general, we see that most witnesses believe that their testimony has had a positive experience on the judicial process. What we still would like to know, however, is what factors can help us understand why some witnesses are more satisfied than others. In the second half of this chapter we endeavor to explain both the beginning and the end of the judicial process from the witnesses' perspectives. We first analyze in greater depth why witnesses are motivated to testify, and then conclude by examining why some witnesses are more likely than others to believe their testimony has had a positive impact on the international justice.

MODELLING MOTIVATIONS TO TESTIFY AND SATISFACTION WITH TESTIMONY

While we have a broad understanding of what motivates witnesses to testify and how satisfied they are with their testimony, little research has explored what the relationships are between demographic factors and experiences and how these can have an impact on witnesses' perceptions about the testimonial process. Individuals are asked to testify before the ICTY by Prosecution or Defence attorneys, or may even be invited to (re)appear by the Trial Chamber judges. We also know that the emotions and beliefs inspiring witnesses to testify and animating their appearances on the witness stand are a diverse mix of personal and altruistic motivations. Witnesses want to tell their story and to help the judges make a decision. They want to put the wars of the past behind them and speak for the dead. Indeed, as we saw there are several motivational forces that nearly all witnesses agree upon as important, such as helping the judges reach an accurate decision and not wanting the war events in the former Yugoslavia to ever happen to anyone else.

Practically speaking, it is also useful for international tribunals and national courts to understand what motivates witnesses to testify. Those who testify for personal reasons more so than larger concerns for justice may be more likely to be frustrated by the testimonial experience when they are not always given the opportunity to tell their story. Those who see a larger purpose in testifying may be better able to weather the difficulties of testifying and, especially, cross-examination. Theoretically, we should like a deeper understanding of witness motivations to understand how their courtroom experiences in the context of these motivations may influence their assessments of international justice (Gibson 2007; Tyler 1990; Tyler and Darley 2000).

Likewise, witness satisfaction with the testimonial process is also important for better understanding whether they perceive their experiences as positive or negative (Clark 2014; Horn et al. 2009b; Stepakoff et al. 2014; Stover 2005); cathartic or traumatizing (Brounéus 2010; Mendeloff 2009; Dembour and

Haslam 2004; Stover 2005); important in truth-telling (Findlay and Ngane 2012; Doak 2011b); or important for telling a personal narrative ("tell my story") (Hodžić 2010; Horn et al. 2009b). The ability of transitional justice mechanisms to maintain legitimacy depends in no small part on whether there is criticism of the impact that the mechanisms have on witnesses, and this can be reflected in their satisfaction with the process.

We suggest that one key factor that can help us understand witness motivations and satisfaction is the concept of *resilience*. Resilience has been widely used in the fields of psychology, sociology, and political science, and is defined as a "process of patterned adjustments adopted by a society or an individual in the face of endogenous or exogenous shocks." This definition recognizes that resilience is not a "quality, a paradigm, or a theory ... [but rather is] an inherently dynamic and complex process" (Bourbeau 2015: 376).[6] It is intended to capture the capacity of societies and, more importantly for us, individuals to adapt, and possibly grow stronger, given some traumatic experience. Resilience may not be the same across all persons surviving trauma, nor is the aftermath of violent trauma all destruction and negative consequences. Generally, resilience research finds that there are often more positive than negative consequences (Winter et al. 2016; Linley and Joseph 2004) for many individuals. The concept of resilience has been used in a myriad of contexts to study the aftermath of a natural disaster or environmental devastation (Caló-Blanco et al. 2017; Cassar et al. 2011; Park et al. 2011; Goldstein 2012; Sendzemir et al. 2013); urban violence (Davies 2012; Muggah et al. 2011); post-election violence (Becchetti et al. 2014); political and ethnic violence (McAdam 2013; Winter et al. 2016; Hobfall et al. 2011); and United Nations peacekeeping missions (Williams 2013). These positive benefits accrue to communities (e.g., violent crime victims are more likely to engage in political and community activities [Bateson 2012]) and individuals (exposure to violent conflict fosters cooperative behavior [Bauer et al. 2016]). Resilience is more likely to be associated with higher education, younger age, particular personality traits, and social support (Winter et al. 2016; Hobfall et al. 2011).

This development of resilience within individuals may be a direct function of their war experiences, and not only their personal motivations and satisfaction with testifying. Witnesses experienced multiple forms of trauma during the wars in the former Yugoslavia (Hodžić 2010; Hukanovic 1996), such as torture, sexual assault, destruction of homes, loss of loved ones, and ethnic cleansing. It is a central tenet of the "testimony as catharsis" school that

---

[6]   Norris et al. (2008: 130) similarly define resilience as "a process linking a set of adaptive capacities to a positive trajectory of functioning and adaptation after a disturbance."

because of this trauma, being given the opportunity to tell one's story may make individuals feel vindicated, and give them a sense of satisfaction from seeing the defendant in a submissive role facing justice and, most importantly, a sense of closure (Mendeloff 2009; Brounéus 2010; Stepakoff et al. 2014, 2015; Cody et al. 2014). Traumatic experiences can also motivate witnesses for multiple reasons: to tell their story; so that justice will be done; to honor loved ones; to put the past behind them; and so that the truth will be known (Stepakoff et al. 2014; Stover 2005). If witnesses are unable to tell the story of what happened, it can mean that the testimonial process may take on negative consequences, interfering with coping and healing (Henry 2009; Clark 2014; Dembour and Haslam 2004; Cody et al. 2014). We suggest that those witnesses who have experienced greater levels of wartime trauma will be more passionate about their reasons for testifying and will be more likely to feel they have made a positive contribution to justice and the discovery of the truth.

We expect that those resilient individuals who have suffered greatly have a strong intrinsic motivation to testify and would be more apt to feel positively about their role in international justice. At the same time, however, we also recognize that there are critical caveats that must be attached to these expectations. First, we note here, as we have described earlier, the simple but essential truism that all individuals do not emerge resilient from wartime trauma. Instead, they may grapple with anger, loneliness, and post-traumatic stress disorder (PTSD). Ideally, we might measure witnesses' level of resilience through real-time measurements and independent assessments of witness well-being, but unfortunately given the timing (years after the experiences), the in-depth nature of narratives from witnesses about the extent of the trauma, and the length of the survey (a more extended battery of questions designed to measure resilience), this was not practically possible.[7] Therefore, we predict that those who indicate they have experienced a broader range of traumatic experiences during the war will be more likely to be motivated to testify and feel positively about their testimony. The statistical tests will help

---

[7]   The topic of asking witnesses about the extent of their trauma was discussed by the VWS focus groups. The concern here was that we would be directly forcing witnesses to recall deeply traumatizing experiences that could trigger emotional and physical difficulties. Consequently, the Harvard Trauma Questionnaire was used to measure the range of different types of trauma witnesses may have experienced, which is consistent with other research on trauma (Ringdal et al. 2008). Apart from this, there are practical reasons related to how one might quantify the depth of any given type of trauma and whether any measure would be accurate. One witness may be more reticent to discuss the experience in great detail, while others who might not have experienced as great a trauma could provide an extended account. For reasons related to witness well-being during the interview process, more probing questions about trauma were not asked.

demonstrate whether this expectation has any traction. Second, we must also note that those individuals who are highly motivated and positive may also have a strong desire to perceive their motivations and testimony in a positive light. For those individuals who have endured much, there may be a strong internal need to perceive their judicial experience positively so as to avoid cognitive dissonance, especially in light of the time, energy, and sacrifice that typically accompany a journey to give evidence in The Hague. As always, we must be cautious in the interpretation of our results.

Further, we suggest that in addition to the hypothesized impact of the level of wartime trauma on witness motivation and satisfaction, this same type of explanation will hold for other types of trauma and difficulties witnesses have experienced. Those who have experienced other types of problems in the postwar era and through the testimonial process may also be more likely to be highly motivated and more positive. First, we include a binary variable measuring whether the individual experienced a social harm (e.g., criticism, ostracism), economic consequences (e.g., damage to property), or verbal and physical threats as a result of testifying before the ICTY (these variables are discussed in depth in Chapter 4). We also include our standard measures of: (1) ethnicity; (2) gender; (3) education; and (4) age. Finally, we include a variable measuring whether the individual testified for the prosecution to determine if these witnesses were more likely to be motivated to testify to right injustices or confront the defendant in court.

For our first models of witness motivation we focus our analyses on four particular motivating factors to account. The reasons are: (1) "I believe it was important for me to testify because I had an obligation to speak for the dead"; (2) "I believe it was important for me to testify so I could put the events from the wars in the Former Yugoslavia behind me"; (3) "I believe it was important for me to testify because I wanted to confront the defendant(s) in court"; and (4) "I believe it was important for me to testify because I wanted to tell my story." Because almost all witnesses agreed that they testified to help the judges reach an accurate decision, as a moral duty toward all victims of war, and because they did not want the war events in the former Yugoslavia to happen to anyone else, we did not test our model on these questions. The dependent variables each contain four values, where "4" represents those who strongly agreed with the reason; "3" is for those who agreed; and "2" and "1" represent those who disagreed and strongly disagreed with the reason proffered, respectively.

The results are quite varied. As we look across Tables 3.2 through 3.5 we see first that the ethnicity variables do not exercise a consistent impact. When predicting witness views on testifying to "speak for the dead," "put the

TABLE 3.2. *Strength of witness motivation to "speak for the dead" – ordered probit estimates*

Variable	Coefficient	Standard error	Z statistic	P value
Bosniak	0.358	0.257	1.390	0.163
Serb	−0.182	0.247	−0.740	0.462
Bosnian Serb	0.071	0.258	0.280	0.782
Croat	0.011	0.247	0.040	0.966
Albanian	−0.076	0.322	−0.240	0.814
Experiences	0.068	0.015	4.620	0.000
Female	0.322	0.244	1.320	0.187
Prosecution witness	0.759	0.175	4.330	0.000
Consequence	0.369	0.183	2.020	0.043
Education level	−0.080	0.050	−1.600	0.109
Age	0.002	0.008	0.240	0.807

n=265

TABLE 3.3. *Strength of witness motivation to "put the past behind" – ordered probit estimates*

Variable	Coefficient	Standard error	Z statistic	P value
Bosniak	−0.067	0.229	−0.290	0.770
Serb	−0.247	0.245	−1.010	0.313
Bosnian Serb	0.022	0.251	0.090	0.929
Croat	−0.049	0.230	−0.210	0.830
Albanian	0.123	0.314	0.390	0.695
Experiences	0.049	0.014	3.510	0.000
Female	−0.135	0.210	−0.640	0.522
Prosecution witness	0.200	0.167	1.200	0.230
Consequence	0.070	0.165	0.430	0.671
Education level	−0.127	0.045	−2.820	0.005
Age	0.000	0.007	0.010	0.989

n=251

past behind me," "confront the defendant," and "tell my story" (Tables 3.2 through 3.5, respectively) we find that none of the coefficients for the ethnicity variables exercises a statistically significant impact, with one exception. Bosniaks are more likely to indicate they are motivated to testify because they wish to confront the defendant. Gender also rarely seems to make a difference.

TABLE 3.4. *Strength of witness motivation to "confront defendant" – ordered probit estimates*

Variable	Coefficient	Standard error	Z statistic	P value
Bosniak	0.442	0.217	2.040	0.042
Serb	−0.290	0.239	−1.210	0.224
Bosnian Serb	−0.337	0.245	−1.370	0.170
Croat	0.031	0.220	0.140	0.889
Albanian	0.195	0.287	0.680	0.496
Experiences	0.039	0.013	2.930	0.003
Female	−0.147	0.207	−0.710	0.476
Prosecution witness	0.611	0.165	3.690	0.000
Consequence	−0.128	0.157	−0.810	0.415
Education level	−0.081	0.044	−1.840	0.066
Age	−0.001	0.007	−0.140	0.888

n=262

TABLE 3.5. *Strength of witness motivation to "tell my story" – ordered probit estimates*

Variable	Coefficient	Standard error	Z statistic	P value
Bosniak	0.067	0.232	0.290	0.772
Serb	−0.109	0.242	−0.450	0.654
Bosnian Serb	−0.307	0.244	−1.260	0.209
Croat	0.295	0.246	1.200	0.232
Albanian	0.296	0.327	0.900	0.366
Experiences	0.060	0.014	4.250	0.000
Female	−0.065	0.214	−0.300	0.764
Prosecution witness	−0.055	0.170	−0.320	0.748
Consequence	−0.064	0.171	−0.380	0.706
Education level	−0.166	0.048	−3.490	0.000
Age	0.000	0.007	−0.050	0.959

n=274

What is most striking is the consistent and powerful impact of wartime experiences on witness motivations. In each of the four models we find that the coefficient for the variable measuring the total number of traumas witnesses report experiencing is positive and statistically significant. Those who have suffered the most are more likely to indicate a greater motivation to testify regardless of the nature of the reason, from "telling my story" to "confronting the defendant." Indeed, as others have found (especially Bauer et al. 2016) there are those who emerge from the crucible of war steeled for the challenges of life. These individuals are especially likely to be motivated to testify, whatever their specific reasons may be. There is less evidence, however, that undergoing further trauma – the social, economic, and security consequences that can result from testifying – is associated with strong motivations for testifying. The coefficient for this variable reaches statistical significance only in the models measuring whether a witness was strongly motivated to testify to "speak for the dead." We also utilized each of the component variables to the threat measure (social, economic, and physical threats) to determine if individually they influenced witness motivation, but found no supporting evidence. Additional stress in the form of consequences resulting from testimony would not appear to further motivate individuals to appear before the ICTY for any reason.

We find that those who appear for the prosecution are more likely to express a greater desire to testify when the reason offered is either to speak for the dead (Table 3.2) or confront the defendant (Table 3.4). The latter finding certainly makes sense as Defence witnesses are generally brought in to support the case of the accused rather than undermine it. We are less certain about why OTP witnesses seem particularly motivated to testify in order to speak for the dead. However, as "speaking for the dead" is more of an external motivation that encompasses a larger community outside oneself, one could make the argument that prosecution witnesses who are called by the side representing the "international community" are more inclined toward such other-regarding motivations. The other two motivations regarding "putting the past behind oneself" and "telling one's story" are factors more internal to the witness's own mental makeup and well-being.

Finally, in three of the four models we find that education is negatively related to the reason in question. Higher levels of education are associated with a decreased likelihood of indicating that putting the past behind oneself (Table 3.3), confronting the defendant (Table 3.4), and telling one's story (Table 3.5) are strongly motivating individuals. Again, all three are largely personal reasons. We might have speculated that better-educated individuals would feel a stronger compulsion to testify because of larger societal concerns as education is intended to broaden one's horizons and make one more aware of human similarities. But we do not find such a result. More educated witnesses are just less likely to feel strongly about personal reasons for testifying.

Two findings stand out in our analysis of witness motivations. First, most witnesses agree that all of the reasons proffered were important in their desire to testify. Hence, witnesses are motivated by a plethora of internally oriented and externally oriented reasons to appear before the ICTY. Second, those who suffered the most during the wars of the former Yugoslavia are more likely to indicate they are especially compelled to testify for all the reasons we examined whether personal or societal. Clearly, these witnesses (and one wonders whether such findings would hold up across analyses of witnesses at other tribunals) are committed to making their voice heard and contributing to international justice. Because of the traumas these individuals have suffered international courts like the ICTY rely on them to bear witness. The desire of these individuals to appear in court comports well with the needs of international justice. We next turn to an examination of how witnesses feel about their contributions to international justice and the discovery of truth.

Witness Satisfaction with Testimony

Two of the final questions witnesses were surveyed about ask them whether they believe their testimony contributed to justice and the discovery of the truth. As we saw earlier most witnesses do believe their testimony helped to achieve these goals. Very few witnesses disagreed with such sentiments, although a number of individuals were not sure or did not offer an opinion. In this penultimate section of the chapter we seek to understand why some witnesses are more satisfied with their testimony than others. Because of the larger number of individuals who did not express an opinion about their testimony we analyze this question in two ways. First, like in the prior analysis we use an ordinal probit model to estimate the model on the four-value dependent variables, where "4" represents those who strongly agreed that their testimony contributed to providing justice or discovering the truth; "3" is for those who agreed; and "2" and "1" represent those who disagreed and strongly disagreed, respectively, that their testimony contributed to truth or justice. Because we lost a number of cases due to a lack of opinions on these issues among a number of witnesses, we also created a dichotomous dependent variable that is coded "1" for those witnesses who either agreed or strongly agreed with the statement, and "0" for all others.

We use the same set of variables as we used in the prior analysis, but also include two additional factors. First, we include a variable measuring whether the witnesses believe the OTP had been fair to them. This variable functions more as a control as we would expect that those individuals who believe they were treated fairly would have a more positive experience overall on the witness stand. Second, we include a measure of the intensity of the individual's motivations for testifying. We count the number of instances in which individuals indicated they "strongly agreed" with one of the seven reasons for

TABLE 3.6. *Ordered probit estimates of witness perception of their contribution to justice*

Variable	Coefficient	Standard error	Z statistic	P value
Bosniak	0.275	0.255	1.080	0.281
Serb	−0.474	0.303	−1.570	0.117
Bosnian Serb	−0.268	0.310	−0.860	0.387
Croat	0.328	0.269	1.220	0.222
Albanian	0.061	0.327	0.190	0.852
Experiences	−0.007	0.016	−0.470	0.641
Female	−0.468	0.235	−1.990	0.047
Prosecution witness	−0.248	0.208	−1.190	0.234
Consequence	0.106	0.184	0.580	0.564
OTP fair to me	0.847	0.235	3.600	0.000
Reason intensity	0.092	0.039	2.380	0.017
Education level	0.020	0.054	0.370	0.711
Age	−0.006	0.009	−0.650	0.518

n=211

testifying. This variable ranges from "0" for individuals who never strongly agreed with one of the motivation questions to "7" for those who strongly agreed with each motivating factor.

When we assess the results for Table 3.6 (ordered probit model) and Table 3.7 (dichotomous probit model) pertaining to the individual contributions to justice we find that the impact of ethnicity differs depending on whether we measure the dependent variable as an ordered or a dichotomous measure. In the ordered probit model (Table 3.6) we see that ethnicity does not appear to exercise a statistically significant or substantively meaningful impact on whether witnesses believe they contributed to justice. In Table 3.7, which contains the results for the probit model where those who agree or strongly agree are coded "1," and all of the rest are coded "0," we see that Bosniaks are statistically more likely to believe that they have contributed to justice, as are Croats and Kosovar Albanians. The coefficients for the gender variable do not reach levels of statistical significance in the dichotomous probit model (Table 3.7), although it is negative and statistically significant in the ordered probit model, and neither does the variable measuring the level of trauma experienced by individuals during the war.

In both Table 3.6 and Table 3.7 the coefficients for the "OTP Fair to Me" variable are statistically significant and positive. Not surprisingly, those individuals who believe they were treated with fairness tend to come out of the

TABLE 3.7. *Dichotomous probit estimates of witness perception of their contribution to justice*

Variable	Coefficient	Standard error	Z statistic	P value
Bosniak	1.034	0.281	3.680	0.000
Serb	−0.326	0.270	−1.210	0.227
Bosnian Serb	−0.032	0.277	−0.120	0.907
Croat	0.514	0.267	1.930	0.054
Albanian	0.741	0.371	2.000	0.046
Experiences	0.008	0.016	0.500	0.614
Female	−0.291	0.247	−1.180	0.239
Prosecution witness	−0.297	0.202	−1.470	0.141
Consequence	0.088	0.197	0.450	0.656
OTP fair to me	0.799	0.211	3.800	0.000
Reason intensity	0.038	0.042	0.900	0.366
Education level	−0.021	0.054	−0.380	0.701
Age	0.000	0.008	0.000	1.000
constant	−0.379	0.629	−0.600	0.547

n=283

testimonial experience with greater levels of confidence that their testimony contributed to justice (Stepakoff et al. 2014). We also tested to see if the witnesses' perceptions of the fairness of their treatment by the Defence made any difference, but the coefficients for this variable were consistently statistically insignificant. In Table 3.6 we see that those individuals who expressed a stronger motivation to testify are also more likely to believe they contributed to justice. The greater the number of times a witness indicated that a reason for testifying was very important to them, the more likely she is to believe that her testimony contributed to the provision of justice. In Table 3.7, however, the coefficient for this variable fails to reach statistical significance in the dichotomous probit model. None of the other coefficients in these two models reaches conventional levels of statistical significance.

In Tables 3.8 and 3.9 we present the ordered and dichotomous probit results for estimating individual attitudes regarding their contribution to the discovery of the truth. In the ordered probit model in Table 3.8 we see that while the coefficients for the Bosniak and Croat variables are positive, they both miss statistical significance. In the dichotomous probit model in Table 3.9 the coefficient for the Bosniak variable is positive and statistically significant. Bosniaks are, in general, more likely to believe that their testimony contributed to the discovery of the truth. None of the coefficients for the ethnicity

TABLE 3.8. *Ordered probit estimates of witness perception of their contribution to truth*

Variable	Coefficient	Standard error	Z statistic	P value
Bosniak	0.404	0.259	1.560	0.119
Serb	−0.278	0.319	−0.870	0.383
Bosnian Serb	−0.227	0.298	−0.760	0.447
Croat	0.406	0.273	1.490	0.137
Albanian	0.422	0.331	1.270	0.202
Experiences	−0.007	0.016	−0.450	0.651
Female	−0.374	0.233	−1.600	0.109
Prosecution witness	0.017	0.214	0.080	0.935
Consequence	0.061	0.187	0.330	0.744
OTP fair to me	0.722	0.236	3.060	0.002
Reason intensity	0.122	0.041	2.990	0.003
Education level	0.035	0.053	0.660	0.511
Age	0.003	0.009	0.380	0.704

n=216

TABLE 3.9. *Dichotomous probit estimates of witness perception of their contribution to truth*

Variable	Coefficient	Standard error	Z statistic	P value
Bosniak	0.599	0.280	2.140	0.032
Serb	−0.315	0.272	−1.150	0.248
Bosnian Serb	−0.063	0.277	−0.230	0.819
Croat	0.453	0.278	1.630	0.104
Albanian	0.614	0.396	1.550	0.121
Experiences	0.006	0.017	0.350	0.728
Female	0.006	0.257	0.020	0.981
Prosecution witness	0.084	0.198	0.420	0.672
Consequence	0.177	0.202	0.870	0.383
OTP fair to me	0.483	0.208	2.320	0.020
Reason intensity	0.117	0.042	2.770	0.006
Education level	0.026	0.056	0.460	0.647
Age	0.000	0.008	−0.030	0.980
Constant	−0.708	0.644	−1.100	0.272

n=283

variables is statistically significant. We see here too that neither gender nor level of wartime trauma appears to exercise any meaningful impact on individuals' perceptions about their contribution to the discovery of the truth. The only commonalities we see, beyond the lack of statistical significance for the coefficients for all of the other variables, concern the results for the "OTP Fair to Me" and "Reason Intensity" variables. The coefficients for both variables are positive and statistically significant in both tables.

We find two important results that generally hold across all four sets of results. First, individuals are clearly influenced by their perceptions of treatment by the OTP. Fair treatment would seem to imply that the individual had a positive courtroom experience, with all of its collateral benefits. The positive impression of the OTP seems to help influence or perhaps solidify individuals' positive assessments of their own performance. These perceptions of OTP fairness may suggest that for these witnesses at least, they were able to say what they came to say, which leaves them feeling more efficacious. We also find in all but one set of estimates that those witnesses who are strongly motivated to testify are also more likely to feel positive about their contributions. Perhaps they are so invested in their testimony that they are motivated to believe that they have turned in a positive performance. As well, individuals who believe their testimony is important are highly motivated witnesses who are apt to arrive in The Hague with high levels of determination. This may be their form of resilience. While we believe it is important to point out such a possibility, without data on individuals' psychological makeup (e.g., outlook on life, general sense of control or efficacy over one's life), we should refrain from reaching any final conclusions.

In general, the models predicting witness attitudes on their contribution to justice and contribution to the discovery of the truth are not as strong as we would like. While we would not exonerate our model from blame for these less than stellar results, we wonder if the concepts of justice and truth may be overly abstract or subjective, which may be leading to different interpretations of their meanings. While we readily utilize such concepts in the study of courts and politics, they may have very different meanings for the witnesses, as they often do for scholars and practitioners. Justice may have more to do with whether witnesses feel made whole again after the experience of testifying, or whether they think that the sentences given in the cases in which they testified were fair. Diverse interpretations by the witnesses of these concepts may ultimately lead to more unpredictable results. This type of "blame the concept" explanation is rather unsatisfying, however, and clearly, understanding witness satisfaction with their testimony is an issue that requires greater and more focused attention.

CONCLUSION

The survey of those who have testified before the ICTY has helped us gain much insight into the unique experiences of the individual witnesses. Despite some work that has suggested witnesses were not always positive about their interactions with the Yugoslav Tribunal (Stover 2005), we see here that most witnesses had a positive, personal experience. First, the vast majority of witnesses indicated they had sufficient time to prepare for testimony and had adequate information about testifying. The data also show that interviewees testify for a number of reasons, but most of them pertain to the need to contribute to a greater good for the societal whole, whether by contributing to truth and justice or helping to reduce the chance of future violence. Third, and most importantly, witnesses indicate they are highly satisfied with their reasons and motivations for having testified. Given the wartime trauma interviewees endured and the challenges of appearing before an unfamiliar court far from home, the findings indicate that witnesses care about the legal, moral, and personal implications of testifying. Moreover, both OTP and Defence witnesses were about equally likely to be satisfied with their experience testifying (93% and 90%, respectively). Witness satisfaction with their testimony is also a positive sign for the ICTY and larger international justice arena. Even given the great demographic diversity of the interviewees, the types of trials they testified in, and their motivations for doing so, the witnesses generally came away from the experience of testifying with some level of personal satisfaction regarding their contribution to international justice.

The models we developed in this chapter to help understand witness motivations for testifying and their level of personal satisfaction with their contributions have also been insightful. We must acknowledge, however, that the results for the statistical analysis of the latter fell short of our expectations for a thorough accounting of the forces that explain why some individuals are more satisfied with their testimony than others. When we estimate models to help explain the reasons why individuals are motivated to testify we find most prominently that those who suffered the most during the wars of the former Yugoslavia were more likely to indicate they felt compelled to testify for a number of reasons, both personal and societal. We see here the fascinating and powerful role that resilience can play in helping some individuals endure the violence of war and the testimonial process. However, the evidence indicated that there was no statistically significant relationship between the amount of trauma a witness endured and their satisfaction with their testimony.

The findings of this section capture one side of interviewees' dual perspectives on international justice. We find here that the witnesses personally felt fairly treated by the Tribunal and felt they had contributed to justice and truth telling. As we shall see in Chapter 6, however, the witnesses have much more divided views on the macro-level of performance of the ICTY, such as the duration of the trials and the punishment imposed on those convicted. We turn next to an analysis of the kinds of threats and harms witnesses experience from individuals who are opposed to their testimony.

4

The Witnesses and Human Security: The Social, Economic, and Security Consequences of Testimony

INTRODUCTION

In 1994, the United Nations began articulating the contours of "human security" in the context of international relations. Broadly defined as having two components – "freedom from fear" (absence of violent conflict) – and a much broader dimension – "freedom from want" (socioeconomic security), both are vital in post-conflict societies (Kaldor 2007; Lautensach and Lautensach 2013; UNDP 1994). Human security exists when individuals can live without threats of violence to their personal and bodily integrity, and when they can live in conditions where basic human needs are met, including work, health, security, and employment. These issues of human security are especially critical in the context of witnesses testifying before international courts, for not only are nearly all of these individuals victims of war who have needs resulting from these conflicts, they are also courageous individuals who have stepped forward to contribute to national and international justice. The act of testifying brings with it human security consequences that are critical to witness well-being, as well as the ability of international tribunals to conduct trials. One only has to look at the problems the ICC has faced regarding witness safety and its subsequent decision to suspend the Kenyatta trial involving election violence in Kenya[1] to understand that witnesses are a sine qua non of international criminal justice.

In this chapter, we examine the impact of witnesses testifying in the context of human security issues and consequences to better understand the degree to which they face social, economic, and physical consequences and which

[1] In September 2014, President Uhuru Kenyatta had his trial suspended because of witness intimidation and allegations of murder (http://bbc.in/2gLYan2). In April 2016, Deputy President of Kenya, William Ruto, had charges dropped by a 2–1 vote, with the judges in the case citing witness interference (http://nyti.ms/2gFouco).

factors are most associated with the occurrence of threats to human security. In the first section of this chapter we review the findings of the survey to document the problems faced by witnesses, the sources of these problems, and the steps taken by witnesses to address them. In the second section of the chapter we analyze the role of the three theoretical lenses on human security – wartime trauma, ethnicity, and gender – to better understand how these three factors shape the witness experience. We find that while ethnicity can help us gain a better understanding of which witnesses are most likely to experience threats to human security, the level of wartime trauma and whether the individual is an ethnic minority in their community are among the more powerful factors associated with such threats.

HUMAN SECURITY AND THE WITNESS EXPERIENCE

Social Consequences of Testimony

Intimate relationships. Particularly important for the individual and society in nations emerging from wartime violence and human rights atrocities are the community relationships and trust that were harmed during conflict and that need to be rebuilt (Clark 2014). These relationships with family, friends, and the community are important for witnesses who are called, subsequently testify, and then return to their communities, where they may face the consequences of testifying (Hodžić 2010; Bloomfield et al. 2003). The impact of testifying may be felt by friends, family, and intimate partners, who may not understand the ordeals and difficulties the witnesses have experienced or comprehend why the witnesses feel compelled to testify. The impact of testifying is not just confined to the present generation as the scars of this social mistrust may also be felt by the next generation that bears the burden of these dysfunctional societal relationships and distrust (Björkdahl and Selimović 2014; Meernik et al. 2016).

Based on VWS experience, some family members or friends may oppose the witness's decision to testify out of fear of possible testimonial consequences, a desire to forget the past, or distrust toward the ICTY. In some cases, VWS personnel observed that witnesses decided not to inform family members of their testimony either because witnesses did not want to reveal some war trauma or because relatives were against their participation in the judicial process. Problems may also arise in the local community, especially in small towns or close communities where everyone knows what their neighbors are doing. Some witnesses have indicated that their testimony might be perceived as helpful or harmful to an entire ethnic group, and thus, regardless of the reasons why individuals testify, they are concerned that others may perceive them as a traitor or an apologist for a particular group.

The potential consequences to witnesses who testify begin even before they go to The Hague, when the calling party (OTP, Defence, or Chambers) reaches out to them. The testimonial process is fraught as there are numerous potential points in the witnesses' interactions with the Tribunal and a variety of ways in which there can be human security consequences, as we describe later in the chapter. These effects can be long lasting. The interpersonal impact on witnesses can be most consequential when there is criticism or disassociation from those with whom the witnesses have the most private and intimate relationships (spouse, family, and friends). Likewise, the acceptance or ostracism of others around witnesses (community leaders, religious leaders, and other persons in the community) can enhance or undermine justice, reconciliation, and the process of rebuilding communities after mass conflict (Spini et al. 2013). Yet, unless the consequences of war and international justice on personal and societal relationships are forthrightly addressed, there may be detrimental consequences for the short- and long-term mental health of witnesses (Stepakoff et al. 2015).

To gauge the consequences of testifying on community relationships and human security, witnesses were asked if and how testifying had an impact on their marriage and their perceptions about how they were treated by family, friends, and other people in their communities. In terms of marital status, the vast majority of witnesses in our survey sample were either married (n=244), involved in a relationship (n=3), or widowed (n=22), with a small number single (n=14) or divorced (n=13) (Figure 4.1).[2] Regarding the potential for positive or negative consequences on their intimate relationships, virtually all witnesses report no impact (n=260), and a few (3.7%) even report testifying had a positive impact on their relations with their partner (n=11) (Figure 4.2). As one interviewee noted eloquently, "when you tell the truth, no matter how difficult it is, it always leaves a favorable impression on your partner to expect the same in mutual relations." Two interviewees reported negative changes to their relationship, with one noting the spouse had been opposed to testifying out of concern that the Tribunal would not be impartial and fair. After the judgment came down in the case where the interviewee testified, there was an adverse impact on their marriage (both were

---

[2] War crimes trials take time, and two witnesses had their relationship status change over the course of testifying. One witness was married, and subsequently lost a spouse (passed away). The second witness classified his/her status as both "divorced" and "in a relationship." Neither witness noted that there had been a negative impact on their relationship.

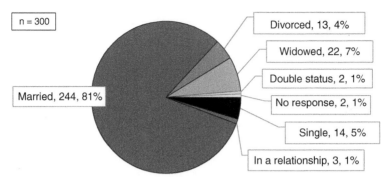

FIGURE 4.1. Relationship status.

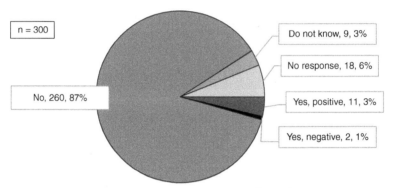

FIGURE 4.2. Impact on intimate relationships.

still married when the witness took the survey). Approximately 9% (n=27) of persons did not respond or were not sure about the impact of testifying on their relationships.

Community relationships. Reconciliation and the ability to move beyond the divisions of war depend on individuals' ability and willingness to repair and sustain relations in their communities. Particularly where there are lingering ethnic tensions (Halpern and Weinstein 2004; Clark 2014) and when there are concerns about the next generation's perceptions of the conflict (Meernik et al. 2016; Spini et al. 2013; Hjort and Frisén 2006), addressing such relationships in the face of traumatic experiences can contribute to a sense of community, which can facilitate long-term understanding (Hutchison and Bleiker 2008). Therefore, it is critical to assess how witnesses perceived their treatment by their community as a result of testimony because it can be one long-term indicator of the challenges to reconciliation (Clark 2014).

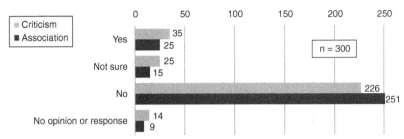

FIGURE 4.3. Criticism, disassociation, and testifying. "I believe I was criticized because of my engagement with the ICTY."
"There are some people who *do not associate/interact* with me because of my testimony."

Interviewees were asked whether they experienced criticism and disassociation as a result of testifying. There was a diverse array of answers including overlap regarding the different types of treatment that witnesses received by others. This criticism and disassociation mean that some witnesses continue to be shunned in some manner by the community for having appeared at the ICTY. In Figure 4.3, we see that there were 35 interviewees (12%) who indicated they were criticized as a result of testifying before the ICTY, while 75% indicated they suffered no such problems. The remainder did not know, had no opinion, or did not respond. We also see in Figure 4.3 that there were 25 individuals (8.3%) who suffered a loss of association with those in their community because of testifying, while 84% reported no such problems. Thus, for a small, but critical number of witnesses, the post-testimonial phase is one in which they feel disparaged and excluded from the community.

Two important caveats need be made about these data. First, there is overlap between the two categories of criticism and disassociation because some witnesses perceived that they were subject to both. Overall, 47 witnesses indicated they believed others criticized or ostracized them because of testifying, with 12 witnesses saying they had experienced both types of negative consequences (results not shown). Second, we note that there are 25 witnesses (8.3%) and 15 persons (5%) who were not sure whether they had been criticized or ostracized. As one witness put succinctly, "there is doubt." Yet five of these witnesses identified, nonetheless, those groups of persons who they believed had either criticized them or no longer associated with them. We report those results here because this is a "witness-centered survey," and because the witnesses took the time to answer the question in detail, our perspective was that we should include their answers in Figure 4.3.

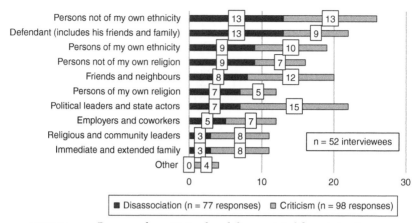

FIGURE 4.4. Persons who criticized and disassociated from interviewees.

Figure 4.4 provides data on which persons issued threats.[3] Witnesses identified multiple categories of persons who they believed acted negatively toward them as a result of their testimony. The results – sorted from highest to lowest in terms of disassociation – indicate that interviewees report the greatest levels of ostracism and criticism by persons of a different ethnicity, with ostracism from the defendant (including his friends and family) being the second largest group of persons. It is striking that in terms of criticism, interviewees face ostracism from persons of their own ethnicity, as well as those who are *not* of their religion (n=9). It is also striking that political and state employees are perceived as being the most critical of all the groups (n=15), and even religious and community leaders seem to have been critical and disassociated from witnesses. These findings are especially significant because political conditions in post-conflict society are important for reconciliation (Clark 2014). One of the most important findings here is that witnesses do not just face exclusion from others outside their ethnic and religious group, but confront such problems from persons who are of their *own* ethnicity and who are from their *own* religion, as well as their friends, neighbors, and family members. Most critically, to the extent that witnesses face multiple threats to the social fabric, these witnesses may be more (or less) likely to support the work of the ICTY.

---

3 The "other" open-ended answers included in "criticism" one each for "envious people," "victims," "Tribunal critics," and "war deserters." In "disassociation" the same interviewee who identified "war deserters" for criticism noted he felt ostracism as well.

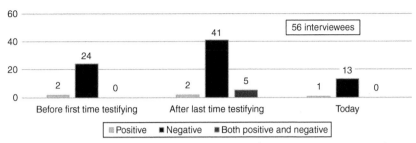

FIGURE 4.5. Positive and negative economic changes across time periods.

Economic Impact of Testimony

Witnesses can also experience adverse economic consequences because they testify at the ICTY (Clark 2014; Cody et al. 2014; Stover 2005). In the aftermath of mass conflict, economies can be destroyed, slowing economic recovery that can further limit economic opportunities (Blattman and Miguel 2010; Kondylis 2010). Thus, it is important to gauge interviewee perception about their economic losses vis-à-vis their testimony, which can range from loss of income and other business opportunities, to government limitations on their income and the destruction of assets. The consequences of being unable to recover financially can fuel continuing tensions.

As with other types of threats to human security, witnesses can experience the economic consequences of testifying over a period of time – not only before they testify, but well into the future after they testify as there are ramifications that come after others learn that the witness has testified. Witnesses were asked whether they (or their families) experienced positive or negative economic changes: (1) before they testified; (2) immediately after they testified for the last time; and (3) today (Figure 4.5).

A sizeable number of witnesses – a total of 56 (18.7%) – reported some type of positive or negative economic consequences before the first time they testified, following the last time they testified, or today. There is overlap for some witnesses who experienced economic change because they may or may not experience change in all time periods. For most of the 56 interviewees who indicated some type of change, the vast majority experienced exclusively negative consequences (n=52). These results lend support to concerns about the negative short-term and long-term economic impact of testifying before war crimes tribunals (Stover 2005; Clark 2014). The scope of this impact cannot always be accurately measured because this survey is based on witness perception, which may not always be correct. The results highlight, however, the importance of examining more accurately the economic changes that happen to witnesses because they testified. It is also in contrast to ICC witnesses who seem mostly neutral on whether they experienced financial losses as a result of testifying (Cody et al. 2014).

Before turning to the economic threats that witnesses face, two caveats are important because the richness of the witness experience and the data are as fascinating as they are complicated. First, as with ostracism and criticism in the community, there is a small, but important number of witnesses who, while they did not indicate positive or negative change, still noted losses.[4] Second, there is significant overlap between witness categories who experience losses over multiple periods. Of the 52 who had losses over some part of three time periods, 7 witnesses experienced losses over all three, with 11 experiencing losses between the first time (during testimony) and today, while 14 encountered negative losses during testimony and after the last time they testified.

What types of losses do witnesses experience? Economic insecurity for interviewees ranged from lost income and deprivation of government benefits, to lost opportunities for additional income and losses of property and agrarian assets. We see in Figure 4.6 that of those reporting, loss of income is the greatest problem during testimony (n=20), after the last time testifying (n=17), while a number of witnesses indicated they experienced such losses through the present because of their testimony (n=11) (Figure 4.6). Finally, for witnesses who testified in more than one trial, eight individuals indicated that they noticed differences in their economic status between trials (results not shown). One noticed more problems in the workplace, while another noted that he did not get salary increases after testifying the second time. For these witnesses, the long-term impact of testifying has had marked consequences. To the extent there are continuing economic harms to witnesses, this may affect their level of satisfaction with the ICTY and its mission (Miller 2008).

Through its directive on allowances for witnesses, the ICTY provided for payment of monetary assistance for expenses incurred by fact witnesses and expert witnesses in order to minimize adverse economic effects they endured while being away from home and work when testifying. Meals, daily allowances, and compensation for witnesses for time away from home and work are set at the United Nations' rates for the country where a witness resides

---

[4] During testifying three marked income, while five noted income after testifying for the last time, and two noted income today. The remaining categories combined resulted in one person noting government intervention on livelihood and loss of livestock after the last time interviewed (the latter witness indicated "not sure" – the story was described in an open-ended interview).

FIGURE 4.6. Economic losses attributed to testifying across time periods.

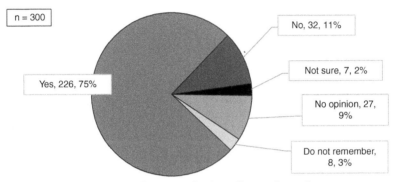

FIGURE 4.7. Satisfaction with ICTY financial entitlements
during testimonial process.

(attendance allowance). In some cases (upon a proper showing and assessment), the ICTY may provide additional compensation to witnesses for extraordinary losses they have experienced because of the testimonial process. About three out of four interviewees were satisfied with ICTY financial entitlements (the per diem compensation they were given during the time of their testimony), with approximately one out of 10 dissatisfied (Figure 4.7).[5] The findings here also mirror the ICC witness survey, where witnesses overall were satisfied, but a small number were dissatisfied with their compensation (Cody et al. 2014).

---

[5] Before 2001, the ICTY was criticized by some witnesses for providing insufficient compensation to cover all of their expenses associated with traveling to testify (Stover 2005). Early on, witnesses who wanted compensation for lost wages due to absences had to: (1) provide a copy of earnings statements if self-employed; or (2) obtain a written statement from their employer that they were not being paid during the testimonial period. Compensation was based on the minimum wage of the relevant countries. Later, concerns about disparate economic losses, fraud, as well as security for witnesses whose employers might not know they were testifying led to the implementation of an attendance allowance based on a flat rate per country of residence regardless of occupation (effective January 2002).

Human Security Impact of Testimony

Human security threats, especially those to the physical security of witnesses, are the most severe of all, and one of the greatest obstacles any transitional justice mechanism has to overcome (Cryer 2014; Stover 2005). Because of the tremendous stakes of international tribunals for the political and military leaders who stand trial, their governments, and other powerful states, as well as the international community, it is not surprising that some defendants, and most especially their supporters back home, may try to coerce, harass, or even threaten witnesses to keep them from testifying. Therefore, it is critical to examine how witnesses perceive their security situation. The existence of threats, intimidation, and fear weakens any judicial process.

The first threats to security for a witness can begin as soon as others think that a witness will be appearing before the Tribunal (Trotter 2013), and continue through travel to and from testifying, as well as upon the return home (Stepakoff et al. 2014; Stover 2005). Threats to witnesses are not just directed at them personally, but may extend to family, friends, as well as property. This is a critical issue for mental health advocates as individuals who perceive security threats are more likely to be at risk for PTSD and depression (Başoğlu et al. 2005). Issues with insecurity may also impede efforts at reconciliation (Clark 2014).

Pressures to prevent witnesses from testifying include contact by third parties with the witness and his or her family to ask them not to testify, and vandalism to property including homes and workplaces. More serious forms of intimidation come through verbal and physical threats against witnesses and their loved ones as a result of testifying before the ICTY. Tribunal judges themselves have noted that witnesses must feel secure in order to be able to testify effectively, and if they do not, such insecurity reflects negatively on the judicial process (Wald 2002).

Witnesses were asked about their overall security, and about the nature of any threats they might have faced because of their testimony and whether they experienced harm or vandalism because of testifying (Figure 4.8). Approximately 16% (n=48) of the 300 interviewees report some sort of vandalism, extrajudicial contact, threat, or harm regarding their testimony.[6] The

---

[6] We note that these counts are only for the witnesses who answered "yes." As with the economic consequences category, there are witnesses who report "no" or "not sure" for whether they suffered any of the threats related to Figure 4.8. Nonetheless, they reported a category of persons responsible for the threats, so we include those in Figure 4.9 later in the chapter.

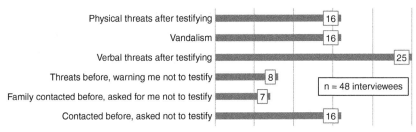

FIGURE 4.8. Threats to security by type.

greatest number of threats are verbal threats following testimony (n=25), followed by physical threats (n=16) and contact with the witness to ask him or her *not* to testify. We note again that there is overlap in witness responses in terms of the contacts and threats that witnesses face.[7]

Of particular concern is when witnesses experience multiple forms of intimidation. As with economic issues, small sections of the interviewee pool remain vulnerable given such multiple challenges to human security. When examining threats made to interviewees (both before and after testifying), of the 25 persons who received verbal threats after testimony, 13 respondents noted that the verbal threats after testifying also meant facing physical threats following testimony (data not shown). Thus, while verbal threats are more common, they are also associated about half the time with more serious threats of physical harm. More alarming is that of eight persons who received threats before testifying, seven interviewees received verbal threats after and six witnesses also received physical threats, indicating a high probability that for those who receive threats before, those threats will continue after testifying. There is also a higher probability of vandalism and harm occurring when contact or threats have been made. Of concern to human rights practitioners and witness advocates, 13 witnesses received physical and verbal threats, and 4 of those indicated harm or injury occurred to either themselves or their family as a direct result of testifying.

The "who" and "how" of witness intimidation is little studied except through high-profile occurrences in war crimes trials (Cryer 2014). Balancing witness protection with defendants' right to a fair trial means providing international courts with the power to provide measures that will help protect

---

7 Note that there are overlapping categories because interviewees could receive multiple threats in different ways. Additionally, there were three write-in answers that are not reflected in the chart. These address whether witnesses experienced some other type of harm as a result of testifying: late-night phone calls; social isolation from people and certain topics; and criminal investigation.

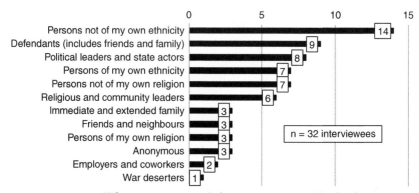

FIGURE 4.9. Whom interviewees believe were responsible for threats.

witness identities and lessen the potential for threat from those opposed to the witnesses' testimony (Bates 2014). This has been an issue with which the ICTY and other tribunals have grappled as there have been problems with witness intimidation, the release of secret witness identity information, and the more general right of public access to war crimes trials (Trotter 2013; Haider and Welch 2008; Elias-Bursać 2015).

To better understand "threats" and their occurrences, interviewees were further asked to identify which persons they believed were responsible for the threats and in what manner threats were delivered (Figure 4.9). The answers given by witnesses reveal that interviewees were unsure about whether they received a threat, while for others, the mere extrajudicial contact with the witness or his or her family constituted a threat. Thus, there were witnesses who reported in the category of persons who were responsible for making contact or threats (n=32), but they may not have indicated that a specific threat was made (recall that there were only 29 witnesses who explicitly said they received some type of threat). Figure 4.9 reports witness perception based on their responses. Witnesses noted that most frequently it was "persons *not* of my own ethnicity," followed by the defendant (including his/her friends or family), along with state employees and political leaders, who were often associated with the threats. Interestingly, witnesses also face threats from those who *are* of the same ethnicity as the witness, indicating that threats to testifying come not just from those who may be ethnically heterogeneous, but homogenous as well.

Threats to physical safety that are delivered in person can be the most directly confrontational and intimidating to a witness (Stover 2005; Clark 2014), but any type of contact with witnesses that involves any kind of threat is of concern not only for protecting international justice, but also for the

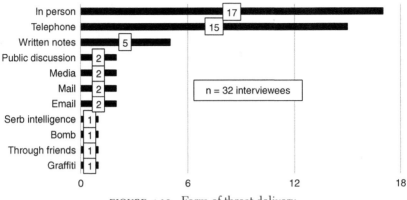

FIGURE 4.10. Form of threat delivery.

security of the witnesses and their families. Interviewees were asked how the threats levied against them were delivered (Figure 4.10). More than one-third of the threats came either in person, over the phone, or through friends and acquaintances. Five witnesses noted that they received both in-person threats and threats *via phone*, while another eight witnesses noted that they received threats in two or more ways (e.g., via email and via phone).

The ICTY, especially in the early years, was accused of not providing enough security to witnesses when threats were being assessed (Walker 1997). Over the years this situation has changed, and consequently, reports of threats can often be referred to a state police force for further investigation and action. In terms of responding to threats, the VWS generally adopts an escalating scale of response to mitigate the risk consisting of: (1) local measures; (2) temporary relocation; and (3) permanent relocation. All of this assumes, however, that witnesses reach out to the ICTY. It has been the VWS experience that some witnesses remain reluctant to involve local authorities. In the aftermath of the conflict, law enforcement in the region had been decimated and a great deal of mistrust existed between agencies and the communities. This appears more prevalent for those from smaller rural areas who are concerned about maltreatment or simply do not wish to draw attention to themselves. As with the ICTY, there has been improvement in local responses to concerns about human security because of increased capacity by local law enforcement agencies in the former Yugoslavia.

When witnesses are threatened, reaching out for assistance can be difficult – particularly if it is authority figures who are making the threats. For those witnesses who answered "yes" they received threats (n=29), the follow-up question asked if they contacted authorities and, if they did not, why not?[8] One indicated that the anonymity of the threats made contacting authorities pointless, while another did not contact authorities because the people he did not trust were in power. Still another expressed resilience "because I am not one of those people who are easily frightened." One witness noted philosophically that he did not contact anyone "because nobody can be technically protected. The point is whether you are afraid or not." These comments from witnesses illustrate the importance of understanding how witnesses experience the impact that threats have on them. Even if mechanisms are in place for security, witnesses may not feel that the authorities will be of any use.

Of those interviewees *who had been* threatened and *who indicated "yes" they did* contact authorities (n=11), witnesses contacted different authorities about assistance, and the majority indicated satisfaction (n=7), while some (n=3) indicated they were dissatisfied (one did not respond). Witnesses were most likely to reach out to the VWS either in The Hague or through the field offices, with the latter being considered the most satisfactory in addressing witness security concerns. Reaching out to the VWS at The Hague offices and reaching out to local officials were both more satisfactory than not, while inquiries to the ICTY Prosecutor resulted in mixed satisfaction (results not shown). Because there was such drop-off between those who indicated there was a threat of some sort against them, and because only one-third of those persons ultimately contacted authorities, more research is needed to look at the critical group of witnesses (ranging from 10%–15% depending on the associated threat) who are affected in both the short- and long-term after having testified.[9] Even if small numbers of witnesses report threats to their human security, it means a core group of witnesses feel insecure today because of having testified, and that harms the viability of trials.

In-Court Protective Measures

Testifying publicly means that witnesses have to reveal their identities to communities back home and face the dual risks of backlash within the community or attacks from those who disagree with them because they are cooperating with the Tribunal (Kravetz 2013). One vital way the ICTY has attempted to

---

[8] Here, 35 witnesses answered the question even though 6 of them did not indicate explicitly they received a threat.

[9] These threats should not be minimized, but the findings contrast with concerns associated with war crimes prosecutions in the local courts where security threats are "widespread" and attempts to deal with such threats are considered inadequate (OSCE 2010: 13; Orentlicher 2008, 2010; Zoglin 2005).

enhance the safety and security of witnesses is by providing in-court protective measures (PMs) through Rule 75 of the Tribunal's Rules of Procedure and Evidence. Such measures may be granted to both prosecution and defense witnesses. Concerns about the use of PMs (they are either too liberal or too conservative) have been raised throughout the history of the Tribunal, and the critical focus has been on whether PMs undermine justice (Trotter 2013; Bates 2014).

Either granting or refusing PMs pits the defendant's right to a fair trial against the need to protect witness security. The ICTY acknowledged this in its very first case, *Prosecutor v. Tadic*.[10] In that case, not only was a rape victim's family so intimidated that she was withdrawn as a witness, but there were also allegations that Bosnian Muslim police coerced another witness into testifying (Walker 1997: 312). Ultimately the *Tadic* Chambers issued a controversial ruling that four witnesses be allowed to remain completely anonymous indefinitely, even to the defendant and his legal counsel. This meant the defendant had no idea who the witnesses were or how they attained their information that was being used against him. While some applauded the Tribunal's willingness to protect the identities of witnesses who were perceived as being vulnerable, the larger criticism was that the legitimacy of the legal process may have been undermined (Haider and Welch 2008).

Since that ruling in *Tadic*, no other witnesses have received complete anonymity. Even if a witness is granted PMs, the defense team and the defendant see and hear the witness as the measures apply only to the viewing public. Only a judge or a Chamber may order appropriate measures for the privacy and protection of victims and witnesses, and different types of in-court protective measures are possible: use of a pseudonym, redaction of the witness's name, voice distortion, facial distortion, closed session testimony, and testimony through one-way closed-circuit TV.[11] Requests for protective measures may not always be granted by the Trial Chamber, and as a result the witness may refuse to testify. Depending on individual circumstances, the witness may

---

[10] *Prosecutor v. Tadic*, IT-94-1-T, http://bit.ly/2huICTY (July 14, 1997).

[11] *Pseudonym*: code used instead of witness's real name and redaction of witness's name from all existing court documents – all identifying information may be sealed or excluded from all Tribunal public records; *voice distortion*: altering the sound of witness's voice; *facial distortion*: altering the image of witness's appearance; *closed session*: witness gives evidence in court session closed to the public (*in camera*) with only the judges, lawyers, the accused, and court officials present in the courtroom; *giving evidence by one-way closed-circuit TV*: witness does not see the accused as the evidence is given in a separate room; the witness is able to hear what is going on in the courtroom, and the judges are able to see the witness on the courtroom television screens on their desks.

be withdrawn from the witness list or compelled to testify without protective measures.

For some witnesses, this mere public anonymity is insufficient to protect those who may be most vulnerable (Peterson 2008). The VWS can also enhance the safety and security of witnesses through a protection program for those individuals who face heightened security risks.[12] In situations where a threat is assessed as imminent and requiring immediate action, an option exists to temporarily remove a witness from the threat area. This is a significant escalation and is only done in the most serious of circumstances. Relocating a witness from their home and employment is yet another extreme measure that causes major disruption. In situations where the threat remains and it is considered unsafe for a witness to return to their community, there may be a permanent relocation, and while the ICTY has the authority and resources to relocate witnesses, it is exceedingly rare. This represents a measure of last resort and is only implemented when no other option exists that adequately addresses the level of threat. In these situations, the ICTY is reliant on the good will of states to resettle a witness, a process established through formal agreements. We note that relocated witnesses were not included in the study out of concern for their safety.

As for the use of PMs by the ICTY, Figure 4.11 reflects the study's findings about how frequently measures are implemented, and it highlights the unique way in which measures are used at the Tribunal. Recall that witnesses may appear multiple times, in the same trial or in multiple trials, and depending on the nature of the testimony and the threat that is posed, a witness may be granted certain types of measures in one trial, and then denied measures in yet another. This leaves up to the witness a decision about whether or not to appear.[13] The 300 witnesses here have had 448 appearances in trials. Of those, more than two-thirds (69.4%) of appearances by witnesses were done *without* any PMs during testimony (data not shown). Note that the findings suggest that the Tribunal is reluctant to grant sweeping measures, and instead tends to give face distortions and pseudonyms most frequently. The Chambers seem to be the most reluctant to grant completely closed sessions that provide the greatest level of protection for vulnerable witnesses.

---

[12] Relocated witnesses and those who experienced heightened security risks were *not* included in the study. Less than 1% of witnesses are relocated by the VWS through its relocation program. Witnesses may migrate on their own initiative to another region or country.

[13] Indeed, one witness who participated in the survey had been granted protective measures in one trial, and when called to testify again, was ready to do so until Chambers denied PMs. He was withdrawn as a witness because he refused to testify without measures.

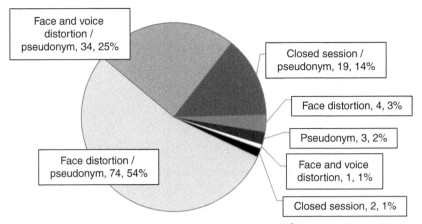

FIGURE 4.11. In-court protective measures of interviewees (using ICTY data on actual PMs).

There has been criticism of the Tribunal for failing to provide in-court protective measures, leaving witnesses feeling vulnerable both during testimony and after they returned home (Stover 2005; Clark 2014). In-court protective measures raise the specter of whether defendants should have the right to confront publicly witnesses or whether that right must be intruded upon to protect a witness's need for security and privacy. Thus, concerns have been raised about whether liberal or conservative usage of the in-court protective measures undermines justice (Trotter 2013; Bates 2014). Chambers or the calling parties may seek PMs, but when witnesses themselves are asking for protective measures, do the security measures make them feel secure? Does it make a difference only when they testify, or does that effect continue in the post-testimonial phase?

Of the 300 witnesses, the ICTY granted in-court PMs of some form to 86 interviewees in one or more of their appearances. Of these, only 64 recalled requesting in-court protective measures on their survey.[14] We focus on those 64 to examine their security at the time they testified and on their return (Figure 4.12). When comparing how secure witnesses felt

---

[14] Differences between interviewee perception and ICTY data may be accounted for by the language of the question that reads "did you ever request protective measures for your testimony?" Interviewees may have perceived that because they *personally* did not request in-court protective measures, they should answer no, which is why there are fewer responses than in the official ICTY record. Regardless, the findings support the need to give witnesses information about the process of requesting measures and that the ICTY may grant those in-court protective measures even if witnesses do not specifically request them.

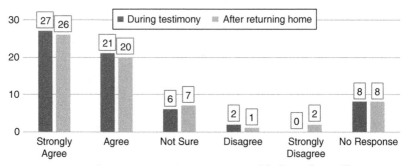

FIGURE 4.12. In-court protective measures and feeling of overall security.

at the time of testifying, and then returning home, there is not much of a decay effect, and witnesses indicate that it does make them feel more secure both during the testimonial process and after they return home for the last time.

Voluntary Migration

Another way to look at human security for witnesses is to examine whether witnesses move from their community in the aftermath of mass conflict. An option for witnesses who do not wish to remain in their communities is voluntary migration (assuming they have the resources and capacity to move), and our results here are based on voluntary moves to a different location. There were 24 interviewees who indicated that they had moved either within their own country (n=17), to another country (n=4), or *both* within their own country and to another country (n=3). One person was not sure if they had moved within his country, while another person was not sure if they had moved within their country or to another country. Given the changing boundaries of the former Yugoslavia perhaps that is not so surprising.

To dig deeper into these decisions, interviewees were asked *why* they moved. Witness migration in a post-conflict environment is complex as the results reveal. Twenty persons indicated they moved inside the country, and of these 18 said that it was not important that they testified when they made their decision to move, while two interviewees indicated that for them, it was "very important." Of the seven persons who moved outside of the country, two indicated that it was "important" they had testified at the ICTY. Figure 4.13 indicates the reasons witnesses gave for why they moved.

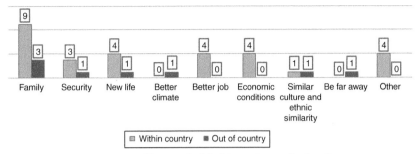

FIGURE 4.13. Reasons behind interviewees' migration.

When it comes to reasons why persons move internally within their country, the majority do it for family (Figure 4.13).[15] The same is true for those who move outside the country.[16] Following behind these are starting a new life, security, and economic conditions. There are also reasons for migrating that pertain to the underlying issues related to the wars in the former Yugoslavia, including wanting to live in an area where there was a similar culture, avoiding war criminals and war perpetrators, and not being able to return to a living situation. As with the granting of protective measures, for a small group of witnesses who have testified, the security threat is very real and significant enough to move (Clark 2014).

Security Today

Threats to security directly endanger justice and the prospects for reconciliation (Bartlett 2015; Spini et al. 2013; Hutchison and Bleiker 2008) if witnesses and their families are harassed and intimidated (Kravetz 2013). In post-conflict societies, the ability of the population to feel secure in their environment is critical for stability. Perhaps then, one of the most important questions regarding witness security is whether *generally* individuals feel secure today. Strikingly, a substantial majority of respondents report they feel very secure (64%) or somewhat secure (13%) today. Nonetheless, 13% of respondents feel (very) insecure still today (Figure 4.14), raising doubts about whether witnesses

---

[15] The "other" reasons given by witnesses include better living accommodations, being unable to return to a former living situation, employment requirements, and "to avoid war criminals."

[16] Of the interviewees who have moved, the majority have only moved once, but there were five witnesses who indicated they had moved two or more times, with one witness having moved five times since testifying. None of the witnesses who had moved more than once indicated that their testimony was important in their decision to move.

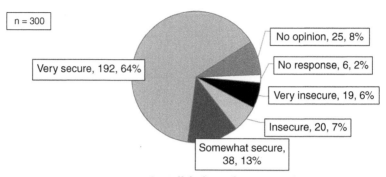

FIGURE 4.14. Overall feeling of security today.

feel secure over the long-term regarding the prospects for renewed violence in the region. Clearly, such perceptions may rise and fall due to events beyond the control of the witnesses and the ICTY, such as elections, protests, and other political events that may call into question the viability of the postwar peace in the Balkans. Such events may affect all peoples of the region in some manner. But for these witnesses who have lived through the violence of the past and have taken such visible steps to confront the violence of the past through testifying, such feelings of insecurity are likely to be especially acute.

UNDERSTANDING THE HUMAN SECURITY CONSEQUENCES OF TESTIFYING

Do the consequences of testifying fall evenly across the witness population? Is it simply a matter of opportunity or happenstance whether one is targeted with loss of property or physical threats? Are there certain dimensions along which we can better estimate the likelihood a witness faces social, economic, or security problems as a result of testifying? The next section of this chapter addresses these questions to evaluate the utility of witness trauma, ethnicity, and gender in shedding light on these issues, and to identify other salient factors. We suggest that threats against witnesses represent a continuation of conflict behavior. Social, economic, and physical threats are made to help produce a desired outcome – witness intimidation – that protects the interests of conflict actors (whether they are major national figures or local actors). Threats and violence may be deployed to produce political outcomes, such as maintaining one group's dominance in a particular town by driving out those who would testify in ways harmful to that group. Threats may also be made to influence judicial outcomes, such as by making guilty verdicts more difficult in the absence of key witnesses. Therefore, it stands to reason that the same factors that are at issue in conflict – ethnicity and gender – will continue to play a role in who is threatened in the post-conflict environment. We would also expect that those who have experienced the most trauma – those individuals who were most affected by the wars – would, by virtue of their experiences, continue to be of interest to the other key decision-makers and participants in the post-conflict environment. Therefore, we suggest that those who experienced the most trauma will be most likely to be targeted with human security threats.

We begin by engaging in some fairly basic descriptive analyses of the relationships among the three types of threats to human security and the factors related to our three theoretical lenses. Then, we develop more fully specified, multivariate models to explain which types of witnesses are most likely to experience these threats.

Ethnicity and Threats to Human Security

We begin by examining the impact of the principal fault line along which the wars of the former Yugoslavia were fought – ethnicity. We examine whether witnesses indicated that, as a result of the testimonial process: (1) they had experienced some sort of social harm and ostracism (disassociation and criticism); (2) they had experienced any adverse economic harm, such as loss of income, missed job opportunity, or destruction of property; and (3) they had experienced some sort of more physical threat, such as vandalism and violence, or verbal threats.

For these analyses, we distinguish among Bosniaks (Muslims from Bosnia); Serbs from Serbia; Serbs from Bosnia-Herzegovina; Croats from Croatia; Croats from Bosnia-Herzegovina; and Kosovar Albanians in order to more accurately measure the effect of ethnicity as it correlates with human security consequences on witnesses. It also more accurately depicts the ethnic identification and tension present in the wars in the former Yugoslavia and the historical reality that geographically the wars did not have the same impact in each region.

Providing ethnicity was optional for interviewees, and 21 individuals did not identify their ethnicity, with two individuals identifying as Macedonian and one person who claimed "Earthling" as his ethnic group. Together, these groups constitute the "Non response / other" category. Turning to the ethnic diversity of the survey population we see that the human security consequences of testifying do not always fall evenly across the different ethnic groups (Figure 4.15). Bosniaks, Croats from Croatia, and ethnic Albanians from Kosovo were the most likely to suffer social harm, with between 19% and 22% of members of

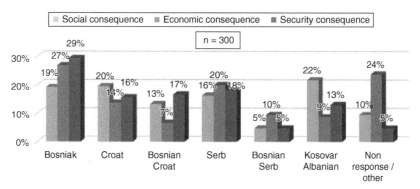

FIGURE 4.15. Ethnicity and testimonial consequences.

these ethnic groups reporting that they felt ostracized, criticized, or socially mistreated in some manner in their communities. Bosnian Croats and Bosnian Serbs were less likely to report social consequences they perceived as resulting from testifying before the ICTY (13% and 5%, respectively).

The results regarding the economic and security consequences in Figure 4.15, however, tell a markedly different story regarding how the consequences of testifying break along ethnic lines as compared to how the results appear if one examines them in the aggregate. Bosniaks are *more* likely to report both economic harm *and* security harm, with nearly 27% of Bosniaks reporting economic harm, while the next highest percentage of those recalling economic harm are those who did not provide an ethnicity, 24% of whom report economic problems. We see again that Bosniaks are much more likely to report such human security problems – 29%, or nearly one-third. Croats from both Bosnia-Herzegovina and Croatia as well as Serbs from Serbia report the next highest levels. Clearly, for the Bosnian Muslim population, the consequences of the war are never far away – the issues that led to the fighting may never be far from the surface. They were traumatized during the war, and some continue to be targeted today. It does bear remembering, however, that the percentage of all witnesses who have experienced these social, economic, and security harms is relatively small. Yet, they are a critical minority for whom the impact of having testified continues to have significant ramifications both before and after testifying.

It was because of the wars in the former Yugoslavia that the term "ethnic cleansing" was coined to describe the expulsion of people from their homes and towns and their replacement by members of another ethnic group who would henceforth lay claim to these lands. Despite the brutality and the success of these forced migrations, a number of individuals either remained or

TABLE 4.1. *Ethnic minority status and testimonial consequences*

	Number identifying as ethnic minority in community reporting consequences	Percentage identifying as ethnic minority in community reporting consequences	Percentage *not* identifying as ethnic minority in community reporting consequences	P value of chi^2
Social consequences	11 of 39	28%	14%	0.02
Economic consequences	11 of 39	28%	16%	0.06
Security consequence	14 of 39	36%	14%	0.01

n=300

returned to their homes. Many of these individuals are now a distinct minority in lands where once they might have been the dominant group. Given the tenuousness and security challenges of their existence, we may find such individuals are more likely to indicate they have experienced threats to their human security. Table 4.1 presents the numbers and percentages of those who identified as ethnic minorities in their communities and reported experiencing some type of human security consequence as a result of testifying.

Those who identify as ethnic minorities are more likely to experience each of the three types of adverse consequences (social, economic, and security), although the chi squared statistic for the economic harm and ethnic minority status variables does not quite reach statistical significance. In fact, 36% of those who are ethnic minorities report that they have experienced threats to their physical security. Most individuals who identify as an ethnic minority are Bosniaks (46%, results not shown, with Croats generally and Serbs generally each contributing about one-quarter of the share of ethnic minorities), which indicates there is still a strong ethnic component to this designation. Bosniaks are the most likely to be ethnic minorities and are more likely to indicate they have experienced economic and security consequences, although not social harm. When individuals who are ethnic minorities in their communities face criticism, ostracism, and threats to their physical security, they are paying a price for having testified. The larger issue for these communities is whether this continuing tension serves to undermine the long-term prospects for reconciliation – especially given the history and events involving ethnic violence in their region (Clark 2014; Orentlicher 2008, 2010).

Gender and Threats to Human Security

We turn next to whether women or men are more likely to experience the various threats to their human security. What is the gender component to these acts of witness intimidation? Are women specifically targeted with increased or enhanced threats to their security as they are often more isolated in communities that have been ethnically cleansed? Perhaps women are targeted more often because of traditional patterns of male patriarchy that imply women are a weak link in social relations and thus more apt to succumb to pressures from males intent on preventing them from testifying (Hudson et al. 2012). Table 4.2 provides the data on gender and threats to human security.

We find, however, that while female witnesses were more likely to report instances of economic harm, there are no statistically significant relationships between gender and social or physical security threats. More than one-quarter of female witnesses reported some type of economic loss they believed resulted from their testimony at the ICTY, while 15% of male witnesses reported such problems. As the reader can see in Table 4.2, however, the percentages of men and women who report social harm and threats to their physical security are fairly similar. It may be that women, who appear much less frequently before the ICTY, do not face the same level of human security consequences that ethnic minorities face, but testifying still has consequences for their economic well-being. It is also worth noting that slightly more than one-fifth of all female witnesses report a threat to their physical security. Thus, future tribunals would do well to consider how there are differences in terms of economic threats for women that are distinctive, and the impact this has in the post-conflict environment.

Wartime Trauma and Threats to Human Security

We now turn to the relationship between the trauma witnesses experience and their human security threats to better understand the impact of mass conflict on those who bear witness. We examine whether the witness burden is made greater because of the consequences some witnesses face based on their identity and personal experiences. Are threats to witnesses' socioeconomic or physical integrity a function of whom the witness is?

To test this, we first ran bivariate correlations between the number of types of wartime traumas witnesses reported experiencing (a cumulative variable indicating the extent of trauma) and each of the binary human security threat variables. Such an approach is consistent with other research highlighting that the range of trauma is a useful indicator of victim trauma (Ringdal et al.

TABLE 4.2. *Gender and testimonial consequences*

	Female	Male	P value of chi²
Social consequences	6 (12.7%)	41 (16.2%)	0.551
Economic consequences	13 (27.6%)	39 (15.4%)	0.042
Security consequence	10 (21.2%)	42 (16.6%)	0.437

n=300

2008). We find in Table 4.3 that there are moderate, positive, and statistically significant correlations between the amount of trauma and whether a witness reported social or security consequences (the correlation coefficients are 0.20 and 0.28, respectively). There is no statistically significant relationship, however, between an economic threat and witness trauma. It may be that witnesses do not perceive economic consequences the same way as other human security consequences, or that economic consequences are in general more difficult to ascertain.

What types of trauma are more associated with the social and security threats to integrity? We ran, as a second step, further correlational analyses to determine if there were specific types of the 26 possible traumas that were linked to the social and security threats.[17] We find that of the types of traumas witnesses experienced, 14 of the 26 traumas were positively and statistically significantly related to social threats. Among the more powerful relationships were those between social threats and imprisonment, physical assault, torture, and psychological abuse, while similar relationships obtained in 18 of the 26 correlations between trauma and security threats (the most powerful relationships were between security threats and lack of food or shelter, physical assault, ethnic cleansing, torture, and psychological abuse). There was only one statistically significant relationship between the traumas and economic consequences (artillery shelling), which was actually negative.

---

[17] Witnesses were also given the opportunity to write in other types of trauma if none of these 26 categories precisely fit their experiences. As this is a first cut at the impact on witnesses and how that correlates with trauma, we did not include the write-in categories to limit the impact this variable might have because some witnesses might be more assertive about write-in responses. In addition, many of these write-in responses were germane to just one or two witnesses. There were 54 witnesses who indicated additional types of trauma they experienced including witnessing or facing executions; sniper fire, grenades, or bombings; homes looted and burned; human shields; removal of bodies; forced labor / travel / removal; escaping captivity; wartime shortages of shelter and food; beatings; exposure to uranium; and military / paramilitary violence.

TABLE 4.3. *Partial correlations between trauma and testimonial consequences*

Wartime trauma	Social consequence	Economic consequence	Threat consequence
Lack of food or water	0.1135^a	0.035	0.1618^a
Ill health without access to medical care	0.1199^a	0.047	0.2142^a
Lack of shelter	0.1174^a	0.037	0.1958^a
Imprisonment	0.1489^a	0.037	0.1731^a
Detention (camp, building, residence, etc.)	0.1379^a	0.006	0.1861^a
Serious injury	0.108	−0.040	0.131^a
Combat situation	0.076	0.017	0.108
Rape or sexual abuse by stranger	0.099	0.034	0.034
Rape or sexual abuse by familiar person	0.049	0.043	0.043
Physical assault by stranger	0.1828^a	0.005	0.2358^a
Physical assault by familiar person	0.2179^a	0.093	0.2629^a
Mine explosion	0.084	0.102	0.102
Ethnic cleansing	0.1318^a	0.053	0.2493^a
Forced isolation from others	0.242^a	0.066	0.1861^a
Being close to death	0.1275^a	0.056	0.1709^a
Forced separation from family members	0.091	0.070	0.1789^a
Family, friends, and relatives went missing	0.064	0.077	0.1131^a
Murder of family or friend or acquaintances	0.023	−0.025	0.046
Unnatural death of family or friend	−0.041	−0.016	0.021
Murder of stranger or strangers	0.062	0.056	0.097
Kidnapped	0.125^a	0.074	0.1414^a
Torture	0.1872^a	0.051	0.2196^a
Exposed to propaganda	0.1897^a	0.103	0.2435^a
Subject to psychological abuse	0.161^a	0.085	0.2142^a
Any other situation that was frightening or life was in danger	0.079	0.008	0.1239^a
Any situation where artillery fire or shelling occurred	−0.015	-0.1607^a	−0.012

[a] $= p < 0.05$

It may be that those witnesses who experienced more trauma have more knowledge of events that make them good witnesses, but also increase the risk that one or more of these experiences involve individuals who might seek to prevent the witness from testifying. In other words, having more traumatic experiences increases the likelihood of testimony, which in turn implies a greater risk of witness intimidation. While these relationships seem logically rational, we must still wonder why there is no relationship between economic threats and wartime trauma. Here, we must make an important distinction between social and security threats where the threat is generally quite obvious (e.g., a person is ostracized or there is physical violence) and economic harms where the individual may be drawing a conclusion between their testimony and some economic loss that may not be so obviously connected. One may suspect that the theft of some property or loss of a job is due to testimony, but those responsible, even assuming they can be identified, may not admit to such actions. Now that we have described the various potential relationships that may exist between our measures of interest and human security consequences, we next turn to developing more richly specified models of human security threats to gain leverage over such questions.

MODELS OF THREATS TO HUMAN SECURITY

To better understand the potential relationships between our key factors of interest and human security consequences, we estimated three separate probit models for social, economic, and security threats where the dependent variable is still the binary measure of whether a witness experienced a particular threat or not. In addition to our focus on ethnicity, gender, and wartime trauma, we introduce several other factors into these models to recognize the personal circumstances involved with witnesses' and victims' experiences. First, we include an indicator of the witness's in-court protection measures (e.g., voice distortion, pseudonym, closed session) to determine if those who *never* had any such protection measures at any of their appearances were more at risk for such threats or whether a lack of protection measures conveys a lack of concern about threats.[18] Second, we include one psychological variable and another measuring whether the individual was an ethnic minority in the community in which they lived. The psychological variable is the individual's current assessment of his or her life situation. As others have found (Meernik 2015a; Meernik and Guerrero 2014), those individuals with more

---

[18] Here, we rely on the official ICTY statistics regarding protective measures granted by the Tribunal.

TABLE 4.4. *Explaining social consequences from the testimonial process*

Variable	Coefficient	Standard error	Z statistic	P value	Marginal impact
Bosniak	0.326	0.328	0.990	0.322	0.069
Serb	0.493	0.394	1.250	0.211	0.114
Bosnian Serb	−0.204	0.467	−0.440	0.663	−0.036
Croat	0.596	0.371	1.610	0.108	0.142
Kosovar Albanian	0.617	0.443	1.390	0.164	0.156
Ethnic minority	0.385	0.315	1.220	0.222	0.087
Female	−0.018	0.311	−0.060	0.954	−0.003
Experiences	0.044	0.018	2.480	0.013	0.008
No protection measures	−0.391	0.244	−1.600	0.109	−0.083
Present personal situation	−0.392	0.144	−2.730	0.006	−0.075
Education	0.072	0.067	1.070	0.283	0.014
Age	0.000	0.011	0.020	0.985	0.000
Constant	−1.001	0.784	−1.280	0.202	

n=265

positive outlooks tend to exhibit greater all-around positive attitudes, and in particular with regard to their views of the ICTY. We suggest that those who are positive will be less likely to report any type of threat. The results of the models are found in Tables 4.4 through 4.6. We caution again here that there are risks of attributing causality to these relationships given that most of these measures all come from witness perception.

We find several commonalities across the estimates of each of the types of threats. For the most part ethnicity appears to make little difference in which witnesses are most likely to report some type of social or economic harm (Tables 4.4 and 4.5).[19] The coefficient for the variable measuring whether a witness is an ethnic minority in the community in which they reside is positive in the model of security threats, although it misses statistical significance. The marginal impact coefficient, which indicates the percentage increase in the dependent variable given a unit increase in the independent variable when holding all other variables constant at their mean value, indicates there is an approximately 14% increase in the probability an ethnic minority will report a threat to their personal security or the security of family and friends.

---

[19] We were unable to run the security model with the Bosnian Serb variable because of insufficient observations.

TABLE 4.5. *Explaining economic consequences from the testimonial process*

Variable	Coefficient	Standard error	Z statistic	P value	Marginal impact
Bosniak	0.171	0.296	0.580	0.565	0.035
Serb	−0.455	0.388	−1.170	0.241	−0.073
Bosnian Serb	−0.683	0.413	−1.650	0.098	−0.098
Croat	−0.056	0.343	−0.160	0.871	−0.011
Kosovar Albanian	−0.364	0.484	−0.750	0.452	−0.059
Ethnic minority	0.375	0.296	1.270	0.205	0.085
Female	0.480	0.278	1.720	0.085	0.113
Experiences	−0.018	0.018	−1.000	0.316	−0.004
No protection measures	−0.168	0.244	−0.690	0.492	−0.034
Present personal situation	−0.371	0.145	−2.560	0.011	−0.072
Education	0.035	0.068	0.520	0.604	0.007
Age	−0.010	0.011	−0.900	0.366	−0.002
constant	0.559	0.790	0.710	0.479	

n=265

The coefficient for the gender variable never reaches statistical significance in the models, although it comes closest in the model of economic threats, where the coefficient is positive. This largely confirms our results from earlier that the consequences for women are not as clear according to the survey results. We cannot be sure if this is a function of the sample used or if there are simply too few women among the Tribunal's witnesses to draw generalizable conclusions. It may be that while war is considered to be "men's work" (Hudson et al. 2012), the business of transitional justice is still seen as male-dominated, and thus any consequences that accrue because of testifying remain focused on male, rather than female, witnesses.

In contrast to the impact on women, the results regarding the range of traumatic experiences a witness has reported, however, are statistically significant and quite strong in two of the models. First, in the model of social consequences (Figure 4.5) the estimates indicate that the greater the range of traumatic experiences a witness had undergone during the wars of the 1990s, the more likely he or she is to report a social consequence to participating in the testimonial process. For every additional wartime trauma a witness indicates he experienced, there is an approximately 0.8% increase in the likelihood of reporting a social threat. Similar results are found in the model of security threats where the coefficient for the trauma experience variable is also positive and statistically significant, with the marginal impact coefficient

TABLE 4.6. *Explaining security consequences from the testimonial process*

Variable	Coefficient	Standard error	Z statistic	P value	Marginal impact
Bosniak	0.291	0.303	0.960	0.336	0.073
Serb	0.288	0.379	0.760	0.447	0.073
Bosnian Serb	na				
Croat	0.201	0.357	0.560	0.573	0.050
Kosovar Albanian	−0.194	0.466	−0.420	0.677	−0.042
Ethnic minority	0.521	0.306	1.700	0.089	0.145
Female	−0.355	0.353	−1.000	0.315	−0.072
Experiences	0.064	0.019	3.420	0.001	0.015
No protection measures	−0.164	0.251	−0.650	0.514	−0.040
Present personal situation	−0.379	0.155	−2.450	0.014	−0.088
Education	−0.024	0.070	−0.350	0.728	−0.006
Age	0.014	0.011	1.330	0.184	0.003
constant	−1.439	0.824	−1.750	0.081	

n=265

approximately 1%. While these predicted increases in the probability of reporting threats are not large they do indicate that for that portion of the witness sample that has already experienced a horrible litany of wartime harms and deprivations, the effects of conflict do not end when peace is declared. Sadly, those who may be more vulnerable (ethnic minorities and those with more traumatic experiences) continue to endure consequences in post-conflict societies that may aggravate ethnic tensions.

There is only one variable that is statistically significant in each of the models – whether the witness reports being satisfied with his or her personal situation at the present. In each of the three models the coefficients for this variable are statistically significant and negative. More satisfied individuals are less likely to report a wider range of harm. The marginal impact coefficients for this variable range from a low of approximately 7% in the model of social consequences to a high of roughly 9% in the model of threats to witness security. We included this variable in these models to serve as a control to determine if an individual's basic outlook on life has any bearing on their perceptions of threats. We might expect that people who have a positive outlook on their personal situation in general may exhibit more positive and supportive attitudes about other areas of their life, or be less likely to recall negative experiences. It is certainly also possible, however, that the correlation is reversed, especially in these models. Individuals who report no harms of any type may be happier because they have not experienced such threats to human security. The lack of problems that might have arisen because of their testimony may be contributing to their positive outlook on life. For these reasons, we do not make too much of these findings at present, but we will subsequently return to this in explaining other attitudes where we would have less reason to suspect the causal arrow may be pointing in the other direction.

While these survey data reveal a great deal about the types of individuals who are most at risk for experiencing some type of threat to their human security, the survey was not designed to retroactively predict these events. What we can learn from witness experience, however, are the types of witness characteristics that seem to suggest that certain types of individuals may be more at risk than others. While ethnicity and gender do not appear to be factors that can greatly aid us in determining which witnesses are most at risk, we are mindful of the importance of one's status in the community. Those who are ethnic minorities in their communities are more likely to report security threats. These individuals may be more defenseless to such threats, and hence those harassing them perceive few, if any, consequences from their actions. They may be individuals who have moved back into communities from which their families had earlier been forcibly expelled, or they may be individuals who chose to remain despite living in such an insecure environment. In either case, they may be targeted both because of their ethnic status and as a signal to others that returning to one's community is not advisable.

When we consider the additional risk factor of the level of wartime trauma a witness endured, we can see that there are a number of individuals who have been living or are living in fraught circumstances. It is a troubling irony that those who suffered the most during the war find themselves still at risk in the post-conflict environment. We note too that there is a small, but positive bivariate correlation between ethnic minority status and the number of wartime traumas a witness experienced (results not shown). These witnesses are especially likely to experience pressure not to testify, and because of the insecure environment in which they live, there are ample reasons for the Tribunal to be concerned about their safety. Other and future tribunals and national courts charged with prosecuting violations of international law should be quite mindful of these results. The most traumatized and vulnerable of potential witnesses are among those most likely to be targeted with threats to human security. As the integrity of the judicial process depends on the ability of witnesses to feel confident to come forward and give their testimony, it is essential that such courts devise means to identify these witnesses and provide them with the type of protection and assistance they require (Eikel 2012).

CONCLUSION

The human security of witnesses at the ICTY is a vital interest. In addition, it has critical moral and political dimensions for the VWS, the ICTY, and those who are advocates of transitional justice mechanisms. The impact is most profound on those who experience threats to their socioeconomic and physical safety, and to the extent that there are groups within the population who remain vulnerable to threats, reconciliation after mass conflict can become more difficult to achieve. Because it is essential both for international justice and witness safety that witnesses testify freely and openly without fear of significant consequences, it is critical to assess how witnesses perceived their treatment by their community as a result of testifying. There is a small, but critical group of witnesses who have endured negative consequences as a result of testifying at the ICTY, and who have faced challenges subsequently in their communities. These negative consequences range from criticism and loss of association, to economic harm and threats to their physical safety and the security of their families. Ostracism and threats to human security directly endanger justice and jeopardize prospects for reconciliation (Clark 2014; Meernik 2005). More critically, these threats to human security continue to this day for witnesses – long after the trials have ended.

We found that more than one in eight interviewees believed that they had endured some negative impact such as criticism or loss of association, and one out of seven reports contact or threats as a result of having testified. Criticism, loss of association, and threats come from a wide range of persons including those who may or may not share the ethnicity of the witness, and include the defendant and those who affiliate with him or her, as well as religious and community leaders. Few of those facing human security threats actually contacted authorities, and five noted that they moved as a result of security issues. This finding is of particular importance because it suggests that witnesses may not feel they have a safety net in their communities in the event of threats to their security. We find as well that 13% of the interviewees continue to feel some level of insecurity today, although whether this is owing to their testimony or continuing tensions in the region cannot be definitively answered with these data. As the international community looks in on the former Yugoslavia, we need to better understand how peace, reconciliation, and human security are interrelated to those who are stakeholders in that outcome.

Our results shed critical light on the impact of three factors in particular on threats to witnesses' human security – ethnicity, gender, and level of wartime trauma experienced by the witness. We found that while Bosniaks in particular are more likely to report experiencing economic harm and threats to their physical security, these relationships did not hold up when we used multivariate analyses. Thus, we cannot conclude that there is consistent evidence of a differential impact rooted in ethnicity. Nonetheless, we find evidence that witnesses who identify as ethnic minorities in their communities are more likely to experience economic and security threats – so ethnicity has a role in better understanding the work of the Tribunal. As well, those individuals who experienced more harm during the Balkan wars of the 1990s are more likely to report threats. Together, these results suggest that one specific group is at risk for threats to their human security – those ethnic minorities who have lived through significant levels of trauma. While this is not a large group, it is a critical group as many of these individuals may well be among the last few of their ethnic group in a town or village who bore witness to human rights atrocities. It will be important for other international and national tribunals to take steps to ensure the security of these vulnerable witnesses, especially if peace becomes fragile again in the region.

The issue of victim and witness security is one of the key issues encountered by transitional justice mechanisms. Due to the potentially serious implications of being found guilty before an international tribunal for the political and military leaders who stand trial, their governments, and other regional states, as well as the international community, it is not surprising that some defendants, and most especially their supporters back home, try to prevent witnesses from testifying. Indeed, such problems have afflicted many of the tribunals including the ICTY, such as in the Haradinaj trial, where there were problems with witness security (Borger 2016). Therefore, it is critical to utilize this research to determine how best to ensure witness safety and human security.

5

The Impact of Testifying

Testifying before a war crimes tribunal can have long-term physical and psychological consequences (Hamber 2009; Stover 2005). The testimonies witnesses give are not just statements about whether there have been violations of international law; typically their evidence pertains to the traumas of war they have experienced, which requires them to recall painful events. One cannot overstate the impact of this trauma in terms of the physiological and psychological health of those persons who are responsible for "bearing witness." It means that not only did they endure significant levels of trauma during the Balkan wars, with which they still need to cope on a daily basis, but the very process of having to testify in one or more trials forces them to recall these memories, to cope with waiting periods (which can last years) before being called to testify, and to deal with the residual impact of having testified. This chapter describes the witnesses' psychological and physical health and how witnesses believe testifying has affected their well-being. There are three key lines of inquiry regarding the factors affecting witness physical and psychological health we explore in this chapter.

First, we examine the central concept of witness well-being through multiple measures evaluating the short- and long-term impact of the wars of the former Yugoslavia on those who have testified, including a battery of questions about their post-traumatic symptoms and perceptions about their health after testifying and today. We will begin by unpacking how well the witnesses are today, which types of post-conflict reactions and psychological concerns they tend to experience, and how the testimonial process has influenced their health.

Second, we examine witnesses' trauma, its impact, and their health to ascertain which characteristics tend to be most associated with psychological and physical health, especially their emotional states before and after testimony. The short- and long-term impact of testifying on ICTY witnesses has been a subject of interest since the beginning of the Tribunal (Wald 2002). VWS personnel can recount years of experience spent working with a diverse witness population, with some witnesses being more fragile during the testimonial process, while others are incredibly self-sufficient and composed despite having to recount horrific events. We contribute to the ongoing debate about whether testimony is considered a cathartic moment or an occasion for re-traumatization (Mendeloff 2009; Hamber 2009; Doak 2011b; Brounéus 2010; Stover 2005). This chapter discusses the reactions witnesses have before, during, and after testifying, together with the external factors that affected them during this critical period.

Third, we examine the witnesses' responses to one of the more intriguing questions in this portion of the survey regarding how well people are doing in their communities. The impact of testifying and the effects of international justice are felt on the witnesses and their relationships with those around them. We are interested in how witnesses perceive these effects on their communities and whether they are optimistic about the quality of relations in their communities. This allows us to gain some leverage on the concept of reconciliation and whether people are able to coexist peacefully in the aftermath of conflict and human rights atrocities. We are especially interested in determining if there are ethnic and geographic dimensions to this issue. We begin, however, by looking at how witnesses have fared more recently in dealing with the traumatic experiences of conflict.

WITNESSES AND RECENT EXPERIENCES WITH TRAUMA

The consequences of dealing with trauma on the scale the interviewees have encountered creates issues associated with re-traumatization, and can present substantial difficulties in obtaining closure (Bandes 2009; Başoğlu et al. 2005). In order to gauge witness psychological health and resilience, the study employed standard measures from psychology to ask witnesses about their well-being within the last six months, as well as questions about the coping strategies they rely upon to handle stressors in their lives. Table 5.1 represents the results from a battery of questions asking interviewees to indicate the extent to which particular feelings associated with traumatic experiences were present in their minds.

Sorted in order from highest to lowest in terms of how frequently the interviewees indicated they experienced the feelings, the results reveal the lasting

TABLE 5.1. *Measures of interviewees' post-trauma symptoms in the last six months*

	Never or almost never	Sometimes	Fairly often or very often
Feeling unable to stop thinking about the persons you lost during the wars in the former Yugoslavia	31.3%	28.7%	37.3%
Feeling unable to put events and experiences of the conflict in the former Yugoslavia out of your mind	40.0%	25.3%	33.0%
Feeling people do not understand what happened to you	31.0%	40.7%	25.3%
Sudden emotional or physical reaction when reminded of hurtful or traumatic events	26.0%	50.3%	22.0%
Spending time thinking about why these events happened to you	36.3%	41.7%	19.3%
Feeling unable to put the events and experiences about testifying out of your mind	58.7%	25.0%	13.3%
Feeling someone you trusted has betrayed you	45.7%	39.3%	12.0%
Difficulty performing work or daily tasks	53.3%	34.0%	11.0%
Feeling hopelessness	65.7%	25.7%	6.0%
Feeling that you have no one to rely on	69.0%	23.3%	5.3%
Feeling others are hostile toward you	72.3%	20.7%	4.3%
Feeling as if you were going crazy	83.7%	10.0%	4.0%
Finding out that you have done something you cannot remember	65.3%	28.0%	3.7%
Feeling guilty for having survived	80.0%	13.3%	3.3%
Feeling ashamed because of the traumatic events	78.7%	15.3%	3.0%
Blaming yourself for things that have happened	74.0%	20.3%	2.7%
Feeling that you are the only one who suffered these events	86.7%	7.3%	2.3%
Feeling you are split into two people and one is watching what the other is doing	87.0%	7.7%	1.3%

impact of the wars in the former Yugoslavia. The three most frequently experienced feelings of interviewees are: (1) being unable to stop thinking about loved ones (37.3%); (2) being unable to put events and experiences from the conflict behind oneself (33%); and (3) feeling as though others do not understand what happened to them (25.3%). For one-third to one-quarter of the interviewees, the impact of the war is still felt. Two other questions prompted at least one in five witnesses to say they "fairly often" or "very often": (1) experienced emotional or physical reactions when reminded of certain events (22%); and (2) spent time thinking about why the events of the past happened to them (19%).

The very act of testifying *itself* has a lasting impact. Of note is that when it comes to "feeling unable to put the events and experiences about testifying" out of witnesses' minds, 13.3% think about it often (fairly or very), with another 25% indicating they think about it "sometimes." Thus, for more than 38% of the witnesses, testifying is part of their post-testimonial emotional well-being. This lends support to a central finding of this study that there is a critical group of witness for whom there is a long-term impact related to testifying. But while the witnesses tell us they continue to think about certain of these experiences, we do not know the extent to which such thinking is "natural" after having undergone such significant life experiences or whether these witnesses may be dwelling on the past in a manner that is not psychologically healthy. On a final note of importance for human rights practitioners concerned about witness well-being, interviewees also expressed feelings of betrayal, difficulty in work, and hopelessness, including some who feel guilty for having survived. Other research has also found similar effects among survivors of war trauma (Palić et al. 2015; Opačić et al. 2006; Van der Kolk 2014; Başoğlu 1999). To the extent that persons in war-torn countries continue to struggle with post-traumatic symptoms, there are important consequences for rebuilding societies in post-conflict contexts (Biruski et al. 2014).

We investigated further whether there were relationships between the top categories of post-traumatic symptoms – (1) being unable to stop thinking about loved ones; (2) being unable to put events and experiences from the conflict behind oneself; and (3) feeling as though others do not understand what happened to them – and our variables for gender, ethnicity, and wartime trauma (results not shown). Notably, there were never statistically significant relationships between gender and any of the three top post-traumatic symptoms. Trauma, as usual, is highly significant – indicating that those who report a broader range of traumatic events are more likely to recall those memories. We find that Kosovar Albanians are more likely to think more frequently about the events and experiences of testifying. Serbs and Bosniaks tend to be less likely to dwell on these events of the past. Understanding more about why certain ethnic groups may be more or less prone to reporting these kinds of feelings, as well as identifying other characteristics associated with post-traumatic symptoms in these post-conflict regions, will be especially important in the provision of proper medical and psychological care.

PHYSICAL AND MENTAL HEALTH BEFORE TESTIFYING AND TODAY

One of the most debated issues within transitional justice networks more generally is whether those who testify before tribunals, truth commissions, and other venues are helped, harmed, or affected in some other manner because of the testimonial process (Doak 2011b; Brounéus 2010; Stover 2005). Attempts to evaluate the impact of testifying can be complicated because of the trauma witnesses have experienced, which also likely plays a significant role in witness reaction to testifying.

Mass conflict, such as the wars in the former Yugoslavia, produces adverse public health consequences that extend beyond the war to the postwar period, and these may be greater than the mortality rates associated with the war itself (Ghobarah et al. 2003, 2004; Poole 2012). Growing efforts to examine the impact of war have relied on multiple psychosocial, physiological, and economic indicators (Shemyakina and Plagnol 2013). Yet among both critics and proponents of the Tribunal, conclusions remain mixed (Clark 2014; Subotić 2009; Hayden 2011; Orentlicher 2008, 2010).

To fairly, objectively, and accurately address this question requires substantial data beyond the scope or capacity of this survey because it would have required independent assessments about witnesses' mental and physical health before, during, and after testifying, although other research has helped fill in some of these gaps[1] at the International Criminal Court (Cody et al. 2014) and the Special Court for Sierra Leone (Stepakoff et al. 2014, 2015). The findings of those studies are that the process of testifying may not necessarily lead to re-traumatization or negative consequences for witnesses, with majorities reporting high levels of positive feelings about the impact of testifying.

Given the relative lack of knowledge about the impact of testifying and legal intervention on crime victims in general (Herman 2003), the results of this study add to the knowledge base with one important caveat. We measure

---

[1] There have been attempts to assess the health of persons in the region of the former Yugoslavia going back in time (Mollica et al. 1999; Cardozo et al. 2000; Salama et al. 2000) and meta-analyses of data regarding the impact on mental and physical health that results for persons who are displaced or who have endured mass conflict (Steel et al. 2009; Percival and Sondorp 2010; Başoğlu et al. 2005).

only witnesses' *perceptions* of their own physiological and psychological states. These are not data from medical reports or trained professionals. Given that witnesses were asked to think back and provide their post-facto recollections about how they "thought" they felt before and after the process of testifying, one must be cautious in interpreting these results. *Nonetheless, witness perceptions about psychosocial health are a valid and important measure because their perspectives matter and these perceptions influence witnesses' behavior and coping.* One of the strengths of the research from Stover (2005), Cody et al. (2014) and Stepakoff et al. (2014, 2015) is that they have endeavored to let the victims speak from their own perspectives. Our study seeks to do the same and to provide a systematic and scientific attempt to quantify these health experiences (Mendeloff 2009; Doak 2011b). The results also contribute to a growing body of work that seeks to understand the impact of significant trauma on persons who survive mass conflict because it can vary substantially depending on the particular conflict and the affected population (Silove 1999; O'Donnell et al. 2004; De Jong et al. 2001).

Relative to studies looking at mental health, there is less research at the micro-level on physical health and the impact of the Yugoslav wars (Shemyakina and Plagnol 2013). The picture that emerges of postwar public health is that there are long-term consequences across multiple indicators (Ghobarah et al. 2003, 2004; Poole 2012; Kerridge et al. 2013; Letica-Crepulja et al. 2011; Mollica et al. 1999; Salama et al. 2000). There seem to be higher levels of mental distress within the population during earlier postwar periods, but this seems to have dissipated over time (Do and Iyer 2012). The nature of the lasting effects of war events on physical health is not fully understood because mental well-being is linked to physical health, and these can be dependent on region, gender, or other factors.

Witnesses face multiple health issues as a result of having experienced wartime trauma, and as with any other aging population, they encounter physiological challenges during the time period(s) when they are testifying. The survey asked interviewees about their physical health by comparing their health before the first time they testified and more recently (Figure 5.1). Witness health is broken down by gender, with the percentages of witnesses in each category reporting the status of their health then and in the last three months.[2]

---

[2]   The reason why witnesses were asked about their health in the period "after the war and before their first testimony" had to do with the many injuries witnesses suffered during the war, which drastically affected their health after the conflict. Additionally, for the purposes of this study, witnesses who testified multiple times were asked to think about the period before the *first* testimony and after their *last* appearance when thinking of before and after testimony.

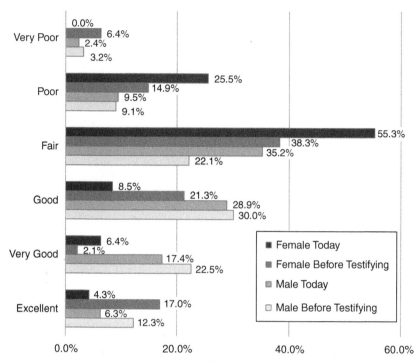

FIGURE 5.1. Interviewee health before testifying and within last three months (by gender).

These results reflect an interviewee pool that is more elderly (the average age of interviewees is 60.3 years for men and 54.3 years for women) and where health is generally in decline – note the differences between men and women especially in terms of the "Fair" and "Poor" categories. An examination of gender and health reveals that there are significant differences in health reports between men and women prior to the first time they testified and today (results not shown). Women more often report their health is worse than do men both before the first time they testified and within the last three months. Ethnicity and trauma do not appear to be related to differences in health over time, although we find that ethnic minorities report significantly higher levels of health wellness before the first time they testified. The same effect does not carry through to the last three months. Overall, women report their health is not as robust as men's, consistent with findings that women in post-conflict societies report great levels of health consequences (Hudson et al. 2012; Eber et al. 2013; Stepakoff et al. 2014, 2015). Men wanting to hide it?

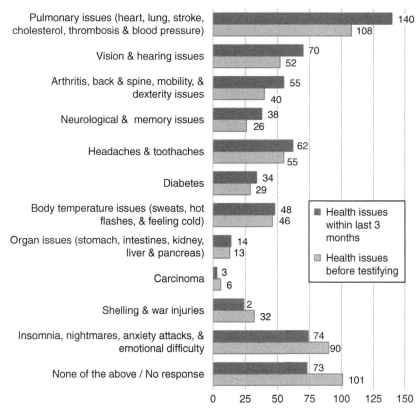

FIGURE 5.2. Health issues before testifying and within last three months.

To delve deeper into witness perceptions about their health vis-à-vis the ICTY, the survey asks witnesses about specific areas relevant to standard measurements of witness physiological health (Figure 5.2).[3] Respondents could (and frequently did) check off multiple health-related issues that applied to them. When examining specific health issues before the first trial at which the witness testified and then within the last three months, interviewees report more health issues today *overall* than they did before the first time they testified – not such a surprise given the aging population.

As with overall health findings, witnesses report their overall health today is not as good as it was before the first time they testified. The highest frequency of health issues within the last three months are also associated with an aging

---

[3] Includes only responses with more than five occurrences. The remaining categories are not included.

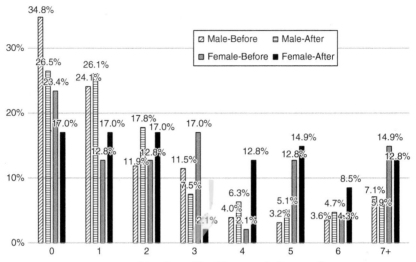

FIGURE 5.3. Number of health issues before testifying
and within last three months.

population – pulmonary issues, vision and hearing issues, along with mobility and dexterity problems. There are a number of health-related issues that are actually *lower in frequency today*, with insomnia, carcinoma, and wounds related to shelling being the top three (results are sorted according to the level of increase in frequency in the last three months). Arguably, these are more likely to be war-related health issues.

Are certain witnesses at risk of greater health issues today? We examined different factors that could contribute to health and well-being across ethnicity, gender, and number of trial appearances, while controlling for interviewee age, health perceptions, and trauma experienced during the conflict (results not shown). Bosniaks, Croats, and Albanians consistently report more health issues than Serbs, today and before the first time they testified. In contrast, Serbs report significantly fewer health issues today than before testifying for the first time. Women report significantly more health issues today than before the first time they testified, and overall, women are more likely to report more health issues in general. We present the bivariate results on gender and health issues in Figure 5.3.

Impact of Testifying on Health

The impact of testifying may be felt long after the witness has left the courtroom (Stover 2005), and given that these witnesses have experienced high

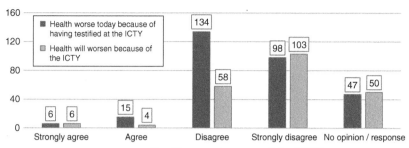

FIGURE 5.4. Health worse because of the ICTY.

levels of trauma, there may be negative consequences that endure to this day. Do witnesses *perceive* that there have been long-term consequences from testifying? Do they think that their health will be worse *because* they testified? Interviewees were asked to self-report about their health today and whether: (1) their health is worse today *because they testified at the ICTY*; and (2) their health *will get* worse *because they testified at the ICTY.* As is clear from the findings in Figure 5.4, interviewees' perceptions that their health is worse today or will get worse are not borne out. The majority of all interviewees (including those who had no opinion and did not respond) – 77.4%–do not think their health is worse today because of having testified at the ICTY. There are some, however – 7%, or 21 individuals – who do (strongly) agree that their health is worse because of having testified at the ICTY. There are some gender effects: women are slightly more likely (13%) than men (6%) to think their health is worse because they testified. Note that about one in five to one in six persons are uncertain about the relationship between their ICTY testimony and their health.

When witnesses look to the future about the impact of testifying over the long-term, almost 73% of witnesses *do not* think that their health will worsen as a result of testifying (Figure 5.4 only 221 persons were able to respond to the future question). Looking more closely at whether the witnesses think the ICTY has contributed to deteriorating health, we ran analyses using our standard measures (results not shown) to explain witness perceptions about the impact of testifying on their health. The only factor that is consistent across both models is witness perception within the last three months about their health (results not shown). Gender and trauma do not appear to be related to such perceptions. Bosniaks and Bosnian Serbs are more likely to disagree that their health is worse because they testified, while Bosniaks (again) and Bosnian Croats were more likely to disagree that their health will be worse because they testified at the ICTY. These findings about traumatic events are consistent with other research about the impact of testifying on witnesses (Stepakoff et al. 2015) and findings that long-term effects of wartime trauma may include an impact on physical health because of bearing witness. Given that many of these studies, including the present one, do not collect data over time on witness health, it is important to continue examining the impact of testifying over the duration of a witness's life, including long after testifying.

PSYCHOLOGICAL REACTIONS BEFORE, DURING, AND AFTER TESTIMONY

Almost all witnesses have some type of reaction to the process of testifying before, during, and/or after their testimony. Articulating traumatic events that may have happened years ago in a formal courtroom setting in the presence of strangers may contribute to re-traumatization of the witness or perhaps a shutdown of emotions. VWS staff have observed that witnesses' reactions in The Hague are frequently stronger when it is their first time testifying because they are recalling difficult and stressful events quite vividly, which they may not have discussed so openly before or talked about in many years. Sometimes witnesses share their thoughts and emotions with VWS staff because they are overwhelmed, or because they have no one back home with whom they can share their emotions about their testimony experience.

There has been increasing research in the last 10 to 15 years on the emotional and psychological well-being of witnesses, victims, and persons who have survived the conflicts in the former Yugoslavia. There has been debate about the impact of testifying on psychological healing (Bandes 2009; Henry 2009, 2010; Herman 2003). Does the process of testifying do more harm than good to the emotional state of those who testify? Some have argued that the process of testifying may provide healing, closure, or catharsis to help individuals overcome traumatic events (Moghalu 2004: 216; Stover 2005). Others argue that evidence is limited and questionable when it comes to the impact on victims (Bandes 2009: 16), and that this is particularly true for the ICTY witnesses (Clark 2009a, 2009b, 2009c, 2009d, 2014: 201). The reality is, however, that we are only beginning to understand "the individual psychological and emotional effects of national truth-telling and accountability mechanisms, or about victims' experiences with criminal justice more broadly" (Mendeloff 2009: 596). However, this is beginning to change.

Scholars have generally found that witnesses experience both positive and negative reactions to the process of testifying regardless of whether the venue is a truth and reconciliation commission (Byrne 2004; Hamber et al. 2000), community justice court (Brounéus 2010), or war crimes tribunal (Stepakoff et al. 2014, 2015; Stover 2014). Moreover, the longitudinal beliefs and attitudes of witnesses about the testimony process may change over time (Backer 2010).

To gauge the emotional states of witnesses before and after testifying, the survey provides witnesses with more than 30 possible emotional responses that ICTY VWS personnel generated based on their interactions with witnesses over the years. Interviewees could select as many or as few feelings and emotions as most accurately reflected their state of mind before going into the courtroom and immediately after testifying. The types of responses were categorized into two categories: (1) positive affect[4] states (n=15); and (2) negative affect states (n=19). It is important to reemphasize that this is a retrospective review by the witnesses about their affect states in the pre- and post-testimony processes. The distribution of individual affect is presented in Table 5.2, where we see wide variation within both positive and negative affect.[5]

Overall, when interviewees reflect back on their testimony experience, comparing positive and negative affect, the results show significant differences between their pre- and post-testimony states (Table 5.2 sorted in order of greatest reduction in affect *after testimony*). A majority of interviewees indicated they felt high levels of positive affect both before and after testifying, and significant numbers of interviewees reported a reduction in negative affect states after having testified for the last time. By far the most frequently occurring positive affect state interviewees reported was feeling "cooperative," with 186 interviewees indicating they felt that way *before* testifying. Interviewees report being less "cooperative" (n=112) after testifying, but this may pertain more to the fact that they perceive their "cooperation" as having successfully concluded with the end of their testimony. Other significant increases in affect experienced by substantial numbers of respondents before and after testimony include feeling "satisfied," "relieved," "positive," and "fulfilled." Figure 5.5 shows there are several affect states in which respondents noted fewer positive affects.

Interviewees could also choose from a range of negative affect states. During the survey development process VWS personnel presumed that there would be *more* negative affect types reported than positive ones, but in fact the opposite is true (Figure 5.6). The interviewees report *significantly* lower levels of negative affect as compared to positive states both before and after testimony, despite the fact that there were more negative affect state options from which

---

[4] "Affect" is here used as a comprehensive term for emotions, moods, and attitudes.

[5] Witnesses could also write in emotions that for positive affect include (total in parentheses) pleased (4); respectful (1); calm (1); curious (1); fighting for truth and justice (1); adrenaline rush (1); want to help (1); focused (1); and contributed (1). These are not included as part of the affect count.

TABLE 5.2. *Distribution of negative and positive affect – before and after testifying*

Negative affect before (alpha)		Positive affect before (alpha)		Negative affect after (alpha)		Positive affect after (alpha)	
Angry	22	Confident	106	Angry	26	Confident	101
Anxious	56	Cooperative	186	Anxious	19	Cooperative	112
Ashamed	9	Courageous	80	Ashamed	0	Courageous	65
Betrayed	11	Energetic	45	Betrayed	15	Energetic	38
Confused	48	Fulfilled	40	Confused	14	Fulfilled	96
Embarrassed	26	Happy	32	Embarrassed	10	Happy	55
Exhausted	13	Hopeful	83	Exhausted	44	Hopeful	78
Guilty	2	Inspired	25	Guilty	1	Inspired	22
Indifferent	15	Positive	76	Indifferent	14	Positive	111
Lonely	16	Powerful	28	Lonely	9	Powerful	31
Obligated	114	Proud	93	Obligated	61	Proud	95
Overwhelmed	11	Relieved	69	Overwhelmed	11	Relieved	129
Panicked	18	Satisfied	88	Panicked	4	Satisfied	128
Powerless	4	Strong	47	Powerless	9	Strong	47
Regretful	3	Vindicated	69	Regretful	5	Vindicated	96
Sad	21			Sad	13		
Scared	19			Scared	9		
Tense	81			Tense	17		
Tired	20			Tired	42		

the interviewees could choose. Moreover, interviewees report significantly lower levels of negative affect states following testimony. Among the negative states interviewees could select, "tense," "obligated," and "confused" were among the top responses. At the same time, however, these are quite likely to diminish significantly after the last time an individual testifies. Immediately after testifying, only "obligated" receives higher response rates, along with "exhausted" and "tired" as we might expect given the nature of human reactions to stressful situations. There are statistically significant differences with "anxious," "tense," and "confused" in terms of a difference of means before and after testimony.[6]

---

[6] Interviewees could provide short answers, and interviewees provided slightly more negative than positive emotions. The range of responses included physical (adrenaline rush, discomfort); psychological (calm, curious, pleased, uneasy, having stage fright, insignificant, regretful, respectful, disappointed), and philosophical (wanting to help, fighting for truth and justice, intolerant, fulfilling a civic duty).

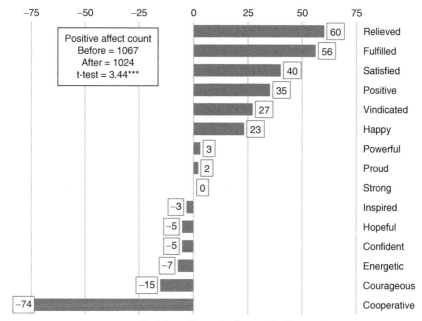

FIGURE 5.5. Positive affect – before and after testimony.

In summary, when comparing self-reported positive and negative affect states by interviewees, there are *more positive* and *less negative* reactions both before and after testifying. This finding contributes to the debate about whether the process of testifying is re-traumatizing or cathartic (Stover 2014; cf. Brounéus 2010). It also suggests that at least in terms of witnesses' recall of their reactions, witnesses are more likely to remember more positive than negative states both before and after testifying.

As we discussed in Chapter 1, it is possible that our sample of witnesses may be a more positive and healthy group of individuals than the witness population as a whole. Since one of the most frequently occurring reasons for declining the opportunity to take the survey was witness health, we want to be sure that our sample is not overly biased toward those in good health and with other positive attributes. Fortunately, we have other data against which to check our results. Since 2009 the VWS has been conducting an internal and anonymous written survey of all witnesses done after they testify. It measures witness perceptions and satisfaction with VWS services immediately following testimony, and thus unlike this study is a more contemporaneous account of witness emotions. These results indicate that the present study mirrors in many ways the VWS internal and anonymous survey results. In both surveys

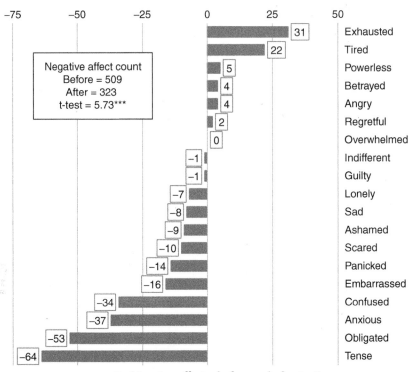

FIGURE 5.6. Negative affect – before and after testimony.

witnesses express significantly higher levels of positive affect and lower levels of negative affect *after* testifying. One key difference is that in the VWS internal anonymous survey, the reduction in negative affect is higher than in this study (results not shown). In all but two categories of negative states, respondents in the VWS survey indicated lower levels of negative affect states in their post-testimony phase. This would seem to suggest that, if anything, the witnesses in our sample may maintain recollections about their feelings after testimony that are more focused on negative affect states. This should also help alleviate concerns that our sample of witnesses is a healthier and more positive group than the witness population more generally.

Explaining Witnesses' Affect

We turn next to assessing why some witnesses are more likely to report positive and negative affect and emotions after testimony. There has been increasing research into this area because of the tremendous interest in determining whether testifying in tribunals and truth commissions produces positive or negative affects (Bandes 2009; Henry 2009, 2010; Herman 2003; Byrne 2004; Brounéus 2010; Stepakoff et al. 2014, 2015; Stover 2014). Indeed, while there is much discussion regarding this issue of whether transitional justice mechanisms are cathartic or re-traumatizing on witnesses when they tell their story before judges and lawyers, we are not yet able to provide as much convincing evidence of their impacts because of the comparative lack of systematic research. There has not been a fully developed account for why there are differences in findings about the impact of testifying on witnesses, especially one that has been tested on a random sample of individuals. Our aim is to begin to address this gap in the research that is of keen interest to scholars and practitioners alike who wish to understand the frequency with which individuals recall positive affect and negative affect states after testimony.

In addition to the standard array of measures we use – ethnicity, gender, and wartime experience – we also include other measures to help explain the extent to which witnesses are likely to report positive and negative emotions at the conclusion of the testimonial process. We include the measures for: (1) how intensely motivated witnesses are to testify using the variable described in Chapter 2; (2) how satisfied the individuals are in their present personal situation; (3) whether the individuals believe they are being treated fairly by the Defence and an equivalent measure of perception of fairness by the OTP; and (4) the number of appearances each witness has made at the ICTY.

We specify a negative binomial regression model because the dependent variables are count variables. Tests comparing Poisson and negative binomial models indicate that the data have both under-dispersion and over-dispersion on our two variables – positive and negative affect. We utilize the negative binomial regression model to estimate the number of positive affects witnesses recall feeling after the conclusion of their testimony, and also the number of negative affect states they recall after testifying in Tables 5.3 and 5.4. Figure 5.7 indicates the dispersion of the dependent variables. T-tests reveal the difference of means is highly significant with the positive affect (mean=4; median=3), outpacing negative affect (mean=1.7; median=0) substantially – the data graphically reveal the same. The range of emotional affect for positive (0–15) and negative (0–11) reveals that witnesses recall fewer negative types of affect, and that overall the range of affect is lower than those given by witnesses for positive affect.

The results presented in Tables 5.3 and 5.4 are quite interesting for both what we find and what we do not find. We first examine the negative binomial regression model for the number of positive emotions witnesses recall feeling

TABLE 5.3. *Model – positive emotions after testimony*

Variable	Coefficient	Standard error	Z statistic	P value
Bosniak	0.1708	0.1584	1.0800	0.2810
Serb	0.0285	0.1858	0.1500	0.8780
Bosnian Serb	−0.2554	0.1967	−1.3000	0.1940
Croat	0.0890	0.1727	0.5200	0.6060
Albanian	0.6409	0.2082	3.0800	0.0020
Experiences	0.0258	0.0098	2.6200	0.0090
Female	0.0200	0.1568	0.1300	0.8990
Reason intensity	0.1614	0.0766	2.1100	0.0350
Defense fair to me	0.0011	0.1233	0.0100	0.9930
OTP fair to me	−0.0577	0.1357	−0.4300	0.6710
Number appearances	0.0122	0.0662	0.1800	0.8540
Present personal situation	0.2197	0.0889	2.4700	0.0130
Education	−0.0123	0.0348	−0.3500	0.7240
Age	0.0050	0.0054	0.9200	0.3560
Constant	−0.1659	0.4942	−0.3400	0.7370

n=275

TABLE 5.4. *Model – negative emotions after testimony*

Variable	Coefficient	Standard error	Z statistic	P value
Bosniak	−0.180	0.266	−0.680	0.499
Serb	−0.260	0.334	−0.780	0.436
Bosnian Serb	−1.073	0.382	−2.810	0.005
Croat	0.485	0.279	1.740	0.082
Albanian	0.262	0.349	0.750	0.452
Experiences	0.020	0.017	1.220	0.223
Female	0.517	0.244	2.120	0.034
Reason intensity	0.116	0.131	0.890	0.375
Defense fair to me	−0.294	0.201	−1.460	0.144
OTP fair to me	−0.434	0.230	−1.880	0.059
Number appearances	0.227	0.109	2.090	0.037
Present personal situation	−0.378	0.130	−2.910	0.004
Education	0.048	0.058	0.820	0.412
Age	−0.005	0.009	−0.530	0.597
Constant	0.726	0.764	0.950	0.342

n=275

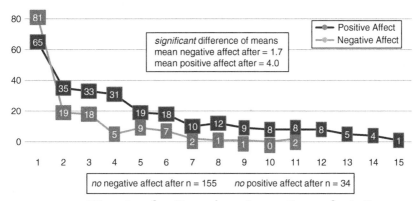

FIGURE 5.7. Dispersion of positive and negative emotions – after testimony.

after the conclusion of their testimony. Ethnicity makes little difference with regard to reporting positive emotions, although we see in Table 5.3 that Kosovar Albanians are more likely to recollect more positive emotions. As we hypothesized, we do find that the greater the number of traumatic experiences a witness endured during the war, the more likely it is that she will recall more positive emotions after testimony. This finding is in keeping with emerging research on positive behaviors that many individuals and communities exhibit after having lived through violence and war. Certainly not all individuals will be as resilient under such circumstances, but there are many (perhaps more than we might have suspected) who do engage in socially and personally positive behaviors. For many of these witnesses who have lived through so much already and then must recount their experiences on the witness stand, it may be that this opportunity to tell their story and find a type of closure in their journey is a largely positive one. A more in-depth examination of how such individuals frame and interpret these experiences would undoubtedly provide a wealth of insight into this fascinating finding.

Two other coefficients are statistically significant in a two-tailed test in the positive emotion model. The coefficient for the variable measuring the intensity of the individuals' motivations for testifying indicates that those who are most strongly compelled to testify for any number of the seven reasons provided in the survey are more likely to recollect positive emotions after testimony. Those individuals who feel more compelled to testify, as distinct from those who may appear reluctantly, are, not surprisingly, more positive about the experience. In addition, witnesses who report a more positive outlook in general on their current life situation are more likely to recall positive emotions. Future research might focus on exploring this relationship in greater depth to better understand the nature of the relationship here and to what degree present circumstances influence individuals' perceptions of past emotions.

In the model estimating the number of negative emotions witnesses recall feeling after testimony, we find some similarities and some differences from the positive emotion model. Here, we find that ethnicity plays a bit more of a role. Croats (from Croatia) are more likely to report negative emotions (although this variable does not quite reach standard levels of statistical significance for two-tailed tests), while Bosnian Serbs are less likely to recollect negative emotions after testimony. And even though Kosovar Albanians were the only group to report more positive emotions after testimony, they are not commensurately less likely to report negative emotions. Also, in contrast to the results in Table 5.3 we find that gender does exercise a statistically significant impact. Female witnesses are more likely to recall negative emotions. We also find that the number of traumatic experiences witnesses suffered during the wars is not related to recollections of negative emotions after testimony. Those individuals who report that they are satisfied with their present circumstances in life are less likely to report negative emotions, which comports with the results in Table 5.3, where one's life satisfaction is positively associated with recalling more positive emotions.

Interestingly, in both models we find that a witness's impression of their treatment by the prosecution or the defense does not usually exercise a statistically significant impact on their recollection of emotions. However, those who believed the ICTY prosecution treated them fairly are less likely to report recalling negative emotions. Given the numerous comments witnesses made about their treatment by counsel we expected these variables would have played a much more prominent role in accounting for the types of emotions witnesses recollected. We checked to determine if multicollinearity might have been playing a role in influencing these estimates, but found no evidence of such. Perhaps witnesses evaluations of their treatment in the courtroom is less tied into their overall experience than we suspected. It is also possible that since most witnesses believe they were treated fairly by both sides this lack of variation may be partially accounting for this result.

Finally, we note that the more frequently witnesses testify, the more likely they are to recall negative emotions. The notion of "witness fatigue" came up repeatedly in our discussions as VWS personnel have found that for many witnesses who journey more than once to The Hague, such frequent appearances create problems and hardships. As well, we would expect that some number of these witnesses have also been called upon to testify in local courts. As repeat witnesses are likely to be more effective in court, it will be critical for future tribunals to take steps to ameliorate the difficulties involved in frequent appearances.

Other Issues Witnesses Experience during the Testimonial Process

Beyond the physical and emotional reactions that witnesses may experience during the process of testifying, witnesses may encounter other more challenging obstacles. Are there certain circumstances or events that make testifying more difficult? Almost one-third (29%) of the interviewees indicated that there are such challenges, as we see in Figure 5.8. Many mentioned postponement or rescheduling of testimony, including long delays and waiting periods, and being away from home, family, and friends.[7] These findings are consistent with other research (Stover 2005, 2014; Stepakoff et al. 2014). Being able to focus at the Tribunal can be difficult if a witness is concerned about the consequences of testifying. In some cases, the presence of other witnesses or persons at the Tribunal may have an adverse impact on witnesses. Interviewees alluded to other logistical issues, the length of proofing sessions, preparation, and cross-examination as issues that concerned them (short-answer responses, noted with "*").

In light of these challenges during the testifying, interviewees were also asked whether there were strategies that would assist with reducing their discomfort (Figure 5.9).[8] As the results indicate, the witnesses rely on a wide range of skills, but clearly the single most prevalent coping mechanism is "assistance from VWS," with more than 56.8% of those responding saying that it alleviated stress. Following that are coping strategies that include "rest periods" and, importantly, the witness's own psychological resolve to be able to testify ("no matter how hard this is, this has to be done"). Additionally, "speaking with family," "having a non-VWS support person present," "talking to someone about the process," or focusing on the ability to survive and concentrate were among interviewees' most reported responses for coping. A number of interviewees (n=53) noted that having an accompanying support person with them helped ease the stress associated with the process of testifying. Spouses (n=21), children (n=8), friends (n=7), and siblings/other family (n=5) are among the most frequently cited among those who selected this response.

---

[7] The same witness might mark multiple categories, thus the numbers for each category do not reflect the actual number of witnesses, who may have marked other categories as well.

[8] There were 951 responses for those provided on the survey, and interviewees gave another 11 responses on the short-answer portion.

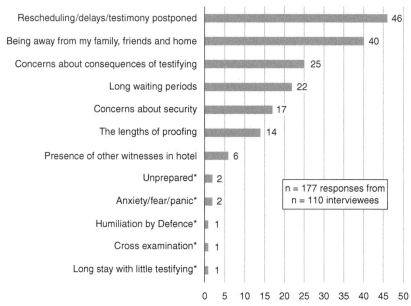

FIGURE 5.8. Issues making testifying more difficult.

SATISFACTION WITH LIFE, SOCIETY, ECONOMICS, AND POLITICS

Another critical element of witnesses' overall health is their general level of satisfaction with the world around them. Interviewees' perceptions of their own lives, their community, and their government influence their willingness to reconcile (Meernik and Guerrero 2014) and their support for the ICTY (Meernik 2015a). How do the interviewees perceive their world and the world around them? To that end, interviewees were asked several questions about their assessment of their own current personal situation, as well as the quality of their relationships in their communities, their economic situation, and the political situation in their country. Interviewees were asked to comment on these circumstances in the present as well as two to five years in the future.

Witnesses often reported to the VWS that war experiences, losses endured, and the consequences thereof are the most important factors influencing their general well-being. Some are still refugees or internally displaced persons who are unable to return to their original homes, while others are minorities or returnees in their local communities. Many witnesses stated that their lives will never be the same as they were before the conflict, although some indicated that for the sake of the next generation and in honor of the lost ones, they need to continue with their lives no matter how bad it might get. Due to

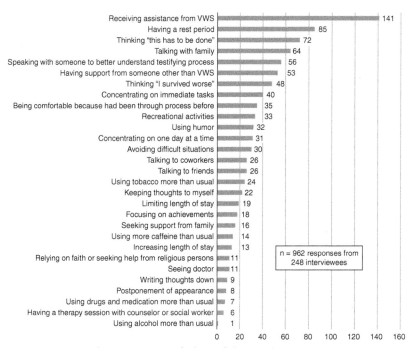

FIGURE 5.9. Relieving emotional/physical distress during testimony process.

the high unemployment rate in many of the regions of the former Yugoslavia[9] and difficulties in finding suitable jobs, witnesses often raised concerns about challenges of ensuring sufficient and regular income to meet the costs of living and for securing funds for their children's education.

In general, the study results show that the interviewees are presently optimistic about their overall life situation (Figure 5.10), but this optimism declines when respondents think of the next two to five years. More than 60% of the interviewees expressed that they were either very satisfied or satisfied with their present life situation, while only 36% expected to be satisfied with their situation in the next two to five years. Part of this issue, however, stems from the number of interviewees who indicated they did not know what the future would hold for them. In fact, of the 248 interviewees who chose one of the three "satisfied" responses in the present, 51 indicated they did not know about the future. What may appear at first glance to be a decrease in optimism is mostly an increase in uncertainty or inability to predict the future.

---

[9] Unemployment data from the World Bank (http://bit.ly/2h5WBU).

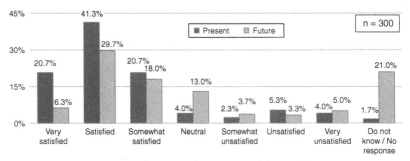

FIGURE 5.10. Satisfaction with present and future life situation.

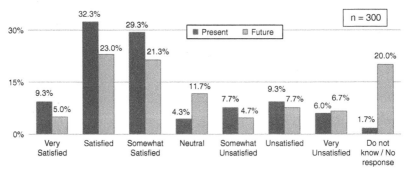

FIGURE 5.11. Satisfaction with present and future economic circumstances.

Figure 5.11 examines interviewees' attitudes about their present and future economic circumstances. Most interviewees are satisfied with their present economic circumstances, but those numbers drop off when they are queried about the future, although some number of the interviewees who are satisfied in the present did not know about the future. In fact, 40 of the respondents who indicated they were satisfied or somewhat satisfied in the present selected the "did not know" response about the future. In general, interviewees are fairly satisfied in the present, but uncertain or unable to predict the future.

The study registered the highest levels of dissatisfaction when interviewees were asked about the present and future political situation in their country. In contrast to the responses to the prior questions, respondents are *much more* likely to believe their present political situation is less than satisfying and tend to more often express greater satisfaction with how they imagine the political situation will be in the future (Figure 5.12). Nearly 70% of the interviewees indicated they were somewhat unsatisfied, unsatisfied, or very unsatisfied with

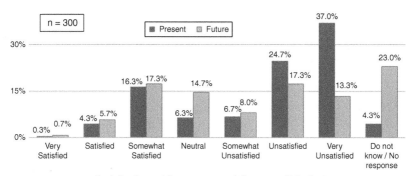

FIGURE 5.12. Satisfaction with present and future political circumstances.

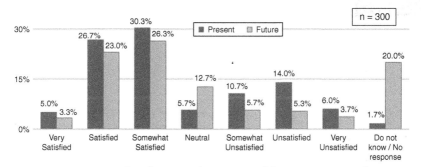

FIGURE 5.13. Satisfaction with present and future interpersonal relations in community. *Could they have high expectations, or disillusioned?*

the present political situation in their country. Whatever else the interviewees may disagree on, most seem to take a fairly dim view of politics and their political leaders. In light of the wars of the past, and the economic and political problems of today, this is not surprising.

Finally, we focus on the issue of interpersonal relations in the community where the witness lives, as we see in Figure 5.13. This is an especially intriguing measure as it pertains indirectly to interviewees' perceptions of the extent to which people in their community are getting along or perhaps reconciling with others. Most interviewees indicate that they are (very) satisfied or somewhat satisfied with the present state of their interpersonal relations in their community (62%), while 52.6% expect to be satisfied in the next two to five years. There are fewer individuals who take a more pessimistic attitude about the future – a total of only 15% expect to be somewhat unsatisfied, unsatisfied, or very unsatisfied in the next two to five years, while 31% are similarly unhappy about the present state of their interpersonal relations in their community. There are also a sizeable number of individuals (19%) who indicated they did not know about the future.

The question about interpersonal relations can also be employed to gain some insight into witnesses' views on reconciliation and what factors correlate with a positive outlook on this variable. Before proceeding, however, it is critical to emphasize two caveats. First, the question does not directly measure reconciliation – the witnesses were asked about "interpersonal relations," which they could choose to interpret however they saw fit. Some may have considered their community holistically, while others may have perceived it more narrowly as concerning just those individuals they knew. Some may have had a great deal of knowledge about community relations, while others may have possessed limited social knowledge or engaged in few social interactions. Second, these opinions are just that – the witnesses' perceptions – and do not speak to the actual state of reconciliation around them. Nonetheless, this measure does provide us with a narrow window into this world of fraught community relations that we describe, while we always bear in mind the limitations of this indicator.

The quest for reconciliation has been central in many nations undergoing a period of transitional justice whether because of government repression (e.g., South Africa, Chile, Argentina) or war (e.g., Rwanda, the former Yugoslavia, Sri Lanka). While systematic and empirical evidence has recently been accumulating (Clark 2014; Hamber 2009; Meernik et al. 2016; Meernik and Guerrero 2014; Olsen et al. 2010), there continues to be theoretical and practical debates over the meaning of this term (Gibson 2004a; Staub 2006). A useful distinction in this research literature for both practitioners and scholars concerns thick versus thin definitions or conceptions of reconciliation. Thin definitions of reconciliation focus on minimal expectations regarding the extent to which formerly adversarial groups coexist together, or minimalist thresholds for defining the existence of reconciliation, such as an absence of violence among groups (i.e., negative peace). Some level of reconciliation may be defined as occurring when civil war violence has ended or when individuals accept the right of their former enemies to exist in the same political space. Little is expected of the individual, the society, or the government. Gibson (2004a: 13) suggests in the context of South Africa, "When people talk about reconciliation, they often mean nothing more than people of different races getting along better with each other – that is, a diminution of racial animosities." A decrease in hostile attitudes, just like a decrease in violence, can certainly signal movement in attitudes in a positive direction, but to what degree must opinions change before we term such changes evidence of reconciliation? Thin definitions are certainly more flexible and better suited to empirical analysis as reconciliation may be defined as occurring when such changes transpire. Thick definitions of reconciliation encompass not only a lack of violence, but also involve changes in attitudes about one's adversaries and changes in behavior, such as a willingness to work with, live next to, and accept marriages with members of the "other." Staub (2006: 868) writes that reconciliation "may be defined as mutual acceptance by groups of each other." In one sense, this sort of reconciliation is marked by a particular state or stage of development in either or both attitudes and government policy. But it presumes that not only behaviors have changed, but attitudes have shifted as well from something like a reactive and begrudging acceptance of the other's right to exist to a proactive embrace of the other. Thick definitions of reconciliation also stress the dynamic and multifaceted nature of this concept, which should encourage ongoing analysis over time as well as diverse indicators of reconciliation.

In the context of the former Yugoslavia the emerging research has been diverse and at times contradictory. Some scholars have been rather pessimistic about the prospects for reconciliation in the region, and especially in Bosnia-Herzegovina, where former enemies must continue to coexist socially and politically. Clark (2009c, 2014) argues that because the peoples of the former Yugoslavia continue to deny the responsibility of their side in committing human rights violations against the other, they are not able to reconcile in a deeper, more positive fashion. Clark (2011: 257) finds that "the denial of truth breeds resentment, anger and frustration, and thus obstructs the reconciliation process." She further argues (2009d: 372), "It is therefore imperative that the problems of denial and multiple truths, which both attest to the absence of, and fundamentally mitigate against reconciliation, are addressed." Other scholars like Mendeloff (2004, 2009) and Snyder and Vinjamuri (2003) are also skeptical about the prospects for reconciliation resulting from transitional justice efforts more generally. Like Orentlicher (2008, 2010), these scholars suggest that a necessary condition for the positive peace is the ability to both shrink the space for denial, but also ensure that justice is achieved through the prosecution of those responsible.

Other research, while not necessarily convinced of the inevitability of reconciliation, has found that reconciliation does exist and can be advanced through various individual, social, and national efforts. Meernik and Guerrero (2014) find that positive attitudes regarding the ICTY are associated with reconciled attitudes – those individuals who support the Tribunal are also more likely to evidence positive attitudes toward living next to, working alongside, or even marrying members of other ethnic groups. Others have found that efforts in public education in other societies can help bridge divides (Cole

2007; Jones et al. 2012; Smith 2005), although some scholars are quite pessimistic about the prospects of the education system to advance reconciliation in the former Yugoslavia (Cole 2007; Freedman et al. 2004). Hewstone et al. (2006: 107) find that in the context of Northern Ireland, those individuals "who reported having more contact with out-group members held a more positive attitude toward mixing with the out-group" (see also Meernik et al. 2016).

In essence, research on reconciliation in the former Yugoslavia as well as in other contexts is making progress, and our understanding of its meaning and determinants continues. Clark (2014) provides an excellent analysis of the challenges of promoting reconciliation in Bosnia-Herzegovina that those readers who are interested in a deeper understanding of the topic are encouraged to consult. For our present purposes, we acknowledge the complexity of the topic, but also the limitations of our measure, which does not expressly measure reconciliation. Our evidence comes from a sample of 300 individuals who testified before the ICTY, and we must rely on other attitudes as revealed through the survey to understand individuals' perceptions of interpersonal relations in their community. Nonetheless, perhaps because the question does not utilize a direct measure with its complex implications and fraught understandings, we may elicit from our survey respondents' more straightforward opinions.

In order to help understand what factors may be associated with positive evaluations of interpersonal relations in communities we develop a probit model for our binary dependent variable and employ our standard measures of ethnicity, experience, and gender. In addition, however, we include several other items from the survey, including: (1) whether one has a positive outlook on one's present situation in life; (2) whether one experienced a social, economic, or security threat; (3) whether the individual believed that local politics interfered with the work of the ICTY; and (4) whether the witness was an ethnic minority in their community. We use this model as a representative measure of the situations witnesses face in the post-testimonial process.

We are particularly interested in whether there are relationships between one's attitudes on interpersonal relations in one's community and the extent of trauma witnesses experienced during the wars of the former Yugoslavia as well as problems they faced afterward. Does having been exposed to a greater range of trauma increase the likelihood that one perceives one's personal situation more positively or negatively? Given the emerging body of research, we might expect to find that the greater the number of wartime traumas individuals report they have experienced, the more likely they will have a positive view of interpersonal relations in their community.

TABLE 5.5. *Understanding witnesses' views on interpersonal relations in their communities*

Variable	Coefficient	Standard error	Z statistic	P value	Marginal impact coefficient
Bosniak	−0.396	0.264	−1.500	0.134	−0.152
Serb	0.244	0.298	0.820	0.414	0.088
Bosnian Serb	−0.152	0.299	−0.510	0.612	−0.058
Croat	0.144	0.285	0.510	0.613	0.053
Albanian	0.166	0.372	0.450	0.655	0.060
Ethnic minority	0.459	0.280	1.640	0.101	0.157
Experiences	0.033	0.015	2.110	0.035	0.012
Female	−0.250	0.250	−1.000	0.317	−0.096
Present personal situation	0.438	0.140	3.120	0.002	0.163
Consequence	−0.488	0.199	−2.460	0.014	−0.186
Local politics	−0.136	0.178	−0.760	0.445	−0.051
Education	−0.139	0.057	−2.450	0.014	−0.052
Age	0.002	0.009	0.280	0.782	0.001
Constant	−0.356	0.683	−0.520	0.602	

n=261

Table 5.5 provides the probit estimates predicting attitudes on interpersonal relations in the community. We see at the top of the table that of all the ethnic groups, only Bosniaks are pessimistic about the state of interpersonal relations in their community. The coefficient for this variable is negative, although it is not statistically significant. None of the other ethnic group variables exercises a statistically significant impact on one's perceptions of community relations. Interestingly, however, individuals who identify as members of an ethnic minority in a community are more likely to evince positive attitudes about interpersonal relations, although the coefficient for this variable is not statistically significant in a two-tailed test. We also sought to determine if a multilevel modelling strategy might work best to evaluate how ethnicity might be a filter through which other variables exercise differential impacts on the dependent variable. The tests for model specification, however, indicated that there was no need for a multilevel model. We also find that women may be less likely to be satisfied with interpersonal relations in their community, although this coefficient also does not reach conventional levels of statistical significance.

The relationship between wartime trauma and attitudes about interpersonal relations is quite interesting. There is a positive relationship between trauma and witnesses' satisfaction with interpersonal relations in their community. The greater the number of traumatic experiences a witness endured during the wars of the 1990s, the more likely he or she is to have a positive outlook on the community. Here again, we find results that support what other scholars have found – there is something about undergoing the crucible of conflict that is associated with the development of positive social attitudes. Whether it is altruism, leadership, or as in this case a greater sense of satisfaction with one's community these individuals somehow emerge stronger and more externally driven.

Bauer et al. (2016) offer several explanations for why these relationships might exist. One is that they arise out of a need for personal safety and security. During war when so much of one's life is thrown into insecurity and chaos, one may develop a greater awareness and need for community support to survive and thrive in the post-conflict environment. It may be that one draws closer to one's community as a matter of survival during wartime, and that such community-focused efforts continue in the postwar environment. Yet this explanation also suggests that while intragroup ties become stronger, relations with other groups may not, and perhaps might suffer as one finds security in the group and danger in the external world (Bauer et al. 2016: 23). It may also be that these wartime traumas lead individuals to reexamine their lives. As Bauer et al. (2016: 27) write:

> After war violence, it is possible to imagine victims changing their priorities in life and placing renewed value on relationships with family and community, and even changing other-regarding preferences. Such changes need not be parochial in nature; the existing literature in this area is silent on this point.

The reasons behind the emergence of these pro-social attitudes are certainly worthy of much more in-depth study. For the present study, we see yet more evidence that for some individuals, trauma is predictive of more positive or pro-social attitudes.

On the other hand, we find that social, economic, and security consequences that occur as a result of one's testimony before the ICTY are negatively related to satisfaction with community relations. It does not appear to be the case that all types of traumatic experiences lead to the development of a positive outlook. It may be that the profound changes and trauma wrought by war are of a different magnitude and impact altogether in shaping people's lives. The kinds of specific problems that occur as a result of the testimonial process at the ICTY may not possess that kind of transformative power. Indeed, individuals may instead simply look to place blame for these specific harms on those responsible locally or at the ICTY instead of reexamining their life or strengthening their kinship ties.

Not surprisingly we find that if one has a positive outlook on life in general, one's satisfaction with community interpersonal relations also tends to be positive. While this finding is not altogether surprising, it suggests that there is a larger construct of a positive attitude or outlook on life that stems from various sources (which we would expect involve family, faith, upbringing, education, and events in one's life that our data mostly do not measure). Future research should investigate these issues to better understand, especially in the context of war-torn or repressive societies, what components make up positive attitudes and which factors are associated with the development of such a mind-set.

Interestingly, education is negatively related to satisfaction with community relations. The more education a witness has, the less likely she is to believe that relations are positive. In fact, as education levels increase across our ordinal measure, satisfaction with community relations declines by approximately 5%. Perhaps the more educated are more pessimistic because of a more realistic view of their community, or perhaps they have a more holistic understanding of what good community relations should be. None of the other coefficients exercises a statistically significant impact on interpersonal relations. Overall, these results suggest that we can construct something of a profile of the more optimistic of our witnesses who perceive positive interpersonal relations in their community. They tend to have suffered greatly during the war, but nonetheless have a more positive attitude in general. They tend not to have experienced any negative consequences regarding their testimony before the ICTY, while they also tend to have less education. Our research can help point toward certain characteristics in the witness sample, but a fuller model of the determinants of reconciliation requires additional data on individuals' contemporary perceptions of the political, economic, and social environment in these communities.

CONCLUSION

Our results suggest that the process of testifying is more complicated than simple conclusions about whether bearing witness is ultimately an act of "re-traumatization" or "catharsis." In general, our study finds witness affect, both before and after testimony, tends to be more positive than negative, lending support to the notion that testifying is not intrinsically traumatic. The difficulties inherent in the process of testifying are helped by the presence of accompanying support persons, VWS staff, and the witnesses' own internal coping strategies.

Given the high levels of trauma (witnessed and experienced) as well as the fact that the interviewee population is aging, the witnesses are rather resilient as reflected in their views of their psychological and physical health vis-à-vis the ICTY. Witnesses utilize a variety of coping strategies to deal with wartime and related trauma, many of which focus on the internal, self-driven coping strategies rather than external support systems. The study, like others, provides additional data that are suggestive on such points, but in no way conclusive. Consistent with other research, there is a percentage of witnesses who continue to experience adverse health effects, and some of them attribute this condition to the process of testifying. Overall, witnesses reported to be satisfied with their present life situation, while they were rather undecided when thinking about the future.

The most interesting finding to emerge from this chapter is the extent to which wartime trauma helps us understand attitudes. As other research is discovering, those individuals who suffer the most from war tend to also be individuals who have pro-social attitudes (Bauer et al. 2016). We find these individuals are more likely to have recollections of positive experiences before and after testimony and are more likely to be satisfied with interpersonal relations in their community. We also found that while those who experienced more trauma, as well as those who were ethnic minorities in their community, were more likely to be optimistic about the state of interpersonal relations in their communities, those who suffered harm as a result of testifying were not as positive. Their negative experiences did not lead to further positive attitudes, but seem to be associated with a more pessimistic attitude about community relations. Given that community members were the ones engaging in this behavior against witnesses their attitudes are quite understandable.

Ultimately, our study findings indicate that a more systematic approach – before, during, and after testifying – is needed to better understand the positive and the negative as well as the short- and long-term effects of testifying on witnesses' psychological and physical well-being. As scholars have begun to do in relation to the ICC, it will be important to collect more "real-time" data on the witnesses rather than the recollections we utilize in this survey (Cody et al. 2014).

Universal approach so that all variables are accounted for
- uniform dataset

6

Perceptions of Justice

INTRODUCTION

The justice cascade (Sikkink 2011) and the increasing resort to international tribunals to confront the atrocities perpetrated during wars and government repression have led to increasing interest in studying the impact of these international institutions and what it means for international justice (Akhavan 2009; Barria and Roper 2005; Clark 2014; Gilligan 2006; Greig and Meernik 2014; Jo and Simmons 2016; Kim and Sikkink 2010; McAllister 2014; Meernik 2005; Simmons and Danner 2010; Stover and Weinstein 2004). In addition to their fundamental mission to provide justice and redress through legalized dispute resolution, these international courts have also been charged with advancing deterrence, promoting peace, and fostering reconciliation. Whether these are appropriate goals for judicial institutions far removed from the scenes of war and atrocity, with no tools beyond the power of their words of condemnation, and in the face of frequent international indifference to their mission, is debatable. Tribunals and their supporters have often embraced these ideals and used them to rally support for international justice. As former ICC President Philippe Kirsch declared, "By putting potential perpetrators on notice that they may be tried before the Court, the ICC is intended to contribute to the deterrence of these crimes."[1] Former Chief Prosecutor of the ICC Luis Moreno-Ocampo asserted that, "Experience has taught us that ... law is the only efficient way to prevent recurrent violence and atrocities."[2] Indeed, as critics of international justice as a mechanism for conflict resolution have pointed out (Mendeloff 2004; Snyder and Vinjamuri 2003), there is

---

[1] Interview with Philippe Kirsch as found at http://archive2.globalsolutions.org/publications/publications_phillipe_kirsch on January 10, 2013.

[2] As found at http://justiceinconflict.org/2011/10/25/international-criminal-law-and-deterrence-%E2%80%93-a-pointless-endeavour/ on January 10, 2013.

no shortage of such expressive idealism from those inside and outside these courts. Is such optimism warranted? Can international justice be an effective means by which to deliver justice, punish the guilty, and deter future violations of international laws?

We examine the subject of the impact of international justice by analyzing the witnesses' perceptions of the work of the ICTY. The perspectives of individuals about international justice are increasingly important in evaluating their prospects of success. As DeGuzman (2012: 268) writes, "the globalization of communications increasingly means that an institution's legitimacy depends on the opinions of ordinary citizens around the world." Survey research on public opinion of international justice has burgeoned, yielding valuable insights into which factors are most determinative of individual support for and evaluations of international justice (Arzt 2006; David 2017; Ford 2012; Hagan and Ivkovic 2006; Klarin 2009; Meernik 2015a; Orentlicher 2010; Subotić 2009), such as the powerful role played by identity. Given the central role played by witnesses in international justice, it is critical to assess the impact and legacy of the ICTY on the stakeholders most closely linked to one of its most central tenets: to do justice.

This chapter examines the interviewees' views about the ICTY's effectiveness in realizing the broader objectives of providing truth, determining responsibility for the crimes committed, punishing those found guilty, and helping deter further violations of international law. It also discusses interviewees' perceptions of the fairness of the Tribunal's procedures and the offices with which they had contact. As with previous chapters, we explore the relationships between ethnicity, gender, and trauma to more fully understand the perceptions of the witnesses. We conclude with a model of witness perceptions about the ICTY and its ability to carry out its core mandates by moving beyond standard analyses to argue that: (1) the intensity of witness motivations in testifying; (2) witness beliefs about their personal contribution to justice; (3) witness experiences in the aftermath of testimony; (4) witness satisfaction with their current life situation; and (5) witness knowledge of the ICTY are all related to witness perceptions about the ICTY's legacy.

OVERVIEW: WITNESS PERCEPTIONS OF ICTY EFFECTIVENESS AND THE ADMINISTRATION OF JUSTICE

This section first examines interviewees' opinions regarding whether they believe the Tribunal has generally done a good job in advancing its most fundamental goals of truth, justice, punishment, and deterrence. We explore in-depth how the lens of identity alters perceptions in the second half of the

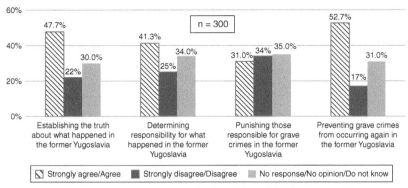

FIGURE 6.1. Interviewees who think the ICTY has generally
done a "good job in …"

chapter, and focus here on reviewing the major findings regarding witness perceptions about the Tribunal's performance (Figure 6.1). To investigate witness perceptions of international justice, we utilize their responses to four questions regarding their opinions of the ICTY's effectiveness in four different areas. Witnesses were asked if they "believe that *in general* the ICTY has done a good job in": (1) "*establishing the truth* about what happened in the former Yugoslavia"; (2) "*determining* who was responsible for the grave crimes committed in the former Yugoslavia"; (3) "*punishing* those responsible for the grave crimes committed in the former Yugoslavia"; and (4) "*preventing* grave crimes from occurring again in the former Yugoslavia." We distinguish between those respondents who either agreed or strongly agreed, and all others, including those who expressed no opinion.

A plurality of interviewees (48%) believe the ICTY has helped establish the truth of what happened in the former Yugoslavia, and has determined who was responsible for committing grave crimes (41%). A majority believe the ICTY has helped prevent such crimes from occurring again (53%), but only 31% believe the ICTY has done a good job in punishing those responsible. Notice that between 30% and 35%, however, do not have an opinion or "don't know" about how well the ICTY has performed, especially when asked about the ICTY's effectiveness in punishing those responsible. The reasons for this are not clear, but it may be due to witnesses' unfamiliarity with the criminal trials, their unfamiliarity with the legal work of the ICTY, or their unwillingness to express a conclusion about such a complex institution and a multifaceted subject.

Survey respondents were also queried about their views on the manner in which the ICTY delivered justice. Strong majorities of men and women

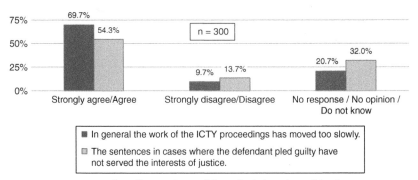

FIGURE 6.2. Perceptions of the administration of justice.

strongly agreed or agreed that the proceedings have moved too slowly (70%). This should come as no surprise because this has been a consistent complaint since the time the first trials began and even by Tribunal judges themselves (Stover 2005; Wald 2002). By 2016, the ICTY had reached the 23-year mark, and it had lasted six times longer than the Nuremberg trials and eight times longer than the Tokyo prosecutions.[3]

Turning to the decisions by prosecutors to seek lower sentences for defendants where a plea of guilty is entered, we see that 54% of witnesses believe that sentences in such cases have not served the interests of justice (Figure 6.2). These guilty plea sentences have aroused controversy, and many of those in the former Yugoslavia believe they have undermined justice (Ivković and Hagan 2011). There were no significant differences between men and women in terms of how they perceive sentences in guilty plea cases.

The VWS has observed that a guilty plea can be perceived differently by victims. Some may be concerned that a guilty plea will result in a significantly lighter sentence and consider it unacceptable in view of the gravity of the crimes committed. Others may be interested in trying to find out what additional information an accused can share with the Prosecutors or Chambers because they are still seeking information about loved ones or they want there to be an acknowledgement of the crimes that have been committed. Notably, witnesses with missing family members might benefit from learning about the circumstances of the death of their relatives or about the location of their remains, if such information is shared as part of the plea agreement.[4] In these

---

3   For an analysis of why the ICTY trials tend to take so long, see Meernik and Aloisi (2008).

4   A total of 34,891 people have been reported to the International Committee of the Red Cross (ICRC) as missing in connection with the conflicts of the 1990s. According to the International Commission for Missing Persons (ICMP), 70% of those missing have been accounted for. For

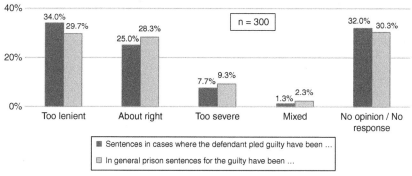

FIGURE 6.3. Perceptions about sentences.

instances, witnesses may or may not recognize that this information is typically provided in exchange for a lesser sentence.

When turning to look beyond the administration of justice and examining the sentences handed down by the ICTY, here we see that witnesses are also critical of the sanctions levied (Figure 6.3). In terms of the guilty plea sentences, the largest percentage (34%) believes the sentences are too lenient, and 25% think they are just right. Interestingly, 29.7% of the sample believe the sentences in general are too lenient, and 28.3% think the length of incarceration is about right. Many interviewees – 32% and 30.3% express no opinion about the sentences for those who plead guilty and for prison sentences in general, respectively. Other than the fact that women (42%) are more likely than men (27%) to think that sentences are too lenient, there are no significant differences in opinions across our three foci.

To dig deeper into witnesses' perception about one issue that has generated much discussion of the ICTY's role in international justice, interviewees were asked about their opinion regarding the impact of international and national politics on the work of the ICTY. In effect, have the institutions and personalities involved in national and international politics interfered with the administration of justice? As the following evidence indicates, most provided negative assessments (Figure 6.4). Most respondents (61%) felt international politics had exercised a negative impact on the work of the ICTY, while a plurality of interviewees (37%) felt the same about national politics.

It is especially striking when we examine the gender breakdown regarding the influence of national and international politics (Figure 6.5). Men are twice as likely as women to think that both national and international politics

more information on missing persons and their families in the Western Balkans visit websites of the ICRC (1999; www.icrc.org) and the ICMP (www.icmp.int).

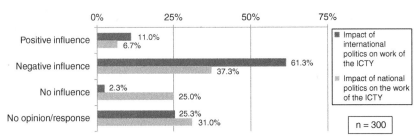

FIGURE 6.4. Impact of international and national politics on the ICTY.

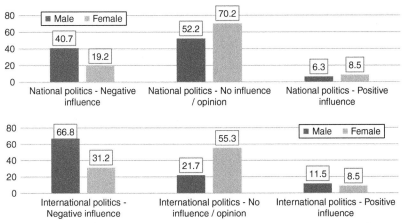

FIGURE 6.5. Gender differences and the influence of international and national politics on the ICTY (in percentages).

have had a negative influence on the work of the ICTY. Women, in contrast, are less likely than men to think or have an opinion about the influence of national or international politics on the ICTY. Neither men nor women think that national and international politics have been a positive influence on the ICTY. Among the ethnic groups (results not shown), Croats are more likely to view national politics as having a negative influence, while Albanians are less likely to hold such beliefs about both national and international politics. Bosnian Serbs are more likely to believe that international politics have had a negative influence. Those who experienced more trauma are more likely to believe that national politics have had a negative influence, perhaps because they have been victims of national politics.

Closely related to the issue of the impact of international and national politics on the work of the ICTY are the interviewees' opinions about whether they think international or national courts are better suited to adjudicating war crimes (Figure 6.6). While a plurality of interviewees (47%) do not believe

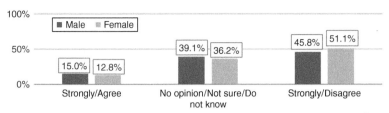

FIGURE 6.6. Local courts are better suited to adjudicate
war crimes (in percentages).

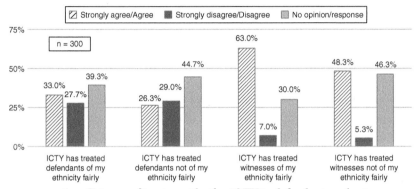

FIGURE 6.7. Fairness of treatment by the ICTY to defendants and witnesses.

local courts are better suited to hearing the kinds of cases that have come
before the ICTY, a substantial percentage also did not respond, had no opinion, or did not know (39%). Unlike the differences between men and women
previously discussed, there are not sharp differences in perceptions about the
local courts. Bosniaks are more likely to believe that national courts would
not be better than the international tribunal, while Serbs, not surprisingly,
believe the opposite. There are no statistically significant relations between
such preferences among the other ethnic groups or between the level of wartime trauma and support of local courts.

Survey respondents were asked about the fairness of treatment of witnesses
and defendants (Figure 6.7). While 33% believe defendants of their own ethnicity have been treated fairly by the ICTY, that number drops to 26% when
the question pertains to whether "other" ethnicities have been treated fairly
by the ICTY. There are similar findings in research on preferential treatment
of other ethnicities (Stover 2005; Clark 2014). There are sizeable numbers in
the former (39%) and the latter group (45%) who are unsure and have no
opinion. On the other hand, 63% believe witnesses of their ethnic group have
been treated fairly, and 48% believe that witnesses from other groups have

been treated fairly. Bosniaks are highly likely to believe the ICTY has treated defendants of their ethnicity fairly (the correlation is 0.35 and statistically significant), while Serbs and Bosnian Serbs are very likely to believe other Serbs were not treated fairly (the correlations are −0.50 and −0.417, respectively). Croats and Albanians are also more likely to believe defendants from their ethnic group were treated fairly, although the correlation is not statistically significant with the latter group. When the question concerns the fair treatment of witnesses of the individual's ethnicity, we find only that Serbs are less likely to believe they were treated fairly.

It is interesting that witnesses are more likely to believe that defendants and witnesses from other ethnic groups were not treated fairly by the ICTY than were those of their own ethnicity. Much research in the context of the former Yugoslavia and in other nations with ethnic divisions has found that members of ethnic groups tend to view themselves as the victimized or aggrieved party that has been treated unfairly in some manner and are often reluctant to perceive such treatment of other groups (Clark 2014). Thus, it is striking that these interviewees perceive the "other" as the party more likely to be treated unfairly, and find treatment of their own ethnicity to be comparatively better.

It is possible that the definition of what it means to "treat a defendant fairly" may have been differently interpreted by the participants in the survey. For example, some interviewees indicated that the ICTY treats defendants fairly when imposing a sentence proportionate to the crimes committed. Some reported in their comments that defendants of "other" ethnic groups have received disproportional positive treatment (detention facilities and living conditions), which they believed creates too much "fairness" and is not deserved. Others indicated that the defendants are fairly treated when they receive proper legal assistance and detention facilities. It is possible that the concept of "fairness" toward the defendant and regarding international justice more generally can both refer to an adequate punishment or to unbiased and fair trial proceedings.[5] The findings here suggest that much work is still

---

[5] There are underlying differences between the civil law systems in the former Yugoslavia with which the witnesses are most familiar, and the common law–civil law hybrid system of the ICTY. An analysis of that is beyond the scope of this study. For purposes of this study, there may be key issues involving differences between the civil and common law traditions that appear in interviewee responses about "fairness." The notion of "guilty pleas," the purpose and role of the Prosecution and Defence, as well as the role of judges as seekers of truth versus seekers of justice are markedly different in the two legal traditions. These differences have consequences not only for the perceptions of whether the defendant was treated fairly, but how the witnesses felt they were treated. For example, a witness may not necessarily understand the role of vigorous cross-examination, and therefore feel unfairly treated, and question why a judge does not stop the hostile questioning.

needed to better understand the construct of fairness within the testimonial process, and what that means for both witnesses and defendants alike.

UNDERSTANDING WITNESS PERCEPTIONS OF JUSTICE

The Powerful Lens of Identity

The courtrooms of the international tribunals are a venue in which it is not just the prosecution and the defense who argue to win the case, but in which there are also competing versions of the truth advanced by ethnic, religious, and social groups fighting over land, government, and even the historical record itself. These actors have waged bloody civil wars in which each side viewed itself as seeking only self-preservation and fighting a just war, while accusing the other side of committing horrific human rights abuses to achieve domination over those standing in their way. These dueling versions of the truth are grounded in and fueled by historical narratives that perceive the current conflict as one more chapter in which each side plays its traditional role of the victim or the villain, the victor or the vanquished. Research from several fields such as psychology, sociology, and political science has found evidence that the power of ethnicity, religion, and nationality shapes individuals' perceptions of war and justice (Elcheroth 2006; Ford 2012; Staub 2006, 2013). When these competing truths clash in the courtroom, the judicial outcomes mean far more to these peoples than a determination of whether the defendant should be acquitted or found guilty – the outcomes can be seen as fundamentally about their very identity and the cultural narratives on which they have been raised. The contemporary and historical accounts offered by the opposing sides are also being judged for their veracity, and hence the verdict represents a judgment on each group's deeply rooted and emotionally laden historical narratives and personal war experiences. The impact of these judicial outcomes, and hence each group's perception of international justice, is tremendous. For many, their opinions regarding the tribunals, like the ICTY, are heavily influenced by whether they believe the judges have vindicated their truth or instead have undermined their version of history.

In the next section, we turn our focus to the role of ethnicity in shaping witnesses' perceptions of the ICTY's performance in achieving its principal mandates and its objectives. It is vital to emphasize, however, that identity will likely play a critical role in shaping perceptions of international justice regardless of whether it is rooted in ethnicity, religion, nationality, or some other deeply felt trait. Wars and political violence, by their very nature, erupt from disputes that divide individuals into groups, and these differences persist into the postwar period when leaders are held to account for their actions at the international tribunals. Whether the dispute concerns the Tutsi versus the Hutu in Rwanda; the Christians versus the Muslims in the Central African Republic; or Bosnian Muslims versus Bosnian Serbs, divisions over identity endure through the violence and can carry on into the courtroom.

Researchers of public opinion and international justice (Arzt 2006; Clark 2009d; Ford 2012; Hagan and Ivkovic 2006; Klarin 2009; Meernik 2015a; Nettelfield 2010; Orentlicher 2008; Subotić 2009) have generally discovered that views about whether the ICTY has fulfilled its objectives depend on which ones are being assessed and which groups are being queried. Researchers typically find that positive evaluations of the ICTY vary considerably across ethnic groups. For example, Bosniaks and Albanians in Kosovo usually register the highest levels of support for the ICTY, followed by Croats and Serbs (Arzt 2006; Hatay 2005; Meernik 2015a; Nettelfield 2010; Peskin 2005, 2008). The majority of those who were indicted by the ICTY and convicted have been Serbs from Bosnia and Serbia proper. Not surprisingly, Serbs have accused the ICTY of overlooking crimes committed by Bosniaks, Croats, and Kosovar Albanians, and of not fully appreciating their "defensive" struggle in which Serbs have sought to check the perceived influence of hostile Islamic and Croatian forces. While Bosniaks have generally been supportive of the ICTY, they too have found fault with the Tribunal when it fails to convict or punish severely enough their adversaries, and have been critical when those perceived as war heroes were prosecuted by the ICTY.

Meernik (2015a) finds, using data from the Southeast Europe Social Survey Project (SEESSP), that almost 90% of Bosniaks support the ICTY; 74% of Kosovar Albanians support the ICTY; 60% of Croatians support the ICTY; and approximately one-third of Serbs agree or strongly agree that they support the ICTY. However, in another survey by the Organization for Security and Cooperation in Europe, it was found that 40% believe that the ICTY was created to "put the blame for war sufferings on the Serbs" (OSCE 2011: 16), and 73% believe that the ICTY has different attitudes toward groups depending on their ethnicity (OSCE 2011: 22). Klarin (2009) and Ford (2012) argue that local elites and the media shape the narratives about group victimization and culpability and that public opinion has often followed these narratives. There is a good case to be made that support for the ICTY is inversely related to the number of those from one's group who have been convicted in The Hague (Klarin 2009). As Ford (2012: 423) argues:

> people's views of themselves are intricately bound up with their social identities. Thus attacks on social or group identities can be treated as attacks on

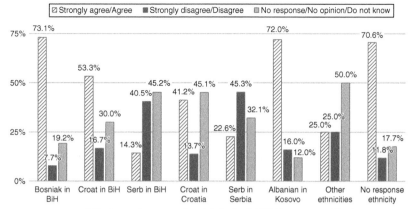

FIGURE 6.8. Interviewees who think the ICTY has generally done a "good job in establishing the truth."

the self that will trigger the same self-defensive reasoning. As a result, group members are resistant to information that is critical of the group.

Given the findings from other research about the ICTY that ethnicity matters, it is not surprising that the results from this analysis regarding ICTY performance vary according to ethnic identification. Here results both confirm and challenge what other major research has found about witnesses at international tribunals and the impact of the ICTY (Cody et al. 2014; Clark 2014). Figures 6.8 through 6.11 highlight that interviewees' views vary according to their self-identified ethnicity. There are consistent patterns among ethnic group perceptions regarding the ICTY and whether the ICTY has fulfilled its mandates in four key areas – establishing the truth, determining responsibility, punishing those responsible, and deterring crimes in the former Yugoslavia.

Figures 6.8 and 6.9 show that support for the most fundamental goals of international justice – establishing the truth and determining responsibility – parallel one another. These are also the two goals that we might argue tie most closely into the historical and contemporary narratives regarding ethnicity, atrocities, and attribution of responsibility. That is, the "truth" and "responsibility" as established by the ICTY will typically be evaluated in terms of their correspondence to the dominant accounts advanced by each of the ethnic groups. The results from this section of the survey are mostly consistent with the findings of previous research (e.g., Ford 2012; Meernik 2015a). Bosniaks are the most supportive of any of the groups on those questions pertaining to the ICTY's effectiveness in establishing the truth (73%) and determining who was responsible for crimes (73%). The differences in approval for the ICTY's efforts

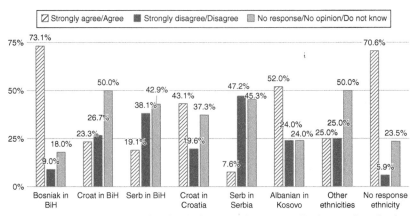

FIGURE 6.9. Interviewees who think the ICTY has generally done a "good job in determining responsibility for grave crimes."

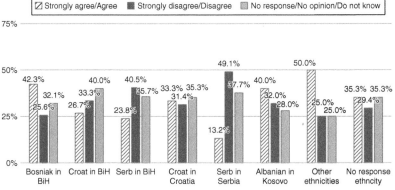

FIGURE 6.10. Interviewees who think the ICTY has generally done a "good job in determining punishment for those responsible."

are the largest on these two measures, although support among Croatians in BiH and Kosovar Albanians is significantly lower on the question of determining responsibility. While some may believe that the ICTY has helped establish the truth of these events, these individuals may also believe that the Tribunal, in the process of doing so, has failed in holding people accountable for their crimes. For example, it is possible that while most Kosovar Albanians believe the ICTY has accurately described the factual truths of their war with Serbia in 1998 to 1999, they may also believe that by acquitting certain individuals for their roles in this violence, such as former Serbian President Milan Milutinović, the Tribunal has not performed as well in assigning blame for these events.

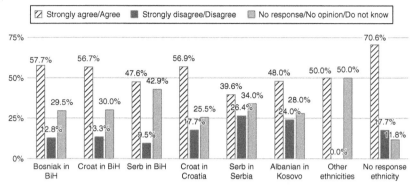

FIGURE 6.11. Interviewees who think the ICTY has generally done a good job in "preventing grave crimes from occurring again in the former Yugoslavia."

The one issue that members of all ethnic groups seem to agree on is their disapproval of the ICTY's punishment of the guilty. Bosniaks provide the closest thing we see to support in Figure 6.10 at 42%. For these witnesses, who have seen so much violence and bloodshed and who have gone through the emotionally draining experience of testifying before the ICTY, the tribunal's punishments may never be commensurate with their pain and suffering. Many witnesses may also object to the severity of the sentences meted out to members of their ethnic group. Only 30% of all witnesses agree or strongly agree that the ICTY has done a good job in punishing the guilty.

When individuals are queried about their perceptions of ICTY effectiveness in deterring the commission of future violations of international law, their support rises markedly. In fact, a majority of respondents agree or strongly agree that the ICTY has generally done a good job in this area. Bosniaks are also the most likely to believe the ICTY has done a good job in preventing crimes from occurring again (58%). Serbs in both Bosnia-Herzegovina (BiH) and Serbia generally are the least supportive, while Croats in both BiH and Croatia evidence fairly high levels of support on the deterrence question (Figure 6.10). Albanian approval of the ICTY's deterrent impact is noticeably lower than in the first two tables, perhaps because despite the establishment of the ICTY in 1993, their region was subject to ethnic cleansing six years later. There are too few respondents in the "Other ethnicities" (4) and "No response" (17) categories to draw any meaningful conclusion. Perhaps because this question does not pertain to deeply held views or perceptions about truth, responsibility, and punishment, the concept of deterrence may not be so value-laden. Deterrence may be a relatively more objective measure of the effectiveness of international justice that pertains to actual events rather than more subjective notions of justice.

TABLE 6.1. *Support for ICTY goals among those who are ethnic minorities in their communities*

ICTY goals	Determine truth	Establish responsibility	Punish those responsible	Prevent crimes from occurring again
Ethnic minority (n=39)	59%	46%	41%	59%
Non-ethnic minority (n=244)	45%	39%	30%	51%

The rich data the witnesses provided permit us to drill down further into identity to examine ethnicity in geographical context. One of the hallmarks of the wars of the former Yugoslavia was the drive by some ethnic groups to create ethnically pure enclaves. While often such strategies were successful on the battlefield, we still find significant numbers of individuals who are ethnic minorities in their communities. Some of these individuals are integrated into these communities relatively well, while others may live a tenuous existence of insecurity. Particularly because the presence of these ethnic minorities testifies to the failure of ethnic cleansing policies in some cases and their relative success in others, their opinions may well differ from their counterparts living in other locales.

The data,[6] shown in Table 6.1, reveal an interesting pattern in which those who are ethnic minorities within their communities express higher levels of support for the ICTY across all four measures than do those who are in an ethnic majority in the communities where they reside. Perhaps it is because ethnic minorities are more acutely aware of the violence and destruction of war as their communities were typically targets of the fighting. They may also live a more insecure existence in the present day, and therefore they are more invested in the success of the Tribunal for human security purposes. Bosniaks, who tend toward more favorable views of the ICTY, are disproportionately overrepresented among those identifying as ethnic minorities, which may then explain part of this trend. At the same time, we also found (results not shown) that Kosovar Albanians, who also exhibit significantly higher levels of ICTY support, are disproportionately underrepresented among ethnic minorities. We explore the possibility of personal investment in the success of the ICTY as a determinant of support later in the chapter.

We make three critical observations from this brief overview of the data. First, and most obviously, approval of the ICTY's job performance varies

---

[6] Some interviewees (n=17) did not identify or did not know whether they were an ethnic minority in their community.

significantly based on ethnicity, especially when the survey items pertain to intensely held values and enduring group narratives. These findings mirror what previous research has found (Ford 2012; Klarin 2009; Meernik 2015a). Second, and more importantly, however, opinions do not move in lockstep across each of the four elements of the Tribunal's missions. While differences across Bosniaks, Croatians, Serbians, and Kosovar Albanians are present in each of the four measures, we see the groups largely in agreement in their negative views regarding punishment, and more positively united in the case of deterrence. This suggests that support for international justice should not be measured just by general approval or disapproval, but that views on these tribunals need to be unpacked. Individual evaluations of those aspects of the Tribunal's work that invoke more intensely held preferences may be more likely to elicit more subjective opinions depending on personal experiences and life situations. Evaluations of relatively more objective measures of success, such as deterrence, or perhaps others, such as the efficiency of the Tribunal, may lead to more dispassionate and perhaps more unbiased views. Third, and finally, given the power of identity in influencing opinions about international justice, how much room is left for other factors? We turn next to examining the role of the witnesses' wartime trauma and their own personal encounters with international justice to help us understand individual evaluations of the ICTY and to unpack what the legacy of the Tribunal is for those who bear witness.

Wartime Trauma and the Evaluation of International Justice

We have explained why and generally found evidence to support the notion that those individuals who experienced the greatest amount of wartime suffering might have more positive attitudes about their own personal encounter with international justice. This section shifts the focus to examine how the degree of trauma witnesses endured may influence their perceptions of the ICTY and its success in realizing the goals set out for it by the UN Security Council mandate. Recall the survey (a modified version of the Harvard Trauma Questionnaire) asked individuals whether they experienced personally 26 different types of traumatic events ranging from deprivation of food and shelter to being subjected to shelling.[7] The witnesses were also given the opportunity to list further experiences – increasing the total number of

---

[7] The study relied on a modified version of the Harvard Trauma Questionnaire, which lists events or activities common in times of conflict (Palić et al. 2015). For more information see http://hprt-cambridge.org/screening/harvard-trauma-questionnaire/.

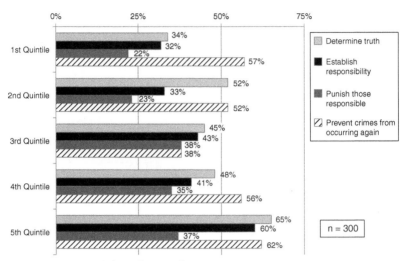

FIGURE 6.12. Range of traumatic wartime experiences
and support for ICTY goals.

possible experiences to more than 40. We then totaled up the number of such
experiences for each individual, which ranged from zero to 25, and then aggre-
gated them into quintiles, with the first quintile indicating the least amount of
trauma suffered and the fifth quintile the most trauma (Figure 6.12).

There is a positive relationship between the number of traumatic experiences witnesses endured and their support for the ICTY, although it is not
strictly linear in each of the four support measures as we see in Figure 6.12.
First, we find that those individuals who suffered the most are the most likely
to approve of the ICTY's efforts to establish the truth. Of those individuals in
the 80th or higher percentile (fifth quintile) of traumatic experiences, 65%
approve of the Tribunal's contribution to establishing the truth, while of those
in the 20th (first quintile), 34% express support. The difference between the
20th percentile and the 80th percentile groups is equally as stark when we
examine approval of the ICTY's contributions toward determining responsibility – 32% versus 60%, respectively. Again, the relationship is not strictly
linear between the two extremes, but generally increasing levels of traumatic
experience correspond with increasing support for the ICTY. The relationship between support for the ICTY's punishment of the guilty and trauma
is not nearly so straightforward. Support is lower among those in the second
quintile group and below, and higher among those above the 40th percentile,
but support within these two groupings does not exhibit much differentiation.
Support for the deterrence mission is even less clear. It is actually highest

among those witnesses in the fifth quintile, while those in the first quintile are not too far behind – 62% and 57%, respectively – and is also high among those in the 6oth to 8oth percentiles at 56%. Once again, we see that support for the ICTY's missions to establish the truth and determine responsibility tracks closely across the variable of interest, while support for the punishment and deterrence mission follows a slightly different pattern, suggesting the latter two are evaluated in a different manner by stakeholders.

Related to our specific arguments about the impact of wartime trauma on witnesses' attitudes, and the findings of research on trauma and positive social behaviors more generally, we suggest that other types of difficult or negative experiences may influence witness opinions about transnational mechanisms and transitional justice (Stepakoff et al. 2015). It is possible that many witnesses may be personally invested in their testimony because of the stressors they have endured prior to testimony and because of their strong desire to speak their truth and tell their story (Stepakoff et al. 2015). This "personal investment" about testifying can be based on the individual's level of trauma experienced during the wars, but here we focus principally on their degree of commitment and expenditure of effort as they relate to the necessity of testifying. We would expect that the greater the personal cost or investment, the more likely individuals will desire that positive and beneficial outcomes will result in order to at least partially "justify" the expenditure of effort made to testify and whatever losses or costs that might have accrued from testifying. In effect, we are suggesting that a perception of "sunk costs" (Garland and Newport 1991) may motivate individuals to evaluate the Tribunal positively to justify to themselves the personal investment in testimony, and by implication, the success of the tribunal. These individuals may be more likely to *want* to see the ICTY succeed. They may also be more positive in their support for the Tribunal's mandate because of their personal circumstances.

Witnesses testify in court for many different reasons, most especially because they are asked to, but for witnesses before international criminal tribunals, the reasons *why* they testify are likely to be especially complex and deeply felt. These tribunals are located in faraway countries, and for many it may be their first experience with international travel or even leaving their village. They are asked to recount some of the most painful and difficult experiences of their lives. In short, the act of testifying is a very intensely personal encounter with the past in a wholly alien environment.

The survey asks witnesses about the importance of their reasons for testifying, as we discussed in Chapter 2, and these range from a desire to tell the truth (which almost all witnesses affirmed) to putting the past behind oneself and speaking for the dead. We have no a priori reason to suppose that any one of

TABLE 6.2. *Support for ICTY goals and level of importance placed*
on reasons for testifying

ICTY goals	Importance of reasons to testify		
	Low level	Mid-level	High level
Determine truth	38%	40%	59%
Establish responsibility	29%	31%	55%
Punish those responsible	27%	24%	39%
Prevent crimes from occurring again	59%	40%	61%

the seven possible reasons influences a witness's assessment of the Tribunal's effectiveness. We suggest that the greater the intensity of one's reasons for testifying – the more powerful the rationale behind one's decision to testify – the more likely such individuals are personally invested in the Tribunal's success. Accordingly, we measured the number of times an individual indicated s/he "strongly agreed" that a particular reason was important to her/him for testifying. We combined the count of these strong reasons into three categories of low (0 and 1), medium (2, 3, and 4), and high (5, 6, and 7) numbers. The results are found in Table 6.2.

The usual pattern of closely tracking trends on the truth and responsibility measures is in evidence here. There is a noticeable difference between those who indicate few, if any, strong reasons for testifying and those who express multiple, intensely felt reasons for testifying on their support for the ICTY's performance in revealing the truth – 38% and 59%, respectively; and for the establishment of responsibility measure – 29% and 55%, respectively. When we examine whether individuals approved of the punishments meted out by the ICTY the differences – 27% and 39% – are still sizeable, while the differences in the low and high categories of intensity of reasons for testifying in the deterrence measure are markedly less – 59% and 61%.

We turn next to examining the relationship between witnesses' perceptions of their own contributions to truth and justice and their assessment of the ICTY's performance in Table 6.3. Those interviewees who believe they have contributed to justice and the discovery of truth are generally, although not consistently, more supportive of the ICTY's efforts to achieve its goals, as we see in Table 6.3. This is most especially apparent when one examines attitudes toward the ICTY's goals of determining the truth and attributing responsibility. Of those who believe they have contributed to justice, 61.5% also believe the ICTY has aided in truth discovery, and 60.6% of those who believe they personally have contributed to truth discovery believe the ICTY has done a

TABLE 6.3. *Support for ICTY goals among those who feel they have contributed to justice and truth*

ICTY goals	Contributed to justice	Did not contribute to justice	Contributed to truth	Did not contribute to truth
Determine truth	62%	20%	62%	17%
Establish responsibility	57%	10%	55%	9%
Punish those responsible	43%	7%	40%	10%
Prevent crimes from occurring again	63%	31%	61%	33%

good job at discovering the truth. Among those who believe they have contributed to justice, 56.7% support the ICTY's job in determining responsibility, while 54.7% of those who believe they have contributed to truth discovery believe the ICTY has done a good job in determining responsibility. However, among those who do not believe they have contributed to justice or truth, support for the ICTY's mission falls off dramatically. For example, only 9% to 10% of those who do not believe they have contributed to truth or justice believe the ICTY has established responsibility. Support for the ICTY's truth mission drops roughly 40% among those who do not believe they have personally contributed to justice or truth.

Support falls off, however, when we turn to examining ICTY success at punishing war criminals. Support for punishment drops to less than 50% regardless of whether one believes one has contributed to justice or truth. ICTY support rebounds and reaches its highest levels when we look at the association between one's contribution and ICTY deterrence. Of those individuals who believe they have contributed to justice, 63% believe the ICTY has been effective in helping to prevent future conflict in the Balkans, while 61% who believe they have contributed to the truth believe the ICTY has been effective in this regard. Two trends are clearly in evidence. First, as we have seen before, attitudes regarding ICTY effectiveness at punishment are again the measure most resistant to influence by the factors we have examined. Second, the tables also reflect that among those individuals who believe they have *not contributed* to justice and/or the discovery of the truth, only a handful of individuals support the ICTY. If an individual doubts her own efficacy, she is hardly likely to believe the ICTY is doing a good job either.

We next turn to our final measure of personal investment – the threats to witnesses' own personal security from testifying. Because of the tremendous stakes of international tribunals, it is not surprising that some defendants, and

TABLE 6.4. *Testimonial consequences and support for the ICTY*

ICTY goals	Experienced social, economic, or security threat	Did not experience social, economic, or security threat
Determine truth	57%	43%
Establish responsibility	49%	37%
Punish those responsible	35%	28%
Prevent crimes from occurring again	59%	49%

most especially their supporters back home, try to threaten witnesses to keep them from testifying. The tribunals take every precaution to ensure witness security, from concealing their identity to the public at large to secretly transporting them to and from their homes, sometimes without even their families knowing what is happening. For those who do not request such protective measures, and even for those who do (but where defendants may illegally pass along their identities to supporters back home) there is always the possibility of some kind of threat or harm.

We examine relationships among the four measures of ICTY effectiveness and our three measures of threat – social harms, economic consequences, and security threats – in Table 6.4. We combine all three testimonial consequences into one binary variable for any type of consequence. We find that support for all four of the ICTY's missions is higher among those who experienced some type of threat. The great difference regards support for the ICTY's mission to establish the truth, where 57% of those who did experience some type of testimonial consequence support the ICTY, while among those who were not so affected support rests at 43%. We find the smallest difference on the punishment goal, where there are only seven percentage points separating those who did and did not experience testimonial consequences.

These descriptive analyses are quite useful in looking at broad trends and developing the beginnings of a multifaceted and generalizable model of support for international justice. We now combine these factors into a series of multivariate models to determine just how much explanatory power each contributes to this development of a holistic model and theory of support for international justice.

MULTIVARIATE ANALYSIS

We use a probit model for each of the four measures of ICTY impact as perceived by the witnesses and our standard variables, as well as: (1) intensity of witness motivations to testify; (2) whether the witness believed they made a personal contribution to justice; (3) whether the individual experienced a consequence to testifying; (4) whether the individual was satisfied with their present life situation; and (5) the level of the individual's knowledge of the ICTY after having testified for the last time. We examined a number of different modeling strategies, and elected to use a series of standard probit models using the same measures of dichotomous support for the ICTY we outlined at the beginning of the chapter.

The overall fit of the models is generally quite good, with the exception of the model regarding witness perceptions of the ICTY deterrence mission. This is not altogether surprising as the first three models of the ICTY goals of establishing truth, determining responsibility, and allocating punishment more directly pertain to matters with which witnesses have some familiarity. These issues revolve around the justice mission, which the witnesses contribute to as well, while the deterrence mission encompasses ICTY influence on political and military events about which witnesses likely have less knowledge, even though it may be that witnesses could draw upon more objective evidence of the relative impact of the ICTY in this area (e.g., the absence of violence). The truth model predicts 75% of the cases accurately (for a 48% proportionate reduction in error over the null model, which would always predict the modal category); the responsibility model predicts 74.3% of the cases accurately (a 37.4% proportionate reduction in error); the punishment model predicts 73.5% of the cases correctly (for a small proportionate reduction in error of 7.7%); and the deterrence model predicts 66.1% of the cases correctly (for a 28.6% proportionate reduction of error).

Ethnicity is a powerful factor in explaining attitudes about the ICTY's effectiveness, but its impact is not consistent across the objectives of the Tribunal. Rather, ethnicity plays an important role in influencing individuals' views regarding ICTY performance with regard to the "establishing the truth" and "determining responsibility" objectives, but is not as powerful in evaluations of the ICTY's punishment mission, nor in its deterrence mission. The lack of diverse measures regarding the effectiveness of international justice has typically forced scholars to rely on single measures (Meernik 2015a) and may have led to more straightforward, but simplistic assessments of group support of the ICTY. The results here indicate that ethnicity plays a much more nuanced role in explaining attitudes. When the respondents are asked questions about subjects that are at the core of the mission of international justice – determining truth and establishing responsibility – we see that ethnicity exercises a critical and consistent influence, as other scholars have found (Ford 2012; Meernik 2015a).

TABLE 6.5. *Establishing the truth model*

Variable	Coefficient	Standard error	Z statistic	P value	Marginal impact coefficient
Bosniak	0.150	0.259	0.580	0.562	0.059
Serb	−1.199	0.316	−3.790	0.000	−0.393
Bosnian Serb	−1.364	0.345	−3.960	0.000	−0.424
Croat	−0.614	0.261	−2.350	0.019	−0.228
Albanian	0.084	0.351	0.240	0.812	0.033
Experiences	0.000	0.016	0.030	0.979	0.000
Female	0.045	0.247	0.180	0.856	0.018
Contributed justice	0.964	0.202	4.770	0.000	0.355
Reason intensity	−0.055	0.127	−0.430	0.668	−0.022
Consequence	0.119	0.200	0.590	0.552	0.047
Present personal situation	0.168	0.142	1.180	0.238	0.066
ICTY knowledge	0.206	0.128	1.610	0.107	0.081
Education	−0.078	0.056	−1.380	0.168	−0.031
Age	−0.002	0.008	−0.190	0.849	−0.001
Constant	−0.935	0.808	−1.160	0.247	

n=279

There are three groups whose members are less likely to believe the ICTY has done a good job in establishing the truth (Table 6.5). The coefficients for the Croat, Serb, and Bosnian Serb variables are all statistically significant and negative. The marginal impact coefficients indicate that these groups are 22%, 39%, and 42%, respectively, less likely to support the ICTY's efforts to establish the truth, holding all other variables constant at their mean value. On the other hand, while there is not a statistically significant relationship between Bosniak respondents and the "truth" metric, Bosniaks are 27% more likely to believe the ICTY has done a good job in determining responsibility (Table 6.6), according to the marginal impact coefficient. Serb witnesses are not favorably disposed toward the ICTY's efforts to determine responsibility – the coefficient for this variable is statistically significant and negative. Serbs are roughly 28% less likely to indicate support for the ICTY on this measure. Serbs are also the only group who are distinctly less likely to believe the ICTY has done a good job in punishing the guilty. The marginal impact coefficient for this variable in Table 6.7 indicates they are 21% less likely to approve of the ICTY's handling of its punishment mission. Finally, in Table 6.8, where we examine support for the ICTY's record in helping to prevent wars again, only

TABLE 6.6. *Determining responsibility model*

Variable	Coefficient	Standard error	Z statistic	P value	Marginal impact coefficient
Bosniak	0.711	0.266	2.680	0.007	0.271
Serb	−0.944	0.379	−2.490	0.013	−0.281
Bosnian Serb	−0.509	0.338	−1.510	0.132	−0.169
Croat	0.066	0.269	0.240	0.807	0.024
Albanian	0.086	0.350	0.250	0.805	0.032
Experiences	−0.014	0.017	−0.850	0.396	−0.005
Female	−0.038	0.267	−0.140	0.886	−0.014
Contributed justice	1.311	0.233	5.620	0.000	0.410
Reason intensity	0.147	0.131	1.120	0.261	0.054
Consequence	0.099	0.208	0.470	0.636	0.036
Present personal situation	0.109	0.144	0.760	0.448	0.040
ICTY knowledge	0.307	0.141	2.180	0.029	0.113
Education	−0.053	0.059	−0.910	0.365	−0.020
Age	−0.008	0.009	−0.880	0.377	−0.003
Constant	−2.075	0.848	−2.450	0.014	

n=280

one ethnicity variable is statistically significant. Here it is the Albanians who are statistically less likely to support the ICTY. The marginal impact for the Kosovar Albanian variable indicates they are approximately 25% less likely to support the ICTY. In light of the fact that Slobodan Milošević's war in Kosovo took place six years after the establishment of the ICTY, this is not altogether surprising. It has long been a criticism that the ICTY failed to deter the violence from recurring (Clark 2014).

Ethnicity clearly plays a role in explaining perceptions of the ICTY's effectiveness, but the effects are much more diverse when we take into account support for the Tribunal's disparate missions. Witnesses' ethnic identity is most relevant in explaining one of the ICTY's most fundamental missions – to establish the truth about the events of the former Yugoslavia – although we see that the Bosniak and Kosovar Albanian support for the ICTY found in other studies is not apparent here. We should note, however, that the impact of these variables is sensitive to the mix of ethnic groups that are included in the truth model. When we experimented with different combinations of ethnic groups we tended to find that the coefficients for the Bosniak variable were generally statistically significant and positive. Overall, the impact of the

TABLE 6.7. *Punishing those responsible model*

Variable	Coefficient	Standard error	Z statistic	P value	Marginal impact coefficient
Bosniak	−0.094	0.262	−0.360	0.720	−0.028
Serb	−0.885	0.382	−2.310	0.021	−0.209
Bosnian Serb	−0.113	0.326	−0.350	0.729	−0.034
Croat	−0.252	0.280	−0.900	0.367	−0.073
Albanian	−0.121	0.361	−0.340	0.737	−0.036
Experiences	0.015	0.017	0.890	0.376	0.005
Female	0.152	0.258	0.590	0.554	0.049
Contributed justice	1.287	0.251	5.120	0.000	0.329
Reason intensity	−0.108	0.131	−0.820	0.412	−0.033
Consequence	0.145	0.207	0.700	0.484	0.046
Present personal situation	0.439	0.156	2.810	0.005	0.136
ICTY knowledge	0.351	0.140	2.510	0.012	0.108
Education	−0.161	0.060	−2.670	0.008	−0.050
Age	0.006	0.009	0.700	0.482	0.002
Constant	−3.248	0.884	−3.670	0.000	

n=280

ethnicity variable is strongest in the truth and responsibility models and less influential in the punishment and deterrence models. As the former group would seem to be more closely related to the competing narratives about the war held by these groups, this makes intuitive sense. The ethnic groups are more similar when the issue concerns punishment, as none seems particularly supportive of the ICTY's work in this regard. When queried about the deterrence mission, the groups are more generally supportive, as we saw earlier. The ethno-nationalist lens comes into sharpest focus when the ICTY's work strikes closest to home. That fits in with our observation that those with a personal investment in the Tribunal are more likely to be supportive of the mission. This clarifies that ethnicity is *also* part of this equation.

The ICTY witnesses interviewed for this project evince an awareness of the international context in which the Tribunal operates. Indeed, it would be nearly impossible for an observer of this tribunal or others to disentangle the decisions of these institutions from their political origins and influence. The ICTY was created in the midst of the Bosnian war when the international community seemed powerless to stem the violence. The political and military facts of the war – namely the disproportionate number of violations

TABLE 6.8. *Preventing crimes from occurring again model*

Variable	Coefficient	Standard error	Z statistic	P value	Marginal impact coefficient
Bosniak	−0.431	0.250	−1.720	0.085	−0.170
Serb	−0.413	0.277	−1.490	0.136	−0.163
Bosnian Serb	−0.201	0.281	−0.720	0.474	−0.080
Croat	−0.257	0.259	−0.990	0.320	−0.102
Albanian	−0.672	0.345	−1.950	0.051	−0.257
Experiences	−0.001	0.015	−0.090	0.928	−0.001
Female	−0.082	0.228	−0.360	0.718	−0.033
Contributed justice	0.836	0.183	4.560	0.000	0.323
Reason intensity	−0.020	0.117	−0.170	0.864	−0.008
Consequence	0.214	0.189	1.130	0.257	0.085
Present personal situation	0.069	0.132	0.530	0.599	0.028
ICTY knowledge	0.029	0.118	0.240	0.808	0.011
Education	−0.110	0.052	−2.110	0.035	−0.044
Age	0.008	0.008	1.040	0.300	0.003
Constant	−0.386	0.750	−0.510	0.607	

n=280

of international law committed by the Serbs – have meant ever since that the ICTY has focused its prosecutorial efforts on the Serbs. While most Bosniaks, as well as some Croats and Kosovar Albanians, view this as entirely appropriate, in the eyes of the Serbs, this is evidence that the ICTY is complicit with NATO (whose 1995 and 1999 air campaigns ended the wars in Bosnia and Kosovo, respectively), and especially with the United States, Great Britain, and France, in ensuring the Serbs are singled out for blame. Thus, while few would deny the role played by the international community in all developments in the former Yugoslavia, especially in Bosnia-Herzegovina, we see how once again ethnicity enters into play and serves as a prism through which international influence is evaluated. In times of conflict, and times of peace and the imposition of transnational justice mechanisms, ethnicity plays a role that shapes perceptions about international institutions.

The influence of the other factors on evaluations of the ICTY is varied; the results here are less predictable. The coefficients for many variables are never statistically significant. We see that neither the level of trauma suffered by a witness nor gender help us explain attitudes toward the ICTY. While previously we saw that those witnesses who experienced greater levels of trauma were more likely to evince positive attitudes on a variety of measures, the bivariate relationships between trauma and support for the ICTY we saw earlier do not hold up in the multivariate analysis. It is likely that the ethnicity variables are absorbing some of the impact of the trauma variable as Bosniaks and Kosovar Albanians tend to report the greatest levels of trauma, while the other groups generally report fewer instances of trauma. Again, this is consistent with the historical record of the conflict that those two groups suffered the highest levels of trauma, while the other groups generally reported fewer instances of trauma (Lacina and Gleditsch 2005).

We also find that the intensity of one's motivation to testify and whether a witness experienced a social, economic, or security threat never exercise a statistically meaningful impact. We do find that those who are satisfied with their present lot in life are more apt to support the ICTY's punishment mission, while those individuals with greater knowledge of the ICTY are more likely to evaluate the ICTY as having done a good job in general in determining responsibility for the crimes committed in the former Yugoslavia and in punishing those responsible.

One factor that is powerful and consistent across all four sets of estimates is the individual's belief that s/he contributed to the provision of justice. Those who believe in the power of their testimony are much more likely to believe the ICTY has done a good job in each of its four objectives. The impact is also quite similar in each of the models, indicating that witnesses' personal "buy-in" in terms of their contribution to the provision of justice is pivotal in understanding their opinions of the ICTY more generally. Again, this highlights that personal investment may drive witness views about whether transnational tribunals have accomplished their goals. These efficacious individuals are 35% more likely to believe the ICTY has generally done a good job in establishing the truth; 41% more likely to believe the ICTY has done a good job in determining responsibility; 33% more likely to support the ICTY's punishment of the guilty; and 32% more likely to believe the ICTY has generally done a good job in helping to prevent such wars from happening again. Those who believe in their own success are generally likely to believe in the success of the ICTY.

This provides us with an important insight into how individuals evaluate an institution like the ICTY. To be sure the objective record of these international tribunals will play a role in these assessments, but we should not overlook how individuals' own personal encounters with justice contribute to their assessments of these international institutions (Stepakoff et al. 2014, 2015). Indeed, as scholars have shown in the domestic context, one's encounters with the justice system as well as the encounters of one's principal identity group more generally with the justice system (e.g., African Americans in the

United States, and especially with regard to the issue of police violence) are highly important in shaping perceptions (see Gibson and Caldeira 1992).

Research on legitimacy and courts has found that the degree to which individuals accord legitimacy to these institutions is premised on their perceived fairness; the respect given to individuals by these institutions; and the individual's sense of efficacy regarding the court (Tyler 1990; Tyler and Darley 2000). Our findings clearly support this third criterion and demonstrate that individuals who believe they have contributed to justice are more likely to believe that the ICTY has been effective across all of its broad objectives. It is possible that individuals who possess such feelings of efficaciousness are more personally invested in the success of the ICTY and so want to believe that the Tribunal is succeeding. In other words, it may be that their own personal investment in the ICTY colors their perceptions and influences their evaluations in the direction of greater support for the Tribunal. On the other hand, these witnesses may simply and strongly believe in the need for international justice and recognize the importance of their witnessing for this important endeavor. Their belief in the need for and importance of justice may inform witnesses' understanding of their critical role in this international undertaking and influence their evaluation of the ICTY. Regardless of what these underlying factors causing this relationship may be, our research supports the idea that personal efficacy is a critical determinant of support for justice.

CONCLUSION

The ICTY witness survey data give us an unparalleled opportunity to explore how the impact of international justice is perceived through the eyes of some of its most important constituents – the witnesses who ensure that justice is done. From these preliminary findings, we make several general observations that are critical for our understanding of not just the ICTY, but the international justice project more generally. First, we have learned that assessments of the Tribunal's efforts to help achieve the goals of the United Nations Security Council mandate differ according to the particular goal. Our findings reveal that broad measures of support for international justice should be broken down into their constituent elements as witness perceptions of international justice differ depending on which aspect of the tribunal's mission is being evaluated. Witnesses do not generally treat these goals – establishing truth; determining responsibility; meting out punishment; and advancing deterrence – as an undifferentiated whole. Rather, they discern critical differences in how the ICTY has approached and advanced these goals and adjust their evaluations accordingly. The truth and responsibility missions tend to garner the most support. Witnesses in general are more likely to give the ICTY high marks on these fundamental and more abstract elements of its mission.

On the other hand, we found that the punishment and deterrence goals attract less support and that witness perceptions are predicated on a different set of criteria. The witnesses in our sample are less likely to support the ICTY's punishment of convicted defendants, while their views of the ICTY's impact on deterrence of future war crimes is much more difficult to predict. We would argue that there are three broad missions on which individuals differentially evaluate international justice – truth and responsibility; punishment; and deterrence. Future research should focus on distinguishing the different elements of support for these missions and determining just which international justice objectives are viewed as most important to witnesses, as well as the general publics in the affected countries.

We find that there are two factors that stand out above all of the other influences on witness perceptions of international justice – ethnicity and efficacy. We see that not only does ethnicity exercise a direct impact on witness perceptions of the ICTY's effectiveness – Bosniaks are more likely to support the ICTY, and Serbs are more likely to not support the ICTY across most dimensions – it is also highly correlated with other determinants of ICTY support such as the number of wartime experiences and whether one is an ethnic minority in one's community. As so much other research has found (Clark 2014; Ford 2012; Meernik 2015a), support for the ICTY tends to vary inversely with the number of one's ethnic brethren in the ICTY detention unit. Ethnicity is a powerful determinant of support for the ICTY. Ethnicity and other key definers of one's identity probably exercise a powerful effect on support for international justice no matter the conflict location whenever war is waged over such differences. Indeed, as Kersten (2016: 194) writes regarding the International Criminal Court, "The primary effect of ICC interventions on ongoing and active conflicts is on conflict narratives – the dominant understandings of the causes and drivers of violence, who is responsible for the conflict, and the appropriate measures to resolve the war."

While ethnicity and other core identity traits will probably always play a role in evaluations of international justice in those nations where conflicts and violence tend to break along these individually and collectively deep-seated traits, it will be critical in the future to survey much larger numbers of witnesses in order to better determine just how influential other individual-level factors are related to ethnicity and opinions regarding international justice. As the ICC expands its investigations into more conflict situations, this need to better understand how ethnicity relates to international justice and especially conflict characteristics that also pertain to justice will become more critical.

While the findings on ethnicity reveal nothing research has not already found, the second principal finding of these analyses does. Witness feelings of efficacy play a crucial role in their attitudes toward international justice. The greater one's belief that one has contributed to the justice mission, and to a lesser extent the truth, the more likely an individual is to support the ICTY. International justice is, in many respects, like domestic justice. Those who take part in it, and those who are affected by it, want to feel that they have made a difference in it. Justice is, after all, a public good, and to the extent the public feels enfranchised or disenfranchised from it, justice either thrives or withers. Given just how new this international justice movement is, it is all the more critical that we understand its determinants if we are to enhance the effectiveness of institutions and the witness experience.

7

Conclusions

Witnesses are indispensable for establishing truth and justice in post-conflict environments. While scholars and practitioners are now studying in earnest the impact of testifying on witnesses' lives, there is still much that remains to be explored and better understood. This study explored how a sample of 300 witnesses perceives they have been affected before, during, and after the process of testifying at the International Criminal Tribunal for the Former Yugoslavia. This chapter presents our conclusions based on the most important findings from the 300 interviews conducted, and offers both recommendations for further advances in research and practical advice for international and national courts on working with witnesses. By delving deeper into witnesses' motivations for testifying, human security concerns, their psychological and physiological health, and their overall perception of international justice, we hope that the results of this study will facilitate the further development of best practices in witness security, health, and the overall witness experience throughout the testimonial process. We also have sought to provide a more comprehensive understanding of what it means to bear witness. We hope that these findings can be used to advance theory development in such areas as international judicial research, studies of witnesses in both international and national courts, and transitional justice more generally.

We organize this chapter by theme. We begin by revisiting the three theoretical themes or lenses – gender, wartime trauma, and ethnicity – we used throughout this study to comment on the importance of the findings for both theory and practice. We also offer recommendations germane to these particular subjects. Subsequently, we discuss findings related to human security, the psychological and physiological impact of testifying, and witnesses' perceptions of their own contributions to international justice and the work of the ICTY.

GENDER ISSUES

The overall number of women who testified before the ICTY is relatively small (approximately 13%), with disproportionate numbers represented in sexual violence cases. Our study purposely oversampled women to ensure sufficient participation of them in the study, and it will be important in future studies to continue to ensure robust numbers of women in surveys, given that they are not called to testify nearly as frequently as men. It is also important to ensure that the contributions made by witnesses to international justice reflect the diversity of the affected populations, especially in the context of the prevalence of crimes of sexual violence. These crimes of sexual violence were frequently committed and widespread in the conflicts in the former Yugoslavia, as well as those situations investigated by other tribunals.

The study found that there are distinctive gender differences between men and women when it comes to the experience of testifying on a number of issues, but especially the impact of testifying on their psychological and physiological health. Women have higher levels of both positive and negative affect about testifying (both before and after). For the female witnesses, the testimonial process elicits a more complex and multifaceted emotional experience. Of special concern is the finding that women report their health is worse than men's both before the first time they testified and within the last three months. Women who report more health issues today are more likely to believe that their health is worse *because of* testifying. We find that female witnesses are somewhat more likely to indicate that they are strongly motivated to testify because they wish to speak for the dead. Perhaps many of these women see themselves as keepers of the torch for their families and communities, especially in situations where the male population has been targeted with extermination or violence. There is also some evidence, albeit weak given the statistical significance of the model coefficients, that women are less likely to believe their testimony contributed to truth or justice. It will be important to further explore this finding to determine if female witnesses in general are more apt to feel less efficacious than their male counterparts, especially in more conservative societies. Finally, gender appears to play little role in influencing opinions regarding how well the ICTY is achieving its political and judicial goals.

Given the substantial gender component to much of the violence (both the crimes that specifically target women, such as sexual assault, and those that deliberately target men, such as the Srebrenica massacres) there remains much work to be done to better understand the impact of gender on human security, testimonial impact, and opinions on international justice. We would like to know more about the perceptions of women who testified in sexual violence cases to understand how witnessing and experiencing such events influences perceptions of ICTY fairness, ICTY impact, as well as these witnesses' views on their reasons for testifying and self-perceived impact of testifying. Furthermore, given the substantial information from the audio-recordings of the open-ended questions (which we did not touch upon in this book), there are outstanding opportunities to evaluate the extent to which there are gendered voices in these wide-ranging discussions of transitional justice. We are especially mindful of the need to broaden the sample population to include sufficient numbers of women from each of the principal ethnic groups to better understand how ethnicity, trauma, and gender intersect and influence the types of problems witnesses experience and their opinions of international justice. We also suggest the following practical recommendations to ensure best practices in gendered issues in the testimonial process.

Practical Recommendations

- Develop witness support policies and services that reflect evolving practices regarding gender-sensitive approaches. The needs of female witnesses may be distinctive and require additional analysis about how and why the testimonial process, as well as the wartime experience, has a differential impact on women. We found that 23% of the female witnesses report experiencing the highest number of wartime traumas, while 16% of male witnesses report such high levels of traumatization. On average, female witnesses report 11.8 wartime traumas, while male witnesses report 9.5 such experiences. Based on findings here and research regarding the role of gender in other post-conflict settings, practices need to be developed to reduce the adverse impact on female witnesses.
- Assess the long-term impact of testifying in cases of sexual violence crimes. The prosecution of wartime sexual violence has been a singular accomplishment of the ICTY. Even though women appear disproportionately in cases charging sexual violence, both men and women in the study indicated they had been victims of sexual violence by either strangers or known acquaintances. Additional research should examine the long-term impact of testifying about sexual violence on both women *and* men.

WARTIME EXPERIENCE AND TRAUMA

The levels of wartime trauma endured by these witnesses are significant and substantial, as the data illustrate. Consistent with one of the largest studies to date in the region that examined wartime experiences,[1] the witnesses in this study have experienced extreme forms of physical and mental trauma. Notably, certain wartime experiences were more prevalent among the sample, with more than 200 interviewees selecting shelling, being close to death, and feeling as if their lives were in danger. Additionally, 185 interviewees indicated they experienced combat situations, as well as a lack of food and water. Indeed, the level of wartime trauma and experiences encountered by the interviewees is substantial and demonstrates that they suffered greatly during the war. In sum, the 300 interviewees reported they directly experienced a total of 2,876 events.[2] Clearly, these individuals have lived through tremendous suffering.

We found that these wartime experiences are powerful in shaping the witnesses' views of justice and many other topics that were raised on the survey. Those individuals who experienced the greatest levels of trauma, as measured by the number of different types of trauma they suffered, are more likely to feel strongly compelled to testify for many reasons, such as speaking for the dead and to tell their story; they are more likely to recall positive affect emotions after testifying; and they are more likely to believe that interpersonal relations are good in their community. They are not, however, more likely to believe their testimony contributed to truth or justice or believe that the ICTY has generally done a good job establishing the truth, determining responsibility for crimes committed, punishing the guilty, or helping to prevent future violence. While their attitudes are noticeably more positive in some areas, those most affected by the violence of the Yugoslav wars are not uniformly positive and optimistic across all the questions we asked. We also found that the coping strategies used by the witnesses to address these traumas in our sample can vary substantially. Interviewees generally indicated relatively low levels of reaching out to friends, family, and coworkers for support. Understanding which types of coping strategies witnesses deploy and why can help us better understand why some individuals emerging from

---

[1] The South-East European Social Survey Project provides social survey data to study the sociology and social history of the Western Balkans (www.svt.ntnu.no/iss/ringdalweb/SEESSP%20 Surveys.html).

[2] Of these, 2,813 were specifically asked about on the questionnaire, and the remaining events were described in short-answers provided by the interviewees.

war are more resilient and positive, while others seem to remain mired in the traumas they endured.

Identifying when and explaining why those who have endured the most trauma are often more positive or optimistic in their outlook and actions will likely generate substantial research for many years. This is a rather embryonic and interdisciplinary field of inquiry that we believe will be a prominent feature of transitional justice research in the years to come. The modestly supportive results we find, coupled with recent work by Bauer et al. (2016), should encourage psychologists, sociologists, conflict scholars, and transitional justice researchers to pursue this line of inquiry more systematically. Of particular interest will be identifying those conditions preceding conflict and violence, and those conditions prevailing in the aftermath of violence that may help explain why some individuals are more likely to be resilient, while others are more physically and emotionally harmed by war.

Practical Recommendations

- **Develop early on and embed witness support structures in international and national tribunals for witness assistance before, during, and after testifying.** This is necessary to ensure adequate care and assistance is provided to victims and witnesses by qualified staff members both at the seat of the court and in the field.

ETHNICITY

Research in psychology, sociology, and political science has found evidence of the power of ethnicity to influence individuals' perceptions of war and justice (Elcheroth 2006; Ford 2012; Staub 2006, 2013). We are interested in how witnesses' ethnicity shapes not just these views, but all the diverse facets of their encounter(s) with international justice. In this regard, it is important to understand that for the affected populations – witnesses included – the ICTY adjudicated not just cases involving the liability of specific individuals for specific crimes, but rather the Tribunal was also passing judgment on a particular version of history. If the judges tended to prosecute and sentence more severely Bosnian Serbs for their role in the conflicts, then in the eyes of many Bosnian Serbs (and probably many Serbs from Serbia as well) the judges were casting doubt, if not aspersions, on their version of present history. For many Bosnian Muslims, efforts made to prosecute members of their group (viewed by many as an attempt to achieve some kind of artificial "balance" in the ethnic composition of the defendant population) or to accept guilty pleas from their adversaries meant that the Tribunal was not supporting their view of justice and history. These dueling versions of the truth are grounded in and fueled by historical narratives with which many of the peoples of the former Yugoslavia perceive the more recent conflicts. The power of these narratives lies in the motivation they inspire in individuals to preserve their ethnic identity in the face of challenges from the other ethnic groups.

It is important to emphasize that interviewees in our sample were drawn from diverse demographic and ethnic backgrounds, with 81 interviewees (27%) describing themselves as Croat; 78 persons (27%) describing themselves as Bosniak; 95 persons (31.7%) describing themselves as Serb; 25 persons (9%) describing themselves as Albanian; and several other identities. Such diversity should enhance the generalizability of these findings. We found some evidence of the impact of ethnicity in opinions, although it was not always as straightforward as many scholars and practitioners might have expected. It was most clearly in evidence when we examined witnesses' views of the performance of the ICTY. Bosniaks and Albanians were generally more likely to express support for the ICTY's performance, while Serbs and Croats were distinctly less likely to do so. Opinions diverged most sharply along ethnic lines when the question concerned the ICTY's performance in establishing the truth and determining responsibility, while they were more alike on the punishment issue (with no group expressing majority support for the ICTY's efforts in this area) and the deterrence question, where there were greater levels of approval of the ICTY's performance across groups.

Bosnian Serb witnesses in our sample were less likely to indicate they were highly motivated to testify because of a need to tell their story, while Bosniaks were somewhat more inclined to wish to testify to confront the defendant. In some of our analyses Bosniaks, along with Croats and Kosovar Albanians, were more likely to believe their testimony contributed to the discovery of truth and the provision of justice. More generally, ethnic minorities in their communities were more likely to experience security threats. Serb witnesses were less likely to recall negative emotions after testifying, while Croats were more likely to do so. Bosniaks were less likely to indicate that interpersonal relations were good in the communities where they lived, while Serbs were less likely to believe they contributed to truth or justice. While there were some indications that Serbs and/or Bosnian Serbs were more negative about the Tribunal and their role in its proceedings, these too were not uniform across all the questions of interest.

Future research should investigate to what extent ethnicity independently explains witness attitudes on these key subjects, and what other factors may also be influential, but closely related to ethnicity. For example, we know that the level of wartime trauma witnesses suffered plays an important role in their attitudes, but we also know that Bosniaks generally suffered the most in the war. Thus, it will be important to disentangle these ethnicity effects from other factors related to both ethnicity and the dependent variable of interest. We would also offer several other suggestions for future research.

There are several groups of witnesses we were not able to include in this survey who should be interviewed to obtain the broadest and most diverse sample of witness opinions and experiences. First, the study did not include witnesses in the cases of Ratko Mladić, Radovan Karadžić, Vojislav Šešelj, and Goran Hadžić to prevent interference with ongoing trials. Many of those testifying in these four trials had also testified in earlier related trials, such as those involving Srebrenica. In order to ensure that we have the best possible sample of witnesses who testify in the great diversity of trials and to ensure that certain crimes (most especially Srebrenica) are accounted for in the types of witnesses in our database, it will be critical to survey witnesses who took part in these four trials. Second, it would be particularly useful in ascertaining the extent of the ethnicity effect to create a larger database with 200 to 300 members per ethnic group in order to reach more robust and generalizable findings.

We next turn to examining the findings and offering recommendations on the topics of: (1) human security; (2) psychological and physiological impact of testifying; and (3) the individual and her micro-/macro-level assessments of the ICTY.

HUMAN SECURITY

Because it is essential for both international justice and witness safety that witnesses testify freely and openly without fear of significant consequences, it is critical to assess how witnesses perceived their treatment by their community as a result of testifying. There is a small, but critical group of witnesses who have endured negative consequences as a result of testifying at the ICTY about wartime events, and who have faced challenges subsequently in their communities. These negative consequences range from criticism and loss of association, to economic harm and threats to their physical safety and the security of their families. Ostracism and threats to human security directly endanger justice and jeopardize prospects for reconciliation.

The study found that more than one in eight interviewees believed that they had endured some negative impact such as criticism or loss of association, and one out of seven reports contact or threats as a result of having testified. Criticism, loss of association, and threats come from a wide range of persons including those who may or may not share the ethnicity of the witness, and include the defendant and those who affiliate with him, as well as religious and community leaders. Only 22 interviewees out of those 44 who received threats contacted authorities, and 5 noted that they moved as a result of security issues. This finding is of particular importance because it suggests that witnesses may not feel they have a safety net in their communities in the event of threats to their security. We note 13% of the interviewees continue to feel some level of insecurity today, although whether this is owing to their having testified or continuing tensions in the region cannot be definitively answered with the results here. Importantly, witnesses report greater levels of satisfaction with the ICTY Field Offices and local authorities regarding security concerns compared to other actors, such as attorneys and the media.

The issue of victim and witness security is one of the key issues encountered by transitional justice mechanisms. Due to the potentially serious implications of being found guilty before an international tribunal for the political and military leaders who stand trial and their governments, as well as the international community, it is not surprising that some defendants, and most especially their supporters back home, try to prevent witnesses from testifying. Therefore, it is critical to utilize this research to determine how best to ensure witness safety and security.

Practical Recommendations

- **Identify factors associated with witnesses that place them "at-risk."** While witness safety and security can never be completely guaranteed, it is critical to take all reasonable steps to protect witness safety and security before, during, and after testifying. It will be especially important to determine which factors may place certain witnesses and their families at higher levels of security threats in order to take whatever precautions may be necessary to prevent attempts at interfering with their testimony.
- **Strengthen local assistance and cooperation with Field Offices.** Witnesses indicate that the Field Offices offer higher levels of satisfactory resolution of security risks, thus efforts should be made to establish and develop strong relationships within the communities where the Field Offices are located and witnesses reside.
- **Determine measures to assist witnesses in exercising their right to reparations.** Witnesses need to be provided with information about and assistance with the legal framework, costs, and the accessibility of legal support to pursue compensation or reparations. Witness support

structures should take steps to ensure that witnesses are fully aware of all of their rights.

PSYCHOLOGICAL AND PHYSIOLOGICAL WELL-BEING AND IMPACT

The impact of the testimonial process on witnesses' emotional and physical health is a critical and enduring concern. While the study adds to the debate over the extent to which testifying has positive or negative consequences for witnesses, further research across international, regional, and local legal mechanisms is needed about the short- and long-term impact of testifying. We return to this theme later.

The consequences of dealing with trauma on the scale the interviewees encountered create issues associated with re-traumatization while testifying, and can present substantial difficulties with obtaining closure about their war experiences. Our results indicated that there are also lasting emotional effects regarding these wartime events for significant numbers of interviewees. Many indicated that they often or fairly often think about loved ones they lost (37%) and events and experiences from the conflict (33%), while a number of interviewees also continue to think about the experience of testifying (13%). Interviewees generally indicated that their coping strategies are more likely to be internally oriented, with approximately half of them often or fairly often relying on their own mental resilience by taking it "one day at a time," avoiding difficult situations, using humor, or focusing on their achievements. Interviewees indicated relatively low levels of external psychosocial support (reaching out to others close to them, seeking assistance from professionals who can help, or finding encouragement from support groups). VWS staff members indicated that in some parts of the former Yugoslavia professional health services may not be available or easily accessible, which may help explain why seeking professional psychological help and social support networks is cited so infrequently. Interestingly, when in The Hague to testify, interviewees indicated that support by VWS and being accompanied by a support person helped to alleviate distress, which leaves unanswered the question of why witnesses do not seek similar support at home upon returning from testifying.

In terms of physical health, a substantial majority of interviewees do not think their health is worse today, nor do they think it will get worse because they testified at the ICTY. Given the relatively advanced age of the witnesses surveyed (the average age of the survey respondents is 59), it is not surprising that they report higher levels of stress-related health problems at the time of testifying, and that today there is a reduction in the overall wellness of the interviewee group as a whole. In particular, women indicate that overall their health is not as robust as is men's, which supports other findings that women in conflict situations report higher levels of health consequences from conflict.

As for the psychological impact at the time of testifying, when interviewees reflect back, their recollections of positive emotions surrounding the process tend to outnumber negative affect recollections. Significant numbers of interviewees report increases in positive affect after testifying and drops in negative affect after having testified for the last time. These results are markedly similar to those of the ongoing internal and anonymous VWS survey that has been conducted for all witnesses appearing at the ICTY since 2009. These results also corroborate findings from surveys conducted at the Special Court for Sierra Leone.

There are however indications based on the experience of the VWS that some witnesses who testified on multiple occasions may experience "testimony fatigue." Almost one in three interviewees had testified more than once (three-fourths of those multiple appearance witnesses testified twice, with a small but critical number of witnesses testifying three or more times). Whether interviewees find it physically and psychologically harder to deal with the experience of testifying or if they face increased security risks given multiple appearances cannot be fully understood based on this analysis. In addition, more than one-third of the interviewees reported logistical issues and problems associated with testifying (delays, rescheduling of testimony, waiting periods, and being away from home, family, and friends), which may be compounded the greater the number of times witnesses are called upon to testify. The linkages between multiple appearances, well-being, and security in particular need further analysis as other research has shown individuals who perceive security threats are more at risk for PTSD and depression (Başoğlu et al. 2005). As there is so little known about how testifying repeatedly affects witnesses, additional inquiry in this area is needed.

The results generally show that the interviewees are presently optimistic about their overall life situation (more than 60% indicate they are "satisfied" or "very satisfied" with their current situation), but this optimism declines when respondents think of the next two to five years. They are also generally satisfied with their economic situation in the present, but less sure about the future. More than 41% of the interviewees express that they are either very satisfied or satisfied with their economic situation, while only 28% expect to be satisfied with their situation in the next two to five years. Part of this issue, however, stems from the number of interviewees who indicated they did not know what the future would hold for them. Witnesses are much more pessimistic about current politics in their communities. Nearly 70% of the interviewees indicate they are somewhat unsatisfied, unsatisfied, or very unsatisfied with the present political situation in their country.

Finally, most interviewees indicate that they are somewhat to very satisfied with the state of interpersonal relations in their community (approximately 62%), while 52% expect to be satisfied in the next two to five years. Our model of these attitudes shows that they tend to correlate positively with the level of wartime trauma suffered and the individual's current satisfaction with their own life situation, while there is a negative relationship between views on interpersonal relations and whether the witness has suffered any kind of testimonial harm.

Researchers should continue to investigate the impact of witness physical and emotional health on survey responses. Among the most prominent reasons witnesses offered for not wishing to take part in the study were health issues. If witnesses who were experiencing more challenges to their physical and emotional health were systematically more likely to choose not to take the survey because of these problems, then the findings here may also be skewed. While an ongoing internal survey by the VWS of all witnesses suggests that witness recollections about the testimonial process in our sample may actually understate the prevalence of positive attitudes, further analysis is required to identify the extent to which such health issues influence witness responses.

Practical Recommendations

- **Standardize pre-testimony needs assessment.** There is a small number of interviewees for whom the experience of testifying was more negative. Additionally, the high levels of trauma experienced and witnessed by the interviewees during the wars calls for awareness of possible vulnerabilities and the need to address psychological, medical, and logistical needs well in advance to minimize negative consequences. Where possible, courts and tribunals should consider engaging the support of local and external organizations for witnesses who require long-term assistance. Additionally, the Field Offices should play a critical role in this phase.
- **Raise awareness of access to services for treatment of war trauma.** The unavailability of adequate support services in war-torn areas creates problems for those who are in need of such services. The survey results confirmed that interviewees who have suffered significant trauma do not tend to seek external professional help and are more inclined to internalize coping strategies. Efforts should be made to raise awareness among witnesses on the latest developments in the field of trauma treatment and redress and the organizations that can provide them with assistance.

Witnesses have a wide range of needs that only one agency cannot easily address. The establishment of relevant points of contact in specific governmental and non-governmental institutions could help address the psychosocial needs of witnesses in the post-testimony phase.

PERCEPTIONS OF INDIVIDUAL TREATMENT AND JUSTICE

The findings of the chapters pertaining to witnesses' views of their own encounter with international justice and their evaluations of the ICTY's performance nicely capture interviewees' dual perspectives on international justice. On the one hand, interviewees tended to provide more critical responses on questions pertaining to the macro-level of performance of the ICTY, such as those involving the duration of the trials and the punishment imposed on those convicted. On the other hand, they personally felt fairly treated by the Tribunal, and most felt they had personally contributed to justice and truth telling. Our results indicate that despite the great demographic diversity of the interviewees, the types of trials they testified in, and their motivations for doing so, they generally came away from the experience of testifying with significant personal satisfaction regarding their contribution to international justice.

A plurality of the interviewees believed the ICTY has helped establish the truth of what happened in the former Yugoslavia, and has determined who was responsible for committing grave crimes. However, only one-third believed the ICTY has done a good job in punishing those responsible. Individuals in the sample were more likely to believe the ICTY had generally done a good job in preventing conflicts from occurring again. The majority of interviewees also indicated that the proceedings have moved too slowly and that sentences where defendants entered into guilty plea agreements had not served the interests of justice. The interviewees were generally critical of sentences in the guilty plea cases, as one-third believed the sentences were too lenient. It should be noted that large numbers of individuals in this section of the study indicated they did not know, had no opinion, or did not respond to these questions. As well, almost half of the interviewees indicated that they did not believe local courts were better suited to hearing the kinds of cases that have come before the ICTY.

Evaluations about witnesses' motivations for and satisfaction with testifying are crucial to ensure their full involvement and preparation in the judicial process. Providing witnesses with the information they need to help understand a new and unique system of international justice, and especially their critical role in it, is an important responsibility for the ICTY, as well as all international tribunals. As expected, while a modest proportion of interviewees (25%) knew a great deal of information even before they testified, a greater and more substantial proportion (50%) knew a great deal after the last time they testified.

Given the wartime trauma interviewees endured and the challenges of appearing before an unfamiliar court far from home, the findings indicate that witnesses care about the legal, moral, and personal implications of testifying. Regardless of demographic and ethnic diversity, and irrespective of the number or types of trials in which they appeared, a large majority of the interviewees think it is important to help judges reach an "accurate decision," as a "duty" to victims, or to "tell their story." Moreover, both OTP and Defence witnesses were about equally likely to be satisfied with their experience testifying (93% and 90%, respectively).

The interviewees generally give the ICTY very good marks for its overall fairness and its fairness toward them individually. Interviewees in general are more likely than not to believe the ICTY has treated witnesses and defendants of their own ethnicity and others fairly. Perhaps what is most striking is that interviewees give very high marks to the ICTY units for their treatment of them personally, with roughly 90% to 95% indicating that the Trial Chambers and the VWS section treated them fairly. There is also strong majority support for the fairness of treatment given by the OTP and Defence, regardless of who called the witness.

Our model of individual evaluations of the ICTY's performance across the four measures of success revealed some especially interesting findings. We first saw that assessments of the Tribunal's efforts to help achieve these goals differ according to the particular goal. Witnesses do not generally treat these goals – establishing truth; determining responsibility; meting out punishment; and advancing deterrence – as an undifferentiated whole. Rather, their support varies across these goals, as well as by other key factors.

We found that ethnicity exercises a direct impact on witness perceptions of the ICTY's effectiveness – Bosniaks are more likely to support the ICTY, and Serbs are more likely to not support the ICTY. As well, the results clearly showed that those individuals who believed they had contributed to justice through their testimony were also more likely to believe the ICTY had generally done a good job across all four metrics.

Practical Recommendations

- **Disseminate information to the wider witness community.** It is important to raise awareness in communities where conflicts occur that the process of testifying provides opportunities to contribute to transitional justice and that the experience need not be viewed as necessarily difficult or negative. Given the hesitancy of many witnesses to testify for various and understandable reasons, it would be useful to provide information from witnesses who have testified publicly about their visit to The Hague.

- **Provide regular updates to witnesses on important developments in the trials in which they have testified.** Given the difficulties involved in understanding the work of international tribunals, all those involved in international justice should make special efforts toward educating the public in general about the trials, and especially critical decisions and outcomes. Witnesses are especially keen to know about and understand the judgments and outcomes of the trials in which they testified. With this in mind, the practice of informing witnesses on judgments and (early) release of the convicted should be further explored.

FINAL PRACTICAL CONSIDERATIONS: POST-TESTIMONY FOLLOW-UP

VWS staff members conducting the interviews for the study found that most witnesses interviewed supported the survey project and its goals, and most especially welcomed the renewed opportunity for contact. Numerous and intense – sometimes positive and sometimes negative – reactions during the participant recruitment calls gave the VWS staff members reason to believe that post-testimony contact fulfilled a need of the witnesses to share their thoughts and feelings about their experiences. Similar reactions occurred during the in-person meetings in which it seemed that many interviewees had been waiting for an opportunity to finally provide feedback. Other interviewees had needs that necessitated further support or referral. Perhaps the ultimate contribution of the study was indicated by those interviewees who told VWS staff that the interview resulted in peace of mind and an opportunity for closure.

These observations, coupled with the higher than expected study participation rate (more than 50% of those individuals with whom the VWS spoke agreed to take part in the survey), indicate that this type of follow-up study is important for international justice and enhancing best practices in effective witness support – something that has already been recommended by the United Nations Interregional Crime and Justice Research Institute's (UNICRI) report (2009). The findings here support and reinforce its recommendations about witness support as a necessary component of the process of testifying and also suggest that even longer-term evaluations of witness well-being should be conducted.

Practical Recommendations

- **All international and national judicial institutions should develop a program of short- and long-term follow-up activities for witnesses.** These programs can be used to ascertain potential issues pertaining to security, emotional well-being, and physical health. These activities should be embedded in the post-testimony service program to provide better insight into witnesses' needs and ensure timely actions are taken, if needed. Such programs will also ensure that witnesses will develop a better understanding of and appreciation for international justice.

- **Standardize usage of post-testimony questionnaire.** To accurately measure the impact of testifying on witnesses' physiological and psychological health as well as their lives in general, it is essential that this type of survey (tailored to the needs of a particular conflict setting) be administered immediately after testifying through witness support structures. This will ensure that witness recollections of various logistical issues, their health, the emotional impact of testifying, and other such measures are as accurate as possible. There should also be a subsequent survey administered 6 to 12 months later to follow-up with witnesses to both ensure their health and welfare and determine if any issues or problems identified in the original survey continue or have been ameliorated. Longitudinal studies over multi-year periods would be ideal.

- **Influence of survey administrator on responses.** It will also be important to investigate the impact of ICTY personnel conducting these surveys on witness responses. Trained VWS staff carried out the survey because of confidential information related to witness well-being and security. It is possible that interviewees' perceptions were skewed as compared to the general population of witnesses because of the administration by VWS staff. Further research should explore whether such an approach biases responses.

CONCLUDING THOUGHTS

The study has sought to thoroughly and scientifically survey, analyze, and understand the nature of the witness population at the ICTY and develop a more comprehensive perspective on the impact of testifying on witnesses. It has sought to contribute to an ever-growing body of research that is, at long last, seeking to document the experiences of these individuals who are often both victims and witnesses, and ultimately citizens who return to war-torn communities. As such, this study contributes not only to a better understanding of witnesses at the ICTY, it also helps advance our knowledge of witnesses across the spectrum of international and national justice mechanisms. For international justice to function best, it is critical to ensure that support services help provide witnesses with the assistance they need to testify most effectively for the sake of both the witnesses themselves and the tribunals. It is also critical that practitioners and scholars understand in-depth the impact of testifying on the lives of witnesses after their time in court has ended. Witnesses often represent their communities by testifying in court about events that have damaged or destroyed these communities, and they can also enlighten others in their community about the process of testifying upon their return. For all these reasons and more, it is fundamental that the international justice and transitional justice community continue to investigate and understand witnesses and the experience of being a witness.

This research provides many critical insights into transitional justice more generally and survey research on international justice more specifically. We identify three theoretical contributions in particular that we believe will advance knowledge in these areas. First, this research has demonstrated that the sample witnesses are strongly influenced in their opinions of international justice by their own personal encounter with the ICTY. Research on legitimacy and courts has found that the degree to which individuals accord legitimacy to these institutions is premised on their perceived fairness; the respect given to individuals by these institutions; and the individual's sense of efficacy regarding the court (Tyler 1990; Tyler and Darley 2000). It is this last factor that we are particularly interested in as we find that individuals who, despite their suffering, the logistical difficulties of testifying, and the anxiety-filled experience of appearing at the ICTY, nonetheless agree to this singular act. Given the degree of physical and emotional investment in testifying, we would expect that individuals will strongly desire that their testimony contribute to truth discovery and justice. We found that those who do feel a sense of personal efficacy as a result of their testimony are more likely to support the ICTY. Thus, while domestic and international courts are generally quite distinct institutions, these findings demonstrate that there is a striking similarity in how individuals perceive these institutions. At both the domestic and international level, most individuals want (perhaps even expect) their testimony to make a difference, and the extent to which these judicial institutions meet such expectations then strongly influences opinions of these courts. Such findings should encourage greater research into assessing how well these models of domestic court legitimacy can be extended to international institutions. It will be especially interesting to determine how the verdicts and sentences issued by international tribunals affect the opinions of witnesses and others, and to what extent opinions may be more grounded in one's own personal encounter with international justice.

We find that our analysis into witness resilience is a second critical area in which our findings can contribute to a burgeoning interdisciplinary research agenda. The reader will recall that we found evidence that many witnesses emerge from the testimonial experience without undergoing re-traumatization. Other research has found that that some societies and individuals tend to emerge from violence in ways that facilitate cooperation and community-building (Bauer et al. 2016). While we cannot speak to the root causes of such positive attitudes and behaviors, we find that witnesses' views of whether testifying is a positive or negative experience is a function of their wartime trauma, their motivation for testifying, and their gender. It will be important for both psychological health reasons and theoretical advancement to develop more sophisticated models of resilience so that we can track this disposition both across time (to assess whether there is something like a gradual progression toward more resilience, or if resilience develops in a nonlinear fashion) and across space (to assess which determinants of resilience may be more culturally based, or pertain to the characteristics of the conflict).

The third area of inquiry where we believe our research provides valuable insights concerns reconciliation. The reader will recall that in Chapter 5 we assessed which factors made individuals more or less likely to see interpersonal relations in their community as satisfactory. Some research has stressed the role of education and contact in fostering positive attitudes regarding reconciliation (Meernik et al. 2016), while other work has stressed the power of cultural narratives and political leaders to detract from such efforts (Clark 2014). Our research highlights several key findings, including the positive roles played by gender, a positive outlook on life in general, and the level of trauma a witness suffered during the war. The latter finding in particular is noteworthy as it ties back into the larger issue of resilience among those who suffered during war and the capacity of some individuals to develop more positive attitudes as a result of (or perhaps in spite of) their trauma. Again, we find important practical and theoretical issues at stake here. Large N research on the determinants of reconciliation is still rather rare. Our model can hopefully serve as a springboard for more research in this area. Especially given the propensity of nations emerging from civil wars toward recidivism (50% by many estimates – see Mason and Meernik 2006), it is critical for local and international actors to identify what conditions are most conducive to reducing the prospects of future violence.

Finally, we are excited about the prospects for future research in this area. The ICTY Witness Survey Project data will provide us and future researchers with critical insight into witness attitudes not only about the international justice mission, but also the impact of testimony on their physical and economic security, their psychological and physical well-being, and the meaning and importance of testimony to witnesses. We encourage further investigation into the experiences and attitudes of witnesses at the other ad hoc tribunals and the permanent ICC, as well as the opinions of all members of the general public in countries that are targeted by war crimes tribunals. By studying these opinions, we understand not just how these institutions acquire and retain support, we also understand just how the administration of international justice works through the views of its most frequent and arguably its most important clients – the witnesses.

Bibliography

Akhavan, Payam. "Are International Criminal Tribunals a Disincentive to Peace? Reconciling Judicial Romanticism with Political Realism." *Human Rights Quarterly* 31.3 (2009): 624–654.

Al-Ali, Nadje Sadig and Nicola Christine Pratt. *What Kind of Liberation? Women and the Occupation of Iraq.* Berkeley: University of California Press, 2009.

Arendt, Hannah. *Eichmann in Jerusalem: A Report on the Banality of Evil.* New York: Viking Press, 1963.

Arzt, Donna E. "Views on the Ground: The Local Perception of International Criminal Tribunals in the Former Yugoslavia and Sierra Leone." *The Annals of the American Academy of Political and Social Science* 603 (2006): 226–239.

Askin, Kelly D. "Prosecuting Wartime Rape and Other Gender-Related Crimes under International Law: Extraordinary Advances, Enduring Obstacles." *Berkeley Journal of International Law* 21.2 (2003): 288–349.

Backer, David. "Watching a Bargain Unravel? A Panel Study of Victims' Attitudes about Transitional Justice in Cape Town, South Africa." *International Journal of Transitional Justice* 4.3 (2010): 443–456.

Bandes, Susan. "Victims, Closure, and the Sociology of Emotion." *Journal of Law and Contemporary Problems* 72.2 (2009): 1–26.

Barberet, Rosemary. *Women, Crime and Criminal Justice: A Global Enquiry.* London: Routledge Press, 2014.

Barria, Lilian A. and Steven D. Roper. "How Effective Are International Criminal Tribunals? An Analysis of the ICTY and the ICTR." *International Journal of Human Rights* 9.3 (2005): 349–368.

Bartlett, William. "Economic Development and Perspectives for Reconciliation." In Martina Fischer and Olivera Simic (eds.), *Transitional Justice and Reconciliation: Lessons from the Balkans.* London: Routledge, 2015: 224–242.

Başoğlu, Metin. *Torture and Its Consequences: Current Treatment Approaches.* Cambridge: Cambridge University Press, 1999.

Başoğlu, Metin, Maria Livanou, Cvetana Crnobarić, Tanja Frančišković, Enra Suljić, Dijana Đurić, and Melin Vranešić. "Psychiatric and Cognitive Effects of War in Former Yugoslavia: Association of Lack of Redress for Trauma and Posttraumatic Stress Reactions." *Journal of the American Medical Association* 294.5 (2005): 580–590.

Bates, Maille Brady. "Balancing Act: The Rights of the Accused and Witness Protection Measures." *Trinity College Law Review* 17 (2014): 143–164.

Bateson, Regina. "Crime Victimization and Political Participation." *American Political Science Review* 106.3 (2012): 570–587.

Bauer, Michael, Christopher Blattman, Julie Chytilová, Joseph Henrich, and TamarMitts. "Can War Foster Cooperation." *Journal of Economic Perspectives* 30.3 (2016): 249–274.

Becchetti, Leonardo, Pierluigi Conzo, and Alessandro Romeo. "Violence, Trust, and Trustworthiness: Evidence from a Nairobi Slum." *Oxford Economic Papers* (2014): 283–305.

Bieber, Florian. "The Construction of National Identity and Its Challenges in Post-Yugoslav Censuses." *Social Science Quarterly* 96.3 (2015): 873–903.

Biruski, Dinka Corkalo, Dean Ajdukovic, and Ajana Löw Stanic. "When the World Collapses: Changed Worldview and Social Reconstruction in a Traumatized Community." *European Journal of Psychotraumatology* 5 (2014): 1–6.

Björkdahl, Annika and Johanna Mannergren Selimović. "Gendered Justice Gaps in Bosnia–Herzegovina." *Human Rights Review* 15.2 (2014): 201–218.

Blattman, Christopher and Edward Miguel. "Civil War." *Journal of Economic Literature* 48.1 (2010): 3–57.

Bloomfield, David, Teresa Barnes, and Luc Huyse (eds.). "Reconciliation after Violent Conflict: A Handbook." Stockholm: International Institute for Democracy and Electoral Assistance, 2003. Available online at: www.un.org/en/peacebuilding/ pbso/pdf/Reconciliation-After-Violent-Conflict-A-Handbook-Full-English-PDF .pdf. Last visited January 5, 2015.

Bonomy, Iain. "The Reality of Conducting a War Crimes Trial." *Journal of International Criminal Justice* 5.2 (2007): 348–359.

Borger, Julian. *The Butcher's Trail*. New York: Other Press, 2016.

Bornkamm, Paul Christroph. *Rwanda's Gacaca Courts: Between Retribution and Reparation*. Oxford: Oxford University Press, 2012.

Botev, Nikolai. "Where East Meets West: Ethnic Intermarriage in the Former Yugoslavia, 1962 to 1989." *American Sociological Review* 59.3 (1994): 461–480.

Bourbeau, Philippe. "Resilience and International Politics: Premises, Debates, Agenda." *International Studies Review* 17.3 (2015): 1,468–2,486.

Brounéus, Karen. "The Trauma of Truth Telling: Effects of Witnessing in the Rwandan Gacaca Courts on Psychological Health." *Journal of Conflict Resolution* 54.3 (2010): 408–437.

Brown, Lyn Mikel and Carol Gilligan. "Meeting at the Crossroads: Women's Psychology and Girls' Development." *Feminism & Psychology* 3.1 (1993): 11–35.

Bunch, Charlotte. "Transforming Human Rights from a Feminist Perspective." In *Julia Peters and Andrea Wolper* (eds.), *Women's Rights, Human Rights: International Feminist Perspectives* 11 (1995): 11–17.

Buric, Fedja. "Becoming Mixed: Mixed Marriages of Bosnia-Herzegovina during the Life and Death of Yugoslavia." University of Illinois Ph.D. Dissertation, 2012. Available online at: http://hdl.handle.net/2142/31178. Last visited December 23, 2014.

Byrne, Catherine C. "Benefit or Burden: Victims' Reflections on TRC Participation." *Peace and Conflict Journal of Peace Psychology* 10.3 (2004): 237–256.

Calo-Blanco, Aitor, Jaromír Kovářík, Friederike Mengel, José Gabriel Romero. "Natural Disasters and Indicators of Social Cohesion." *PLoS ONE* 12(6) (2017): e0176885. https://doi.org/10.1371/journal.pone.0176885.

Cardozo, B. L., A. Vergara, F. Agani, and C. A. Gotway. "Mental Health, Social Functioning, and Attitudes of Kosovar Albanians Following the War in Kosovo." *Journal of the American Medical Association* 284.5 (2000): 569–577.

Cassar, Alessandra, Pauline A. Grosjean, Sam Whitt. "Civil War, Social Capital and Market Development: Experimental and Survey Evidence on the Negative Consequences of Violence (November 10, 2011.)" UNSW Australian School of Business Research Paper No. 2011ECON14. 2011.

Cederman, Lars Erik, Kristian Skrede Gleditsch, and Nils B. Weidemann. "Horizontal Inequalities and Ethno Nationalist Civil War: A Global Comparison." *American Political Science Review* 1.18 (2011): 478–495.

Ciorciari, John D. and Anne Heindel. "Victim Testimony in International and Hybrid Criminal Courts: Narrative Opportunities, Challenges, and Fair Trial Demands." *Virginia Journal of International Law* 56.2 (2016): 1–74.

Clark, Janine Natalya. "Judging the ICTY: Has It Achieved Its Objectives?" *Southeast European and Black Sea Studies* 9.1-2 (2009a): 123–142.

"Plea Bargaining at the ICTY: Plea Agreements and Reconciliation." *European Journal of International Law* 20.2 (2009b): 415–436.

"The Limits of Retributive Justice: Findings of an Empirical Study in Bosnia and Herzegovina." *Journal of International Criminal Justice* 7 (2009c): 463–487.

"From Negative to Positive Peace: The Case of Bosnia and Herzegovina." *Journal of Human Rights* 8 (2009d): 360–384.

"Transitional Justice, Truth and Reconciliation: An Under-Explored Relationship." *International Criminal Law Review* 11.2 (2011): 241–261.

International Trials and Reconciliation: Assessing the Impact of the International Criminal Tribunal for the Former Yugoslavia. New York: Routledge, 2014.

Clark, Phil and Nicola Palmer. *Testifying to Genocide: Victim and Witness Protection in Rwanda.* London: Redress, 2012. Available online at: www.refworld.org/docid/50a3a9002.html. Last visited December 3, 2015.

Cody, Stephen Smith, Alexa Koenig, Robin Mejia, and Eric Stover. *Bearing Witness at the International Criminal Court: An Interview Survey of 109 Witnesses.* Berkeley: University of California, Human Rights Center, 2014.

Cohen, Dara Kay and Ragnhild Nordås. "Sexual Violence in Armed Conflict: Introducing the SVAC Dataset, 1989–2009." *Journal of Peace Research* 51.3 (2014): 418–428.

Cole, Elizabeth A. "Transitional Justice and the Reform of History Education." *International Journal of Transitional Justice* 1.1 (2007): 115–137.

Copelon, Rhonda. "Gender Crimes as War Crimes: Integrating Crimes against Women into International Criminal Law." *McGill Law Journal* 46 (2000): 217–240.

Crawford, James, Alain Pellet, and Catherine Redgewell. "Anglo-American and Continental Traditions in Advocacy before International Courts and Tribunals." *Cambridge Journal of International and Comparative Law* 72.4 (2013): 715–737.

Cryer, Robert. "Witness Tampering and International Criminal Tribunals." *Leiden Journal of International Law* 27.1 (2014): 191–203.

Danieli, Yael. "Massive Trauma and the Healing Role of Reparative Justice." *Journal of Traumatic Stress* 22 (2009): 351–357.

David, Roman. "What We Know about Transitional Justice: Survey and Experimental Evidence." *Political Psychology* 38 (2017): 151–177.

Davies, Arwel. "Scoping the Boundary between the Trade Law and Investment Law Regimes: When Does a Measure Relate to Investment?" *Journal of International Economic Law* (2012): 793–822.

DeGuzman, Margaret. "Choosing to Prosecute: Expressive Selection at the International Criminal Court." *Michigan Journal of International Law* 33 (2012): 265–320.

De Jong, Joop T. V. M., Ivan H. Komproe, Mark Van Ommeren, Mustafa El Masri, Mesfin Araya, Noureddine Khaled, Willem van de Put, and Daya Somasundaram. "Lifetime Events and Posttraumatic Stress Disorder in Four Post-Conflict Settings." *Journal of American Medical Association* 286.5 (2001): 555–562.

Dembour, Marie-Bénédicte and Emily Haslam. "Silencing Hearings? Victim-Witnesses at War Crimes Trials." *European Journal of International Law* 15.1 (2004): 151–177.

Denny, Elaine K. and Barbara F. Walter. "Ethnicity and Civil War." *Journal of Peace Research* 51.2 (2014): 199–212.

Do, Q.-T. and L. Iyer. "Mental Health in the Aftermath of Conflict." In M. Garfinkel and S. Skaperdas (eds.), *Oxford Handbook of the Economics of Peace and Conflict*. New York: Oxford University Press, 2012: 341–360.

Doak, Jonathan. "Honing the Stone: Refining Restorative Justice as a Vehicle for Emotional Redress." *Contemporary Justice Review*. 14.4 (2011a): 439–456.

"The Therapeutic Dimension of Transitional Justice: Emotional Repair and Victim Satisfaction in International Trials and Truth Commissions." *International Criminal Law Review* 11.2 (2011b): 263–298.

"Enriching Trial Justice for Crime Victims in Common Law Systems: Lessons from Transitional Environments." *International Review of Victimology* 21.2 (2015): 1–22.

Eber, Stephanie, Shannon Barth, Han Kang, Clare Mahan, Erin Dursa, and Aaron Schneiderman. "The National Health Study for a New Generation of United States Veterans: Methods for a Large-Scale Study on the Health of Recent Veterans." *Military Medicine* 178.9 (2013): 966–969.

Eikel, Markus. "Witness Protection Measures at the International Criminal Court: Legal Framework and Emerging Practice." *Criminal Law Forum* 23 (2012): 97–133.

Elcheroth, Guy. "Individual-Level and Community Effects of War Trauma on Social Representations Related to Humanitarian Law." *European Journal of Social Psychology* 36 (2006): 907–930.

Elcheroth, Guy and Dario Spini. "Public Support for Prosecution of Human Rights Violations in the Former Yugoslavia." *Peace and Conflict* 15 (2009): 189–214.

Elias-Bursać, Ellen. *Translating Evidence and Interpreting Testimony at a War Crimes Tribunal: Working in a Tug-of-War*. New York: Palgrave MacMillan, 2015.

Enloe, Cynthia. *The Morning After: Sexual Politics at the End of the Cold War*. Berkeley, CA: University of California Press, 1993.

Findlay, Mark. "Activating a Victim Constituency in International Criminal Justice." *International Journal of Transitional Justice* 3.2 (2009): 183–206.

Findlay, Mark and Sylvia Ngane. "Sham of the Moral Court? Testimony Sold as the Spoils of War." *Global Journal of Comparative Law* 1.13 (2012): 73–101.

Fjelde, Hanne and Lisa Hultman. "Weakening the Enemy: A Disaggregated Study of Violence against Civilians in Africa." *Journal of Conflict Resolution* 58.7 (2014): 1,230–1,257.

Ford, Stuart K. "A Social Psychology Model of the Perceived Legitimacy of International Criminal Courts: Implications for the Success of Transitional Justice Systems." *Vanderbilt Journal of Transnational Law* 45.2 (2012): 405–476.

Freedman, Sarah Warshauer et al. "Public Education and Social Reconstruction in Bosnia and Herzegovina and Croatia." In Eric Stover and Harvey Weinstein (eds.), *My Neighbor, My Enemy: Justice and Community in the Aftermath of Mass Atrocity.* Cambridge: Cambridge University Press, 2004.

Gagnon, V. P. Jr. *The Myth of Ethnic War: Serbia and Croatia in the 1990s.* Ithaca: Cornell University Press, 2004.

Garland, Howard and Stephanie Newport. "Effects of Absolute and Relative Sunk Costs on the Decision to Persist with a Course of Action." *Organizational Behavior and Human Decision Processes* 48.1 (1991): 55–69.

Ghobarah, Hazem Adam, Paul Huth, and Bruce Russett. "Civil Wars Kill and Maim People – Long After the Shooting Stops." *American Political Science Review* 97.2 (2003): 189–202.

"The Post-War Public Health Effects of Civil Conflict." *Social Science and Medicine* 59.4 (2004): 869–884.

Gibson, J. L. "Does Truth Lead to Reconciliation? Testing the Causal Assumptions of the South African Truth and Reconciliation Process." *American Journal of Political Science* 48 (2004a): 201–217.

"Truth, Reconciliation, and the Creation of a Human Rights Culture in South Africa." *Law & Society Review* 38.1 (2004b): 5–40.

Gibson, James. "The Legitimacy of the U.S. Supreme Court in a Polarized Polity." *Journal of Empirical Legal Studies* 4.3 (2007): 507–538.

Gibson, James L. and Gregory A. Caldeira. "Blacks and the United States Supreme Court: Models of Diffuse Support." *The Journal of Politics* 54.4 (1992): 1,120–1,145.

Gilligan, Carol. *In a Different Voice.* Cambridge, MA: Harvard University Press, 1982.

Gilligan, Michael J. "Is Enforcement Necessary for Effectiveness? A Model of the International Criminal Regime." *International Organization* 60.4 (2006): 935–967.

Goldstein, Joshua S. *Winning the War on War: The Decline of Armed Conflict.* London: Penguin, 2012.

Greig, Michael and James David Meernik. "To Prosecute or Not to Prosecute: Civil War Mediation and International Criminal Justice." *International Negotiation* 19.2 (2014): 257–284.

Grim, Brian J., Todd M. Johnson, Vegard Skirbekk, and Gina A. Zurlo. *Yearbook of International Religious Demography 2014.* Boston: Brill Publishers, 2015.

Hagan, John and Sanja K. Ivkovic. "War Crimes, Democracy, and the Rule of Law in Belgrade, the Former Yugoslavia, and Beyond." *The Annuals of the American Academy* 605 (2006): 130–151.

Haider, Huma and Timothy Welch. "The Protection of Witnesses in Bosnian War Crimes Trials: A Fair Balance between the Interest of the Victims and the Right of the Accused?" *The Denning Law Journal* 20 (2008): 55–86.

Halpern, Diane E. *Sex Differences in Cognitive Abilities* (Fourth Edition). London: Psychology Press, 2013.

Halpern, Jodi and Harvey M. Weinstein. "Rehumanizing the Other: Empathy and Reconciliation." *Human Rights Quarterly* 26.3 (2004): 561–583.

Hamber, Brandon. *Transforming Societies after Political Violence: Truth, Reconciliation, and Mental Health*. New York: Springer, 2009.

Hamber, Brandon, Dineo Nageng, and Gabriel O'Malley. "'Telling It Like It is': Understanding the Truth and Reconciliation Commission from the Perspective of Survivors." *Psychology in Society* 26 (2000): 18–42.

Harari, Yuval Noah. "Armchairs, Coffee, and Authority: Eye-Witnesses and Flesh-Witnesses Speak about War, 1100–2000." *The Journal of Military History* 74.1 (2010): 53–78.

Haslam, Emily. "Victim Participation at the International Criminal Court: A Triumph of Hope over Experience?" In Dominic McGoldrick, Peter Rowe, and Eric Donnelly (eds.), *The Permanent International Criminal Court: Legal and Policy Issues*. Oxford: Hart, 2004: 315–336.

Hatay, J. "Peacebuilding and Reconciliation in Bosnia and Herzegovina, Kosovo and Macedonia 1995–2004" (2005). Available online at: www.pcr.uu.se/publications/other_pub/Reconciliationreport_jacobsson_050615.pdf. Last visited May 16, 2015.

Hayden, Robert. "What's Reconciliation Got to Do with It? The International Criminal Tribunal for the Former Yugoslavia (ICTY) as Antiwar Profiteer." *Journal of Intervention and Statebuilding* 5.3 (2011): 313–330.

Heckman, James J. "The Common Structure of Statistical Models of Truncation, Sample Selection and Limited Dependent Variables and a Sample Estimator for Such Models." *Annals of Economic and Social Measurement* 5 (1976): 475–492.

Henry, Nicola. "Witness to Rape: The Limits and Potential of International War Crimes Trials for Victims of Wartime Sexual Violence." *International Journal of Transitional Justice* 3.1 (2009): 114–134.

"The Impossibility of Bearing Witness: Wartime Rape and the Promise of Justice." *Violence Against Women* 16.10 (2010): 1,098–1,119.

Herman, Judith Lewis. "The Mental Health of Crime Victims: Impact of Legal Intervention." *Journal of Traumatic Stress* 16.2 (2003): 159–166.

Trauma and Recovery: The Aftermath of Violence – From Domestic Abuse to Political Terror. New York: Basic Books, 2015.

Hewstone, Miles, Ed Cairns, Alberto Voci, Jürgen Hamberger, and Ulrike Niens. "Intergroup Contact, Forgiveness and Experience of 'The Troubles' in Northern Ireland." *Journal of Social Issues* 62 (2006):99–120.

Hjort, Hanna and Ann Frisén. "Ethnic Identity and Reconciliation: Two Main Tasks for the Young in Bosnia-Herzegovina." *Adolescence* 41 (2006): 141–153.

Hobfall, Stevan E., Anthony D. Mancini, Brian J. Hall, Daphna Canetti, and George A. Bonanno. "The Limits of Resilience: Distress Following Chronic Political Violence among Palestinians." *Social Science & Medicine* 72.8 (2011): 1,400–1,408.

Hodžić, Refik. "Living the Legacy of Mass Atrocities: Victims' Perspectives on War Crimes Trials." *Journal of International Criminal Justice* 8.1 (2010): 113–136.

Hoefgen, Anne M. "There Will Be No Justice Unless Women Are Part of That Justice: Rape in Bosnia, the ICTY and Gender Sensitive Prosecution." *Wisconsin Women's Law Journal* 14 (1999): 155.

Horn, Rebecca, Simon Charters, and Saleem Vahidy. "Witnesses in the Special Court for Sierra Leone: The Importance of the Witness Lawyer Relationship." *International Journal of Law, Crime and Justice* 37.1-2 (2009a): 25–38.

"Testifying in an International War Crimes Tribunal: The Experience of Witnesses in the Special Court for Sierra Leone." *International Journal of Transitional Justice* 3.1 (2009b): 135–149.

"Testifying in the Special Court for Sierra Leone: Witness Perceptions of Safety and Emotional Welfare." *Psychology, Crime & Law* 17.5 (2011): 435–455.

Hudson, Valerie M., Bonnie Ballif-Spanvill, Mary Caprioli, and Chad F. Emmett. *Sex and World Peace*. New York: Columbia University Press, 2012.

Hukanovic, Rezak. *The Tenth Circle of Hell: A Memoir of Life in the Death Camps of Bosnia*. New York, NY: Basic Books, 1996.

Human Rights Watch. "Justice for Atrocity Crimes: Lessons of International Support for Trials before the State Court of Bosnia and Herzegovina" (2012): 29. Available online at: www.hrw.org/sites/default/files/reports/bosnia0312_0.pdf.

Human Security Report. Oxford: Oxford University Press, 2005.

Hutchison, Emma and Roland Bleiker. "Emotional Reconciliation: Reconstituting Identity and Community after Trauma." *European Journal of Social Theory* 11 (2008): 385–403.

International Bar Association. *Witnesses before the International Criminal Court* (2013). Available online at: www.ibanet.org/Document/Default.aspx?Document Uid=9c4f533d-1927-421b-8c12-d41768ffc11f.

International Committee of the Red Cross (Greenburg Research). *People on War Survey* (1999).

International Criminal Law Series. "Victims & Witnesses Supporting the Transfer of Knowledge and Materials of War Crimes Cases from the ICTY to National Jurisdictions, Funded by the European Union" (2012).

International Criminal Tribunal for the former Yugoslavia. "ICTY Manual on Developed Practices." Prepared in conjunction with UNIERI as part of a project to preserve the legacy of the ICTY. Italy: Wald, 2009. Available online at: www .icty.org/x/file/About/Reports%20and%20Publications/ICTY_Manual_on_ Developed_Practices.pdf. Last visited February 5, 2016.

Ivković, Sanja Kutnjak and John Hagan. *Reclaiming Justice: The International Tribunal for the Former Yugoslavia and Local Courts*. Oxford, UK: Oxford University Press, 2011.

"Legitimacy of International Courts in the Aftermath of War Crimes and Crimes against Humanity: Victims' Evaluations of the ICTY and Local Courts in Bosnia and Herzegovina." *European Journal of Criminology* (2015): 200–220.

"Images of International Criminal Justice in the Former Yugoslavia." *Transitional Justice: Images and Memories* (2016): 181–204.

Jackson, J. and B. Bradford, Mike Hough, A. Myhill, P. Quinton, and T. R. Tyler. "Why Do People Comply with the Law? Legitimacy and the Influence of Legal Institutions." *British Journal of Criminology* 52.6 (2012): 1,051–1,071.

Jo, Hyeran, and Beth A. Simmons. "Can the International Criminal Court Deter Atrocity?" *International Organization* (2016): 1–33.

Jones, Nicholas A., Stephan Parmentier, and Elmar G. M. Weitekamp. "Dealing with International Crimes in Post-War Bosnia: A Look through the Lens of the Affected Population." *European Journal of Criminology* 9.5 (2012): 553–564.

Kaldor, Mary. *Human Security*. Cambridge: Polity Press, 2007.

Kalyvas, Stathis N. "The Ontology of 'Political Violence': Action and Identity in Civil Wars." *Perspectives on Politics* 1.3 (2003): 475–494.

Kapan, C. "The Politics of Location." In I. Grewal and C. Kaplan (eds.), *Scattered Hegemonies: Post-Modernity and Transnational Feminist Practices*. Minneapolis: University of Minnesota Press, 1994.

Kaplan, R. "The Coming Anarchy: How Scarcity, Crime, Overpopulation, and Disease Are Rapidly Destroying the Social Fabric of Our Planet." *Atlantic Monthly* (February 1994): 44–76.

Kelly, Michael J. "The Tricky Nature of Proving Genocide against Saddam Hussein before the Iraqi Special Tribunal." *Cornell International Law Journal* 38 (2005): 983–1012.

Kerridge, Bradley T., Maria R. Khan, Jürgen Rehm, and Amir Sapkota. "Conflict and Diarrheal and Related Diseases: A Global Analysis." *Journal of Epidemiology and Global Health* 3.4 (2013): 269–277.

Kersten, Mark. *Justice in Conflict*. Oxford: Oxford University Press, 2016.

Kim, H. J. and K. Sikkink. "Explaining the Deterrence Effect of Human Rights Prosecutions for Transitional Countries." *International Studies Quarterly* 54.4 (2010): 939–963.

King, Kimi Lynn and Megan Greening. "Gender Justice or Just Gender? The Role of Gender in Sexual Assault Decisions at the International Criminal Tribunal for the Former Yugoslavia." *Social Science Quarterly* 88.5 (2007): 1,049–1,071.

King, Kimi Lynn, James D. Meernik, and Eliza G. Kelly. "Deborah's Voice: The Role of Women in Sexual Assault Cases at the International Criminal Tribunal for the Former Yugoslavia." *Social Science Quarterly* 98 (2016): 548–565.

Klarin, Mirko. "The Impact of the ICTY Trials on Public Opinion in the Former Yugoslavia." *Journal of International Criminal Justice* 7.1 (2009): 89–96.

Kondylis, Florence. "Conflict Displacement and Labor Market Outcomes in Post-War Bosnia and Herzegovina." *Journal of Development Economics* 93.2 (2010): 235–248.

Kravetz, Daniela. "The Protection of Victims in War Crimes Trials." In Christoph Safferling and Thorsten Bonacker (eds.), *Victims of International Crimes: An Interdisciplinary Discourse*. New York, NY: Springer Press, 2013: 149–163.

Lacina, Bethay and Nils Petter Gleditsch. "Monitoring Trends in Global Combat: A New Dataset of Battle Deaths." *European Journal of Population* 21.3–4 (2005): 145–166.

Lautensach, Alex and Sabine Lautensach (eds.). *Human Security in World Affairs: Problems and Opportunities*. Vienna: Caesar Press, 2013.

Letica-Crepulja, Marina, Ebru Salcioglu, Tanja Frančišković, and Metin Basoglu. "Factors Associated with Posttraumatic Stress Disorder and Depression in War-Survivors Displaced in Croatia." *Croatian Medical Journal* 52.6 (2011): 709–717.

Linley, P. Alex and Stephen Joseph. "Positive Change Following Trauma and Adversity: A Review." *Journal of Traumatic Stress* 17.1 (2004): 11–21.

Mason, T. David and James D. Meernik (eds.). *Conflict Prevention and Peace-Building in Post-War Societies: Sustaining the Peace*. Abingdon on Thames, UK: Routledge, 2006.

McAdam, Jacqueline. "Coping and Adaptation: A Narrative Analysis of Children and Youth from Zones of Conflict in Africa." In Chandi Ferenando and Michael Ferrari (eds.), *Handbook of Resilience in Children at War*. New York: Springer, 2013: 163–177.

McAllister, Jacqueline. "On the Brink: Understanding When Armed Groups Might Be More Susceptible to International Criminal Tribunals' Influence." Paper presented at the 2014 Annual Meeting of the American Political Science Association (2014).

McBride, Dorothy E. and Amy G. Mazur. *The Politics of State Feminism: Innovation in Comparative Research*. Philadelphia, PA: Temple University Press, 2010.

Meernik, James. "Justice or Peace: How the International Criminal Tribunal Affects Societal Peace in Bosnia." *Journal of Peace Research* 42 (2005): 271–290.

"Explaining Public Opinion on International Criminal Justice." *European Political Science Review* 7.4 (2015a): 567–591.

"The International Criminal Court and the Deterrence of Human Rights Atrocities." *Civil Wars* 17.3 (2015b): 318–339.

"What Kind of Bargain Is a Plea?" *International Criminal Law Review* 14.1 (2014): 200–217.

Meernik, James and Rosa Aloisi. "Is Justice Delayed at the International Criminal Tribunals?" *Judicature* 91.6 (2008): 276–287.

Meernik, James and Jose Raul Guerrero. "Can International Criminal Justice Advance Ethnic Reconciliation? The ICTY and Ethnic Relations in Bosnia-Herzegovina." *Journal of Southeast European and Black Sea Studies* 14.3 (2014): 383–407.

Meernik, James and Kimi King. "A Psychological Jurisprudence Model of Public Opinion and International Prosecution." *International Area Studies Review* 17 (2013): 3–20.

Meernik, James, Kimi King, Nenad Golcevski, Melissa McKay, Ayal Feinberg, and Roman Krastev. "Truth, Justice, and Education: Towards Reconciliation in the Former Yugoslavia?" *Southeast European and Black Sea Studies* 16 (2016): 413–431.

Mendeloff, David. "Truth-Seeking, Truth-Telling, and Postconflict Peacebuilding: Curb the Enthusiasm?" *International Studies Review* 6.3 (2004): 355–380.

"Trauma and Vengeance: Assessing the Psychological and Emotional Effects of Post-Conflict Justice." *Human Rights Quarterly* 31.3 (2009): 592–693.

Menkel-Meadow, Carrie. "Portia in a Different Voice: Speculations on a Women's Lawyering Process." *Berkeley Women's Law Journal* 1 (1985): 39–63.

Miller, Zinaida. "Effects of Invisibility: In Search of the 'Economic' in Transitional Justice." *International Journal of Transitional Justice* 2.3 (2008): 266–291.

Minority Rights Group International. "The Status of Constituent Peoples and Minorities in Bosnia and Herzegovina." London: Minority Rights Group International, 2003. Available online at: www.refworld.org/pdfid/469cbfd80.pdf. Last visited June 5, 2015.

Mischkowski, Gabriela and Gorana Mlinarević. *The Trouble with Rape Trials: Views of Witnesses, Prosecutors and Judges on Prosecuting Sexualized Violence during the War in the Former Yugoslavia*. Cologne: Medica Mondiale, 2009.

Moffett, Luke. *Justice for Victims before the International Criminal Court.* New York: Routledge, 2014.

Moghalu, K. Chiedu. "Reconciling Fractured Societies: An African Perspective on the Role of Judicial Prosecutions." In R. Thakur and P. Malcontent (eds.), *From Sovereign Impunity to International Accountability: The Search for Justice in a World of States.* Tokyo: United Nations University, 2004: 197–223.

Mollica, Richard F., Keith McInnes, Marcissa Sarajlic, James Lavelle, Iris Sarajlic, and Michael P. Massagli. "Disability Associated with Psychiatric Comorbidity and Health Status in Bosnian Refugees Living in Croatia." *Journal of the American Medical Association* 282.5 (1999): 433–439.

Mrdjen, Snjezana. "Ethnically Mixed Marriages in the Area of the Former Yugoslavia: 1970–2005." *Zbornik Matice srpske za drustvene nauke* 131 (2010): 255–267.

Muggah, Robert, Elijah Agevi, Joshua Maviti, Paul Mbatha, and Kenneth Odary. *Urban Resilience in Situations of Chronic Violence: Case Study of Nairobi, Kenya.* Cambridge, MA: MIT Center for International Studies, 2011.

Nettelfield, Lara. *Courting Democracy in Bosnia and Herzegovina.* Cambridge: Cambridge University Press, 2010.

Norris, Fran H., Susan P. Stevens, Betty Pfefferbaum, Karen F. Wyche, and Rose L. Pfefferbaum. "Community Resilience as a Metaphor, Theory, Set of Capacities, and Strategy for Disaster Readiness." *American Journal of Community Psychology* 41(2008): 127–150.

No Justice Without Peace. *Making Justice Count: Assessing the Impact and Legacy of the Special Court for Sierra Leone in Sierra Leone and Liberia* (2012). Available online at: www.npwj.org/node/5599. Last visited June 16, 2014.

O'Brien, James C. "The Dayton Constitution of Bosnia and Herzegovina." In Laurel E. Miller and Louis Aucoin (eds.), *Framing the State in Times of Transition: Case Studies in Constitution Making.* Washington, D.C.: United States Institutes for Peace, 2010: 332–349.

Ochoa, Juan Carlos. *The Rights of Victims in Criminal Justice Proceedings for Serious Human Rights Violations.* Boston: Martinus Nijhoff Publishers, 2013.

O'Connell, Jamie. "Gambling with the Psyche: Does Prosecuting Human Rights Violators Console Their Victims?" *Harvard International Law Journal* 46.2 (2005): 295, at 328–336.

O'Donnell, Meaghan L., Mark Creamer, and Phillipa Pattison. "Posttraumatic Stress Disorder and Depression Following Trauma: Understanding Comorbidity." *American Journal of Psychiatry* 161 (2004): 1,390–1,396.

Olsen, T. D., A. G. Reiter, and L. A. Payne. *Transitional Justice in Balance: Comparing Processes, Weighing Efficacy.* Washington, DC: United States Institute of Peace Press, 2010.

Opačić, Goran, Vladimir Jović, Borislav Radović, and Goran Knežević (eds.). *Redress in Action: Consequences of Forcible Mobilization of Refugees in 1995.* Belgrade: IAN International Aid Network, 2006.

Orentlicher, D. *Shrinking the Space for Denial: The Impact of the ICTY in Serbia.* New York: Open Society Initiative, 2008.

That Someone Guilty Be Punished: The Impact of the ICTY in Bosnia. New York: Open Society Justice Initiative, 2010.

Organization for Security and Cooperation in Europe (OSCE). *Witness Protection and Support in BiH Domestic War Crimes Trials: Obstacles and Recommendations a Year after Adoption of the National Strategy for War Crimes Processing* (2010). Available online at: www.osce.org/bih/69314. Last visited December 23, 2014.

Attitudes towards War Crimes Issues, ICTY and the National Judiciary. (2011). Available online at: www.osce.org/serbia/90422?download=true Last visited July 3, 2017.

Palić, Sabina, Jessica Carlsson, Cherie Armour, and Ask Elklit. "Assessment of Dissociation in Bosnian Treatment Seeking Refugees in Denmark." *Nordic Journal of Psychiatry* 69.4 (2015): 307–314.

Park, Jeryang, Thomas P. Seager, P. Suresh, and C. Rao. "Lessons in Risk- versus Resilience-Based Design and Management." *Integrated Environmental Assessment and Management* 7(3) (2011): 396–399.

Percival, Valerie and Egbert Sondorp. "A Case Study of Health Sector Reform in Kosovo." *Conflict and Health* 4.7 (2010): 1–14. Available online at: www.conflictandhealth.com/content/4/1/7. Last visited December 21, 2015.

Perrin, Kristen. "Memory at the International Criminal Tribunal for the Former Yugoslavia (ICTY): Discussions on Remembering and Forgetting within Victim Testimonies." *East European Politics and Societies and Cultures* 30.2 (2015) 1–18.

Peskin, Victor. "Beyond Victor's Justice? The Challenge of Prosecuting the Winners at the International Criminal Tribunals for the Former Yugoslavia and Rwanda." *Journal of Human Rights* 4.2 (2005): 213–231.

International Justice in Rwanda and the Balkans: Virtual Trials and the Struggle for State Cooperation. Cambridge, UK: Cambridge University Press, 2008.

Peterson, Lindsay. "Hared Dilemmas: Justice for Rape Victims Under International Law and Protection for Rape Victims Seeking Asylum." *Hastings International and Comparative Law Review* 31 (2008): 509–510.

Poole, Daniel. "Indirect Health Consequences of War: Cardiovascular Disease." *International Journal of Sociology* 42.2 (2012): 90–107.

Ray, Amy E. "The Shame of It: Gender-Based Terrorism in the Former Yugoslavia and the Failure of International Human Rights Law to Comprehend the Injuries." *American University Law Review* 46 (1997): 793–840.

Ringdal, Gerd Inger, Kristen Ringdal, and Albert Simkus. "War Experiences and War-Related Distress in Bosnia and Herzegovina Eight Years after War." *Croatian Medical Journal* 49.1 (2008): 75–86.

Roper, Steven D. and Lilian A. Barria. *Designing Criminal Tribunals: Sovereignty and International Concerns in the Protection of Human Rights*. Hampshire: Ashgate, 2006.

Runswick-Cole, Katherine. "'The Tribunal Was the Most Stressful Thing: More Stressful Than My Son's Diagnosis or Behaviour': The Experiences of Families Who Go to the Special Educational Needs and Disability Tribunal (SENDisT)." *Disability & Society* 22.3 (2007): 315–328.

SáCouto, Susana. "Victim Participation at the International Criminal Court and the Extraordinary Chambers in the Courts of Cambodia: A Feminist Project." *Michigan Journal of Gender & Law* 18.2 (2012): 297–359.

Salama P., P. Spiegel, M. Van Dyke, L. Phelps, and C. Wilkinson. "Mental Health and Nutritional Status among the Adult Serbian Minority in Kosovo." *Journal of the American Medical Association* 284 (2000): 578–584.

Saxon, Dan. "Exporting Justice: Perceptions of the ICTY Among the Serbian, Croatian, and Muslim Communities in the Former Yugoslavia." *Journal of Human Rights* 4.4 (2005): 559–572.

Sendzimir, J., C. P. Reij, and P. Magnuszewski. "Rebuilding resilience in the Sahel: regreening in the Maradi and Zinder regions of Niger." *Ecology and Society* 16(3) (2011): 1.

Seymour, Lee J. M., Kristin M. Bakke, and Kathleen Gallagher Cunningham. "E Pluribus Unum, Ex Uno Plures: Competition, Violence, and Fragmentation in Ethnopolitical Movements." *Journal of Peace Research* 53.1 (2016): 3–18.

Shemyakina, Olga N. and Anke C. Plagnol. "Subjective Well-Being and Armed Conflict: Evidence from Bosnia-Herzegovina." *Social Indicators Research* 113.3 (2013): 1,129–1,152.

Sikkink, Kathryn. *The Justice Cascade: How Human Rights Prosecutions Are Changing World Politics (The Norton Series in World Politics)*. New York, NY: WW Norton & Company, 2011.

Silove, Derrick. "The Psychosocial Effects of Torture, Mass Human Rights Violations, and Refugee Trauma: Toward an Integrated Conceptual Framework." *Journal of Nervous & Mental Disease* 187.4 (1999): 200–207.

Simmons, Beth and Allison Danner. "Credible Commitments and the International Criminal Court." *International Organization* 64.2 (2010): 225–256.

Smith, Alan. "Education in the Twenty-First Century: Conflict, Reconstruction and Reconciliation" *Compare* 35 (2005):373–391.

Smits, Jeroen. "Ethnic Intermarriage and Social Cohesion: What Can We Learn from Yugoslavia?" *Social Indicators Research* 96.3 (2010): 417–432.

Snyder, Jack and Wright L. Vinjamuri. "Trials and Errors: Principle and Pragmatism in Strategies of International Justice." *International Security* 283 (2003): 5–44.

Spini, Dario, Guy Elcheroth, and Rachel Fasel. *Towards a Community Approach of the Aftermath of War in the Former Yugoslavia: Collective Experiences, Social Practices, and Representations*. New York: Springer, 2013.

Staggs-Kelsall, Michelle and Shanee Stepakoff. "'When We Wanted to Talk about Rape': Silencing Sexual Violence at the Special Court for Sierra Leone." *International Journal of Transitional Justice* 1.3 (2007): 355–374.

Staub, Ervin. "Reconciliation after Genocide, Mass Killing, or Intractable Conflict: Understanding the Roots of Violence, Psychological Recovery, and Steps toward a General Theory." *Political Psychology* 27.6 (2006): 867–894.

"Building a Peaceful Society: Origins, Prevention, and Reconciliation after Genocide and Other Group Violence." *American Psychologist* 7 (2013): 576–589.

Steel, Zachary, Tien Chey, Derrick Silove, Claire Marnane, Richard A. Bryant, and Mark van Ommeren, "Association of Torture and Other Potentially Traumatic Events with Mental Health Outcomes among Populations Exposed to Mass Conflict and Displacement: A Systematic Review and Meta-Analysis." *Journal of the American Medical Association* 302.5 (2009): 537–549.

Stepakoff, Shanee, G. Shawn Reynolds, and Simon Charters. "Why Testify? Witnesses' Motivations for Giving Evidence in a War Crimes Tribunal in Sierra." *International Journal of Transitional Justice* 8.3 (2014): 426–451.

"Self-Reported Psychosocial Consequences of Testifying in a War Crimes Tribunal in Sierra Leone." *International Perspectives in Psychology: Research, Practice, Consultation* 4.3 (2015): 161–181.

Stiglmayer, Alexandra (ed.). *Mass Rape: The War against Women in Bosnia-Herzegovina*. Lincoln, NE: University of Nebraska Press, 1994.

Stover, Eric. *Bearing Witness at the International Criminal Court: An Interview Survey of 109 Witnesses*. Berkeley: University of California, Human Rights Center, 2014.

The Witness: War Crimes and the Promise of Justice in The Hague. Philadelphia: University of Pennsylvania Press, 2005.

Stover, Eric and Harvey Weinstein (eds.). *My Neighbor, My Enemy: Justice and Community in the Aftermath of Mass Conflict*. Cambridge: Cambridge University Press, 2004.

Stover, Eric, Mychelle Balthazard, and K. Alexa Koenig. "Confronting Duch: Civil Party Participation in Case 001 at the Extraordinary Chambers in the Courts of Cambodia." *International Review of the Red Cross* 93 (2011): 503–546.

Subotić, Jelena, *Hijacked Justice: Dealing with the Past in the Balkans*. Ithaca: Cornell University Press, 2009.

Themnér, Lotta and Peter Wallensteen. "Armed Conflicts, 1946–2011." *Journal of peace research* 49.4 (2012): 565–575.

Tickner, J. Ann. *Gendering World Politics: Issues and Approaches in the Post-Cold War Era*. New York, NY: Columbia University Press, 2001.

Trotter, Andrew. "Witness Intimidation in International Trials: Balancing the Need for Protection against the Rights of the Accused." *George Washington International Law Review* 44.3 (2013): 521–537.

Tyler, Tom. *Why People Obey the Law*. New Haven: Yale University Press, 1990.

Tyler, Tom and John Darley. "Building a Law-Abiding Society: Taking Public Views about Morality and the Legitimacy of Legal Authorities into Account When Formulating Substantive Law." *Hofstra Law Review* 28.3 (2000): 707–739.

Tyler, Tom R. and Yuen Huo. *Trust in the Law: Encouraging Public Cooperation with the Police and Courts* . New York, NY: Russell Sage Foundation, 2002.

United Nations Development Programme (UNDP). *Human Development Report 1994*. New York: Oxford University Press, 1994. Available online at: http://hdr .undp.org/sites/default/files/reports/255/hdr_1994_en_complete_nostats.pdf. Last visited December 1, 2015.

United Nations Interregional Crime and Justice Research Institute. "ICTY Manual on Developed Practices. 2009. Available on line at www.unicri.it/services/library_ documentation/publications/unicri_series/ICTY_Manual_on_Developed_ Practices.pdf. Last accessed July 3, 2017.

United Nations International Criminal Tribunal for the Former Yugoslavia. *Information Booklet for ICTY Witnesses*. Victims and Witnesses Section, 2007.

Van der Kolk, Bessel. *The Body Keeps the Score: Brain, Mind, and Body in the Healing of Trauma*. New York: Viking, 2014.

Wald, Patricia M. "The International Criminal Tribunal for the Former Yugoslavia Comes of Age: Some Observations on Day-To-Day Dilemmas of an International Court." *Washington University Journal of Law and Policy* 5 (2001): 87–123.

"Dealing with Witnesses in War Crimes Trials: Lessons from Yugoslavia Tribunal." *Yale Human Rights & Development Law Journal* 5 (2002): 1–21.

Walker, William. "The Yugoslav War Crimes Tribunal: Recent Developments." *Whittier Law Review* 19 (1997): 304, 308.

Walker, Pamela M. and Miles Hewstone. "A Perceptual Discrimination Investigation of the Own-Race Effect and Intergroup Experience." *Applied Cognitive Psychology* 20.4 (2006): 461–475.

War Crimes Justice Project. "International Criminal Law and Practice Training Materials Victims & Witnesses Supporting the Transfer of Knowledge and Materials of War Crimes Cases from the ICTY to National Jurisdictions." European Union Organization for Security and Cooperation in Europe (OSCE) and the International Criminal Law Series (2010). OSCE-ODIHR/ICTY/UNICRI Project-European Union (2008). Available online at: http://wcjp.unicri.it/deliverables/docs/Module_8_War_crimes.pdf. Last visited May 16, 2015.

Williams, Paul D. "Protection, Resilience and Empowerment: United Nations Peacekeeping and Violence against Civilians in Contemporary War Zones." *Politics* 33.4 (2013): 287–298.

Winter, David, Rachel Brown, Stephanie Goins, and Clare Mason. *Trauma, Survival and Resilience in War Zones: The Psychological Impact of the War in Sierra Leone and Beyond*. London: Routledge, 2016.

Woodward, Susan. *Balkan Tragedy*. Washington D.C. Brookings Institution Press, 1995.

World Health Organization. *Reproductive Health During Conflict and Displacement*. Geneva: World Health Organization, 2000.

Youngs, Gillian. "From Practice to Theory: Feminist International Relations and 'Gender Mainstreaming.'" *International Politics* 45.6 (2008): 688–702.

Zoglin, Katie. "The Future of War Crimes Prosecutions in the Former Yugoslavia: Accountability or Junk Justice?" *Human Rights Quarterly* 27.1 (2005): 41–77.

Index

age
  witness sampling process and, 24, 124
Albanians, 38
  belief in ICTY fairness towards Albanian
    defendants, 156
  reporting of health issues before and three
    months post-testifying, 126
  support for deterrence mandate of ICTY
    and, 161

Balkan wars, 38
  civilian deaths and, 47
  ethnicity and, 6, 7
  gender violence in, 8
  sparing of individuals in Croatia and
    Serbia, 49
Bauer, Michael, 146
bivariate correlations
  between ethnic minority status and number
    of traumas experienced, 115
Bosnia, 14, 23, 25
  mixed ethnic marriages in, 41
Bosniaks, 6, 35, 38
  belief in ICTY fairness towards Bosniak
    defendants, 67, 156
  as highest percentage of civilian deaths
    and, 47
  interpersonal relations in their community
    and, 145
  level of knowledge of ICTY after
    testimony, 55
  level of knowledge of ICTY before
    testimony, 55
  motivations to testify of, 60–61
  on national vs. international tribunals for
    adjudicating war crimes, 155

post traumatic symptoms and, 121
  reporting of economic harm and physical
    security threats by, 116
  reporting of health issues before and three
    months post-testifying, 126
  reporting on if health is worse due to
    testifying, 127
  support for deterrence mandate of ICTY
    and, 161
  support for punishment mandate of ICTY
    and, 161
  support for truth and responsibility
    mandates of ICTY and, 159
  trauma experienced and reported by, 47–51
Bosnian Croats, 38
  level of knowledge of ICTY before
    testimony, 55
  motivations to testify of, 60–61
  reporting on if health is worse due to
    testifying, 127
  satisfaction with information and assistance
    from VWS of, 58
  support for deterrence mandate of ICTY
    and, 161
Bosnian Serbs
  belief in ICTY unfairness towards Bosnian
    Serb defendants, 156
  level of knowledge of ICTY after
    testimony, 55
  level of knowledge of ICTY before
    testimony, 55
  motivations to testify of, 60–61
  reporting of negative emotions after
    testifying and, 136
  reporting on if health is worse due to
    testifying, 127

Bosnian Serbs (*cont.*)
  satisfaction with information and assistance
    from VWS before testimony, 58
  support for deterrence mandate of ICTY
    and, 161

catharsis, testifying as, 9, 72, 128
civil conflicts and wars. *See also* post-conflict
    societies
  ethnicity and, 6–7
Clark, Janine Natalya, 143, 144
closure
  difficulty obtaining post-trauma, 119
  providing witnesses with ICTY as goal of
    study, 19
  testifying as, 9, 34, 73, 128
Cody, Stephen Smith, 3, 57, 123
community relations. *See also* relationships
  consequences of testimony on, 88–91, 116
  education and, 147
  ethnicity and satisfaction with interpersonal
    relations, 144–45
  gender and satisfaction with
    interpersonal, 145
  human security threats and issues as
    negatively related to satisfaction in, 146
  need to strengthen local assistance from
    field offices in, 185
  positive outlook on life and, 147
  satisfaction with for ethnic minorities in
    their communities, 145
  trauma and witness satisfaction with
    interpersonal, 145–48
Conference Language Services Section
    (CLSS), 12
criticism and disassociation in community, as
    consequence of testimony, 88–91, 116
Croatia, 14, 23
  mixed ethnic marriages in, 41
Croats, 6, 38, *See also* Bosnian Croats;
    Serbian Croats
  belief in ICTY fairness towards Croatian
    defendants, 156
  level of knowledge of ICTY after
    testimony, 55
  level of knowledge of ICTY before
    testimony, 55
  motivations to testify of, 60–61
  reporting of health issues before and three
    months post-testifying, 126
  reporting of negative emotions after
    testifying and, 136

support for deterrence mandate of ICTY
    and, 161
support for truth and responsibility
    mandates of ICTY and, 160
Cunningham, Kathleen Gallagher, 7

deGuzman, Margaret, 150
deprivation as trauma, 56
deterrence mandate of ICTY, 35, 159–63, 176
  belief in efficacy of testimony and, 174–75
  experiences of human security threats
    and, 167–68
  levels of importance of reasons for testifying
    and, 165–66
  probit model of influence of ethnicity on
    witness perception on, 169–73
  support for by ethnicity, 161, 161f6.11.
  trauma and, 163–65
  witness perceptions of their contributions to
    truth and justice and, 166–67

economic consequences of testifying, 9, 10,
    91–94. *See also* human security threats;
    social consequences of testifying;
    testimony and testimonial process
  Bosniaks reporting of, 117
  economic losses attributed to across time
    periods, 92
  ethnicity and, 105–06
  gender and, 108
  as negatively related to satisfaction with
    community relations, 146
  positive and negative changes across time
    periods, 91, 92
  satisfaction with ICTY financial
    entitlements during testifying
    and, 92–94
  witness satisfaction with present and future
    economic circumstances, 139, 140
education
  as negatively related to satisfaction with
    community relations, 147
  positive outlook and, 147
  reconciliation and, 143
  witness educational attainment levels, 24
  witness motivation for testifying and, 77
effectiveness of ICTY, 34–35, 189–91
    See also deterrence mandate of
    ICTY; punishment mandate of ICTY;
    responsibility mandate of ICTY; truth
    mandate of ICTY
  ethnicity and witness perception of, 176–77

gender and impact on national and international politics on perception of, 153–54
probit model of influence of ethnicity on witness perception of, 169–73
witness belief in efficacy of testimony and perception of, 52, 174–75
witness perception on, 150–51
witness perception on ICTY sentences, 152–53
witness perception on impact of international and national politics on, 153
witness perceptions on proceedings having moved too slowly, 152
ethnic cleansing, 6, 72, 106, 162
ethnic minorities in their communities, 144. *See also* by specific ethnic group; ethnicity
human security threats and, 105–08, 112, 115, 117
as more likely to have positive attitudes about community interpersonal relations, 145
support for ICTY mandates and, 162
trauma and, 50, 115, 117
ethnicity, 182–84. *See also* by specific ethnic group; ethnic minorities in their communities
in Balkan wars, 6, 7
breakdown of by gender in witness survey, 38, 40f2.3.
civil conflicts and wars and, 6–7
critical role of in shaping perceptions of international justice, 157–58
criticism and disassociation in community as consequence of testimony and, 88–91
economic consequences of testifying and, 105–06
ethnic identification among key ICTY nationalities in witness survey, 39f2.2.
ethnic self-identification in witness survey, 26, 39f2.1., 183
general lack of support for punishment mandate of ICTY and, 160f6.10., 161
health of witnesses before testifying and three months post-testifying, 123–27
human security threats and, 96, 105–6, 115
ICTY support and, 158–59
ICTY witness motivations to testify, 60–61, 74

influence of on witness perception of ITCY effectiveness, 176–77
interethnic marriages and, 39–42
level of knowledge of ICTY after testimony by ethnic group, 55
level of knowledge of ICTY before testimony by ethnic group, 55
on national vs. international courts as better for adjudicating war crimes, 154–55
perceptions of fairness of ICTY toward witnesses of own ethnic group, 67, 155–57
post traumatic symptoms and, 121
probit model of influence of on witness perception of ITCY effectiveness, 169–73
religion and, 6
reporting of negative emotions after testifying and, 136
reporting on if health is worse due to testifying, 127
satisfaction with interpersonal relations in their community and, 144–45
on satisfaction and preparation before testifying, 57–58
sexual violence and, 8
social consequences of testifying and, 105–06
support for deterrence mandate of ICTY and, 161, 161f6.11.
support for responsibility mandate of ICTY and, 159–60
support for truth mandate of ICTY and, 159–60
trauma as disproportionately felt along ethnic lines, 37
witness experience and, 5–7, 37

fairness of ICTY, 34–35, 189–91, 193
gender and, 67
negative and positive emotions model and, 136
perceptions of by ethnic group, 67, 155–57
witness perception of, 65–69
witness perceptions of OTP fairness, 78–82
female witnesses, 3. *See also* gender; male witnesses
ethnicity of in witness survey, 38
human security threats and, 112–13
on ICTY proceedings having moved too slowly, 152
as less likely to be satisfied with interpersonal relations in their community, 145

female witnesses (*cont.*)
  level of knowledge of ICTY before and
    after testimony, 54–55
  as more likely to report trauma than
    male witnesses, 50, 51
  on motivations for testifying, 60
  perception of fair treatment by ICTY, 67
  reporting of negative emotions after
    testifying, 136
  on satisfaction with their assistance from
    VWS, 58
  sexual violence and, 179, 180
  on sufficient time and information to
    prepare for testimony, 57
Ford, Stuart K., 158

Gagnon, VP Jr., 7
gender. *See also* female witnesses; male
    witnesses
  breakdown of by ethnicity in witness survey,
    38, 40f2.3.
  differences between in post-trial
    phase and, 3
  economic consequences of testifying
    and, 108
  gender ratio and representation in witness
    survey, 14, 25, 26f1.8., 37
  health of witnesses before testifying and
    three months post-testifying, 123–27
  human security threats and, 108
  on ICTY proceedings having moved too
    slowly, 152
  ICTY witnesses motivation for testifying
    and, 60, 75
  impact on national and international politics
    on ICTY effectiveness and, 153–54
  interethnic marriages and, 42
  level of knowledge of ICTY before and
    after testimony, 54–55
  level of trauma by quintiles, 46–47
  perception of ICTY fairness and, 67
  perceptions about the local courts and, 155
  post traumatic symptoms and, 121
  post-conflict societies and, 7, 124
  proportion of male to female witnesses, 25,
    26f1.8., 37, 179
  reporting of negative emotions after
    testifying, 136
  reporting on if health is worse due to
    testifying, 127
  satisfaction with interpersonal relations in
    their community and, 145

sexual violence and, 8, 179, 180
social consequences of testifying
    and, 108
trauma as disproportionately felt along
    gender lines, 37
witness experience and, 7–8, 37
witness perceptions of their contributions to
    truth and justice and, 3
witness support policies and, 180
Guerrero, Jose Raul, 143

Hadžić, Goran, 184
Harvard Trauma questionnaire, 163
healing, testifying as, 9, 128
health of witnesses. *See* physiological
    health of witnesses; positive
    outlook; post traumatic symptoms;
    psychological health of witnesses; sexual
    violence; trauma
Herzegovina, 14, 23, 26
  mixed ethnic marriages in, 41
human security threats, 10, 85–86, 94–98, 104–5,
    184–86. *See also* deterrence mandate
    of ICTY; economic consequences of
    testifying; punishment mandate of ICTY;
    responsibility mandate of ICTY; social
    consequences of testifying; testimony
    and testimonial process; truth mandate
    of ICTY
  Bosniaks reporting of, 117
  ethnic minorities in their communities and,
    105–08, 112, 115, 117
  ethnicity and, 96, 105–06
  form of threat delivery, 97
  gender and, 108, 112–13
  human security defined, 85
  as impediment to reconciliation and,
    94, 116
  in-court protective measures (PMs)
    and, 98–102
  as negatively related to satisfaction in
    community relations, 146
  overall feeling of witness security
    today, 103–04
  positive outlook and, 112
  positive outlook and satisfaction with
    current situation and, 114–15
  reporting of and assistance for, 97–98
  trauma and, 108–11, 112–14, 115
  types of threats experienced, 94–95
  voluntary migration and, 102–03
  who and how of threat delivery, 95–96

ICTY. *See also* deterrence mandate of
ICTY; effectiveness of ICTY; fairness of
ICTY; punishment mandate of ICTY;
responsibility mandate of ICTY; truth
mandate of ICTY
ethnic minorities in their communities
support for mandates, 162
history of the establishment of, 10–12
in-court protective measures (PMs)
of, 98–102
knowledge of and the level of trauma, 56
preparation process for witnesses and, 53
Prosecutor v. Tadic case of, 99
support for and ethnicity, 158–59
witness knowledge of before and after
testifying, 53–54
witness knowledge of before and after
testifying by ethnicity, 5655f3.3.
witness knowledge of before and after
testifying by gender, 54–55
in-court protection measures, 111
Institutional Review Board (IRB), 2, 12
International Criminal Court (ICC), 85, 122,
148, 149, 176
International Criminal Tribunal for the
Former Yugoslavia (ICTY). *See* ICTY
international justice and tribunals, 149–50
need for post-testimony service programs
in, 192

Karadžić, Radovan, 184
Kenyatta trial, 85
Kirsch, Philippe, 149
Kosovar Albanians, 6
level of knowledge of ICTY before and
after testifying, 55
motivations to testify of, 60–61
perceptions of fairness of ICTY toward
witnesses of own ethnic group, 67
post traumatic symptoms and, 121
reporting of emotions after testifying
and, 136
support for truth and responsibility
mandates of ICTY and, 160
trauma experienced and reported by,
47–48, 50, 51
Kosovo, 14, 23

life satisfaction
human security threats and, 114–15
negative and positive emotions models
and, 136

witness satisfaction with present
and future economic circumstances,
139, 140
witness satisfaction with present and future
life situations, 139–40
witness satisfaction with present and future
political situation in their country,
140, 141
local courts
gender perceptions on, 155

Macedonian, 38
male witnesses, 3. *See also* female
witnesses; gender
on ICTY proceedings having moved too
slowly, 152
as less likely to report trauma than female
witnesses, 50, 51
level of knowledge of ICTY before and
after testimony, 54–55
on satisfaction with their assistance from
VWS, 58
sexual violence and, 179, 180
on sufficient time and information to
prepare for testimony, 57
Meernik, James, 143, 158
Milosevic, Slobodan, 7
Milutinovic, Milan, 160
Mladić, Ratko, 184
Moreno-Ocampo, Luis, 149
Muslims from Bosnia. *See* Bosniaks

national courts, vs. international for
adjudicating war crimes
ethnicity and, 154–55
negative affect. *See* negative emotions model;
post traumatic symptoms; psychological
health of witnesses; trauma
negative binomial regression models, 133
negative emotions model
ethnicity and reporting of negative
emotions, 136
frequency of testifying and, 136
gender and reporting of negative emotions
after testifying and, 136
life satisfaction and, 136
perception of fair treatment by ICTY
prosecution and, 136
Negotiating the Memorandum of
Understanding (MOU), 2
Northern Ireland, 144
Nuremburg trials, 58

Office of the Prosecution (OTP), 5
Organization for Security and Cooperation in
　　Europe, 158

partial correlations
　　between trauma and testimonial
　　　consequences, 109
physiological health of witnesses, 118–19,
　　179, 186–89
　　before testifying and three months
　　　post-testifying, 123–27
　　coping strategies for stress during
　　　testimony, 137–38
　　impact of trauma on, 9
　　witness reporting on if believe have
　　　worsened health due to testifying, 126–28
Poisson regression model
　　of trauma experienced, 49, 51
political situation
　　witness satisfaction with present and future,
　　　140, 141
positive affect. *See* life satisfaction; positive
　　emotions model; positive outlook;
　　psychological health of witnesses
positive emotions model
　　life satisfaction and, 136
　　motivations for testifying and, 135
　　perception of fair treatment by ICTY
　　　prosecution and, 136
positive outlook, 135
　　education and, 147
　　human security threats and, 111, 114–15
　　as unexpected consequence of trauma,
　　　9–10, 145–46
　　witness satisfaction with community
　　　interpersonal relations and, 147
post-conflict societies, 103. *See also* civil
　　conflicts and wars
　　post traumatic symptoms and, 121, 122
　　post-war public health and, 122, 123
　　women in, 7, 124
post traumatic symptoms, 119–22
　　ethnicity and, 121
　　gender and, 121
　　impact of testifying and, 121
　　table of measures of from last 6 months, 119
　　trauma and, 121
probit models, 78, 144, 168
　　on attitudes of community interpersonal
　　　relations, 145
　　for social, economic and security threats, 111

witness support for ICTY mandates
　　and, 169–73
Prosecutor v. Tadic, 99
psychological health of witnesses, 4, 10, 118–19,
　　179, 186–89
　　coping strategies for stress during
　　　testimony, 137–38
　　during witness survey interviews, 20, 21fi.4.
　　impact of testifying on, 121
　　impact of testifying on healing and, 9
　　positive outlook as unexpected
　　　consequence of trauma, 9–10
　　positive and negative affect before and after
　　　testifying, 128–32
　　question of whether testifying is re-
　　　traumatizing for witnesses, 131, 133
punishment mandate of ICTY, 35,
　　159–63, 176
　　belief in efficacy of testimony and, 174–75
　　experiences of human security threats
　　　and, 167–68
　　general lack of support for by ethnicity,
　　　160f6.10., 161
　　levels of importance of reasons for testifying
　　　and, 165–66
　　probit model of influence of ethnicity on
　　　witness perception on, 169–73
　　trauma and, 163–65
　　witness perceptions of their contributions to
　　　truth and justice and, 166–67

rape. *See* sexual violence
recommendations. *See also* research
　　to advance theory in international judicial
　　　research, 178
　　for best practices in witness security, health,
　　　and witness experiences throughout
　　　testimonial process, 3, 4, 115, 148, 178
　　for early development of witness support
　　　structures in international tribunals
　　　before, during, and after testifying, 182
　　to examine impact of testifying over
　　　duration of witness' life, 128
　　on examining economic consequences of
　　　testifying, 92
　　for further understanding on ethnicity and
　　　reporting of post-traumatic symptoms, 122
　　for future tribunals to ameliorate difficulties
　　　with frequent appearances, 137
　　for gender sensitive witness support
　　　policies, 180

for human security threats, 185
on including witness voices in
  understanding of impact of international
  tribunals, 23
on informing witnesses on judgments and
  (early) release of convicted, 191
to investigate impact of ICTY personnel
  conducting witness surveys, 192
need for future research on ethnicity and
  witness attitudes, 183
need to better understand construct of
  fairness within testimonial process, 157
to raise awareness on benefits of
  testifying, 190
to standardize pre-testimony needs
  assessment, 188
for standardized usage of post-testimony
  survey, 192
to strengthen local assistance and
  cooperation with field offices, 185
for testifying on sexual violence, 179, 180
for witness support structures providing
  awareness of rights, 186
for witness survey on those who took part
  in Mladić, Karadžić, Šešelj, and Hadžić
  trials, 184
for witness well-being post-testimony, 122
reconciliation, 38, 119, 194
  community relations and, 88
  education and, 143
  human security threats and, 94, 116
  research on in former Yugoslavia, 143–44
  thick versus thin definitions
    of, 142, 143
relationships. *See also* community relations
  consequences of testimony on community
    relationships and, 88–91
  consequences of testimony on intimate
    relationships and, 86–88
religion
  ethnicity and, 6
  witness affiliations in witness survey, 26
research. *See also* recommendations
  on emotional and psychological well-being
    of persons post-Balkan wars, 128
  on impact of testifying in international
    tribunals on psychological health, 10, 133
  lack of on gender in transitional justice
    research, 7
  need for on ethnicity and witness
    attitudes, 183

need for on support for ICTY
  mandates, 176
need to better understand components and
  make up of positive attitudes, 135, 147
need to utilize on best practices for witness
  safety and human security, 117
on perceived respect and fairness of and
  legitimacy of tribunals, 175
on positive experiences with testifying, 3
on positive outlook as unexpected
  consequence of trauma, 9–10
on reconciliation in former
  Yugoslavia, 143–44
resilience, 22, 72–74, 82, 83, 119, 135, 194
  defined, 72
responsibility mandate of ICTY, 35, 159–63,
  175, 176
  belief in efficacy of testimony and, 174–75
  experiences of human security threats
    and, 167–68
  levels of importance of reasons for testifying
    and, 165–66
  probit model of influence of ethnicity on
    witness perception on, 169–73
  support for by ethnicity, 159–60
  trauma and, 163–65
  witness perceptions of their contributions to
    truth and justice and, 166–67
Rwandan witnesses
  research on motivation for testifying
    of, 59, 60

Serbia, 14, 23
  mixed ethnic marriages in, 41
Serbs, 6, 35, 38
  belief in ICTY unfairness towards Serbian
    defendants, 156
  level of knowledge of ICTY after
    testimony, 55
  level of knowledge of ICTY before
    testimony, 55
  motivations to testify of, 60–61
  on national vs. international tribunals for
    adjudicating war crimes, 155
  post traumatic symptoms and, 121
  reporting of health issues before and three
    months post-testifying, 126
  support for deterrence mandate of ICTY
    and, 161
  trauma experienced and reported by, 47–48
Šešelj, Vojislav, 184

sexual violence, 5, 8, 9, 46
    ethnicity and, 8
    liability for, 5
    motivation for testifying for victims of, 59
    need for research on impact of testifying, 179, 180
Seymour, Lee JM, 7
social consequences of testifying. *See also* economic consequences of testifying; human security threats; testimony and testimonial process
    ethnicity and, 105–06
    gender and, 108
    impact on community relationships and, 88–91
    impact on intimate relationships and, 86–88
    as negatively related to satisfaction with community relations, 146
South Africa, 142
Southeast Europe Social Survey Project (SEESSP), 158
speaking for the dead, 179
Special Court for Sierra Leone (SCSL), 3, 58, 59, 61, 122
Stepakoff, Shanee, 59, 123
Stover, Eric, 2

testimony and testimonial process. *See also* economic consequences of testifying; human security threats; social consequences of testifying; witness motivation for testifying; witness motivations for testifying (ICTY witnesses)
    belief in efficacy of testimony and perception of ICTY effectiveness, 52, 174–75
    as closure, healing and catharsis, 9, 34, 72, 73, 128
    coping strategies for stress during, 137–38
    criticism and disassociation in community as consequence of, 88–91, 116
    negative emotions model and frequency of testifying, 136
    partial correlations between trauma and, 109
    post-testimonial emotional well-being and, 121
    preparation process for witnesses, 53, 57
    psychological health of witnesses before and after, 128–32

question of whether testifying is re-traumatizing for witnesses, 131, 133
reasons for testifying, 59–60
research on positive experiences with, 3
voluntary migration after, 102–03
witness knowledge of ICTY before and after, 53–54
witness knowledge of ICTY before and after by ethnicity, 56 55f3.3.
witness knowledge of ICTY before and after by gender, 54–55
witness perception of effectiveness of, 69–71
witness perception of effectiveness of and resilience, 72–74
witness preparation, knowledge, and satisfaction before trial, 53–58
witness reporting on physiological health and, 126–28
witness satisfaction with testimony and, 62–65
witnesses with long-term impact related to, 121
transitional justice, 72, 117
    human security threats as obstacle to overcome in, 94
    lack of research on gender and, 7
    need for research on witness experience and, 193
    question of whether testifying is cathartic or re-traumatizing on witnesses, 122, 131, 133
trauma, 181–82. *See also* economic consequences of testifying; human security threats; physiological health of witnesses; post traumatic symptoms; psychological health of witnesses; sexual violence; social consequences of testifying
    Bosniaks and, 47–51
    deprivation as, 56
    as disproportionately felt along ethnic lines and gender, 37, 49
    for ethnic minorities in their communities, 50, 115, 117
    experiences of reported in witness survey, 43–46
    human security threats and, 108–11, 112–14, 115
    ICTY witness motivation to testify and, 61, 74, 78
    knowledge of ICTY and level of, 56
    Kosovar Albanians and, 47–48, 50, 51

level of by gender by quintiles, 46–47
partial correlations between testimonial
process and, 109
Poisson regression model of, 49, 51
positive outlook as unexpected
consequence of, 9–10, 145–46
post traumatic symptoms and, 121
question of whether testifying is re-
traumatizing for witnesses, 131, 133
recollections of negative emotions after
testimony and, 136
Serbs and, 47–48
support for ICTY mandates and, 163–65
witness experience and, 8–10, 37
witness satisfaction with interpersonal
community relations and, 145–48
truth mandate of ICTY, 35, 159–63, 175, 176
belief in efficacy of testimony and, 174–75
experiences of human security threats
and, 167–68
levels of importance of reasons for testifying
and, 165–66
perceptions of their contributions to truth
and justice and, 166–67
probit model of influence of ethnicity on
witness perception on, 169–73
support for by ethnicity, 159–60
trauma and, 163–65
Tudjman, Franjo, 7

unemployment rate, in former Yugoslavia, 139
University of North Texas. *See* UNT
UNT, 2, 3, 12, 13, 14, 19, 23

victim and witness security, 117, 185
Victims and Witnesses Section. *See* VWS
voluntary migration, 102–03
VWS, 4, 131, 192
assistance from as coping mechanism from
stress during testimony, 137
Policy on Privacy and Confidentiality of, 18
reporting of and assistance for human
security threats and, 97–98
testimony preparation process for
witnesses, 57
witness survey project and, 12, 13, 14, 19,
20, 21, 23

wars of the former Yugoslavia. *See* Balkan wars
witness experience
ethnicity and, 5–7, 37

gender and, 7–8, 37
trauma and, 8–10, 37
witness fatigue, 136, 187
witness motivation for testifying, 58
research from Rwandan prosecution and
defence witnesses, 59
research from Special Court for Sierra
Leone (SCSL), 3, 58, 59, 61, 122
for victims of sexual violence, 59
witness motivations for testifying (ICTY
witnesses), 52–53, 61, 77
confronting the defendant
and, 74–78
education and, 77
ethnicity and, 60–61, 74
gender and, 60, 75
ICTY mandates and, 165–66
positive emotions after testifying
and, 135
putting the past behind oneself
and, 74–78
reasons for testifying, 59–60
resilience and, 72–74
speaking for the dead and, 74–78
telling one's story and, 74–78
trauma and, 61, 74, 78
witness support structures, 4, 193
gender and, 180
need for before, during, and after
testifying, 182
for witness awareness of rights, 186
witness survey, 29, 194
average age of witnesses, 24, 124
Bosniaks reporting of trauma in, 47–51
breakdown of ethnicity by gender, 38,
40f2.3.
cases not included in, 184
development of, 12–14
education levels and, 24
eligibility for inclusion in, 13
ethnic and religious minorities and mixed
ethnic marriages in immediate family,
41f2.4.
ethnic identification among key ICTY
nationalities, 39f2.2.
ethnic self-identification in, 26,
39f2.1., 183
experiences of trauma reported in, 43–46
gender ratio and representation in, 14, 25,
26f1.8., 37
geographic diversity in, 23–24

witness survey (*cont.*)
  ineligibility for inclusion in, 13
  interethnic marriages and, 39–42
  interview process and, 19–21
  interviewee appearances as proportion of
    all witnesses per trial, 31f1.14.
  interviewee appearances by year, 28f1.11.
  interviewee trial appearances, 28f1.12.
  interviewees by trial and the side for which
    individual testified (OTP, Defence or
    Chambers), 29, 30f1.13.
  level of trauma experienced by gender by
    quintiles, 46–47
  locations of interviews in, 19
  number of interethnic marriage by
    geographic region, 41, 42
  possible selection bias of healthy witnesses'
    participation in, 22, 131, 132
  post-interview procedures, 20–21

  protecting the identity, security, and
    confidentiality of witnesses as critical in,
    2, 3, 12, 14, 19, 20, 21
  reasons for refusal to participate, 17, 22
  recruitment process outcome, 16f1.2.
  religious affiliations in, 26
  selection effects, 22–23
  table of witness sampling goals &
    interviewees surveyed, 23
  table on witness roles and trial
    appearances, 29
  typical witness ethnicity, gender and
    trauma level, 51
  UNT and VWS and, 23
  witness behaviors and emotions during
    interview process, 20, 21f1.4.
  witness recruitment process, 14–19

Yugoslavia, wars of the former. *See* Balkan wars